MW01039850

SOUTHERN WOMEN IN
REVOLUTION, 1776–1800

H. Dec. 28. 1791

The Honorable the General Assembly of the State of N. Carolina

Now in Session at Newbern. —

The memorial of Jennet Spurgen Humbly

Sheweth

That during the late war She furnished the regular Troops and Militia of this State with Provisions and for Carriage Some part of which, the Officers that took it gave her certificates for — But the greater part that was taken from her She never got any vouchers for, owing to her husbands being disaffected to the government and owing to the Same reason, the Vouchers She did obtain would not be received and audited by the auditors of Salisbury District to whom they were presented for that Purpose. And tho it was your memorialists misfortune to be married to a man who was Enimical to the revolution it was an evil that was not in her power to remidy and as she has always behaved herself as a good Citizen and well attached to the government. She thinks it extreamly hard to be deprived of the common rights of other Citizens. Your memorialist is advanced in life and very much failed and has Six Children to provide for and no one to afist or help her, and is also in very low Circumstances. her husband not having lived with her Since the war. She has therefore Stated her account for Such articles As she obtained Vouchers for and humbly hopes your honorable body will grant her Such relief in the premifes as you in your great wisdoms may think her entitled to — And your memorialist

as

Petition of Jane Spurgin of Rowan County, North Carolina, 28 December 1791.
(Courtesy of the North Carolina Division of Archives and History.)

SOUTHERN WOMEN IN REVOLUTION, 1776–1800
Personal and Political Narratives

Cynthia A. Kierner

UNIVERSITY OF SOUTH CAROLINA PRESS

Copyright © 1998 University of South Carolina

Published in Columbia, South Carolina, by the
University of South Carolina Press

Manufactured in the United States of America

02 01 00 99 98 5 4 3 2 1
Library of Congress Cataloging-in-Publication Data

Kierner, Cynthia A., 1958–
    Southern women in revolution, 1776–1800 : personal and political
narratives / Cynthia A. Kierner.
        p.   cm.
    Includes bibliographical references (p.   ) and index.
    ISBN 1–57003–218–1
    1. United States—History—Revolution, 1775–1783—Women—
Sources.   2. Southern States—History—Revolution, 1775–1783—
Women—Sources.   3. Women—Southern States—History—18th
century—Sources.   4. Petition, Right of—Southern States—History—
18th century—Sources.   I. Title.
    E276.K54   1998
    305.4′0975′09033—dc21   97–33890

In memory of
Teena Kierner
and
Helen Di Sturco

CONTENTS

ACKNOWLEDGMENTS

This project originated as part of a more general attempt to discern women's relationship to public life in eighteenth-century America. While women in the southern states and elsewhere participated in a variety of public and quasipublic activities ranging from ceremonial balls to religious revivals, petitioning was the only formal political activity in which they could engage. Between 1776 and 1800, more women than ever before petitioned the southern legislatures. The petitions they presented were largely autobiographical narratives that often told compelling stories of sacrifice, hardship, and perseverance. In addition, the language and logic of these petitions subtly revealed much about how women in the revolutionary era understood their relationship to government and to the larger political community.

Many people have offered suggestions and insights to enhance my understanding of these documents and their significance. W. W. Abbot and Dorothy Twohig taught me most of what I know about documentary editing. Joan Gundersen, Sally McMillen, Susan Miller, Mitchell Snay, and Albert Tillson commented, either formally or informally, on a paper I gave at the Southern Historical Association meeting in 1993, in which I first attempted to analyze the language of women petitioners. A conversation with Warren Slesinger at that same conference convinced me that the petitions were worth editing for publication. Constance Schulz strengthened that conviction with a helpful and encouraging review of my initial proposal as well as an enthusiastic endorsement of the finished manuscript. At the University of South Carolina Press, Fred Kameny saw the project through to fruition.

Other individuals and institutions have assisted me financially and intellectually in the course of completing this study. Thomas Buckley, S.J., kindly shared his research on divorce in early Virginia. Cita Cook and Leslie Griffin offered southern hospitality in Atlanta and Columbia, respectively. Paula Stathakis was my roommate and fellow researcher during several trips to Raleigh. Faculty research grants from the Foundation of the University of North Carolina at Charlotte funded the transcription of documents and some of the research required for annotation. A Summer Stipend from the National Endowment for the Humanities allowed me to devote an entire summer to writing at a critical stage.

Anyone using public documents depends on state archivists for a variety of services, but the prospective editor of such documents relies especially heavily on their expertise, efficiency, and cooperation. Without the informed assistance of the staffs of the state archives in Georgia, North Carolina, South Carolina, and Virginia, this book would have taken much longer to complete. At the North Carolina Division of Archives and History in Raleigh, Ed Morris was especially helpful in tracking down obscure documents, Earl Ijames procured the illustration for the frontispiece, and William H. King generously supplied some important last-minute citations.

My husband, Thomas Bright, whose work took us both to Sweden, gave me an ideal place to produce this book and the necessary time to do it. Finally, I dedicate this volume to the memory of my grandmothers, who were born in an era when gender constructed the rights and obligations of American citizenship much as it did for the petitioners whose stories follow.

EDITORIAL METHOD

Because this book seeks to recover the voices and concerns of eighteenth-century women, the documents in it have been transcribed and reproduced as literally as possible. Spelling, grammar, and syntax reveal much about the education, speech, and perceptions of those who use them and therefore remain unchanged, though superscript characters are lowered and new paragraphs consistently indented, despite the varied usage of eighteenth-century writers. Punctuation has not been modernized, except for the deletion of superfluous dashes and commas and the silent insertion of a period, when necessary, to end a paragraph.

This book contains five thematic chapters, each chronologically organized, and employs several editorial devices to make its contents more accessible and meaningful to modern readers. Interpretive essays introduce each chapter, situating the petitions in their broader historical context. A separate introduction to each petition provides information about its author and the resolution of the case she submitted for the assembly's consideration. Within each document, annotation in the form of footnotes defines obscure or obsolete terms and identifies people, places, events, and laws not discussed elsewhere. Square brackets indicate editorial insertion of words when a text is illegible or torn or the expansion of abbreviations for the purpose of clarification. At the end of each document, abbreviations identify the archival source of the petition and indicate whether it was written and signed by the petitioner.

ABBREVIATIONS

Short Titles

AHR	*American Historical Review*
Biog. Dict. of S.C. House, 1775–1790	Louise N. Bailey and Elizabeth Ivey Cooper, eds., *Biographical Dictionary of the South Carolina House of Representatives*, vol. 3: *1775–1790* (Columbia: University of South Carolina Press, 1981)
Biog. Directory of S.C. House, 1719–1774	Walter B. Edgar and Louise N. Bailey, eds., *Biographical Directory of the South Carolina House of Representatives*, vol. 2: *1719–1774* (Columbia: University of South Carolina Press, 1974)
Boatner, *Ency. of Amer. Rev.*	Mark Mayo Boatner, *Encyclopedia of the American Revolution* (New York: D. McKay, 1966)
Claghorn, *Women Patriots*	Charles Claghorn, *Women Patriots of the American Revolution: A Biographical Dictionary* (Metuchen, N.J.: Scarecrow Press, 1991)
Clark, *Loyalists*	Murtie June Clark, *Loyalists in the Southern Campaign of the Revolutionary War*, 3 vols. (Baltimore: Genealogical Publishing Company, 1981)

Clemens, *Marriage Recs.*   William Montgomery Clemens,
                                         North and South Carolina Mar-
                                         riage Records: From the Earliest
                                         Colonial Days to the Civil War
                                         (Baltimore: Genealogical Publish-
                                         ing Company, 1987)

DAB   *Dictionary of American Biography,*
                                         1936 ed., 10 vols.

Davis, *Ga. Citizens and Soldiers*   Robert S. Davis Jr., *Georgia Citi-*
                                         zens and Soldiers of the American
                                         Revolution (Easley, S.C.: Southern
                                         Historical Press, 1979)

DeMond, *Loyalists in N.C.*   Robert O. DeMond, *The Loyalists*
                                         in North Carolina during the Revo-
                                         lution (Durham, N.C.: Duke Uni-
                                         versity Press, 1940)

Dict. of Ga. Biog.   Kenneth Coleman and Charles
                                         Stephen Gurr, eds., *Dictionary*
                                         of Georgia Biography, 2 vols.
                                         (Athens: University of Georgia
                                         Press, 1983)

Dict. of N.C. Biog.   William S. Powell, ed., *Dictionary*
                                         of North Carolina Biography,
                                         6 vols. (Chapel Hill: University of
                                         North Carolina Press, 1979–95)

GASR   General Assembly sessions records

GHQ   *Georgia Historical Quarterly*

[Hay et al.], *N.C. Soldiers*   [Gertrude Sloan Hay et al.], *Roster*
                                         of Soldiers from North Carolina in
                                         the American Revolution (Durham:
                                         North Carolina Daughters of the
                                         American Revolution, 1932)

Heads of Families . . . in the Year 1790: N.C.	*Heads of Families at the First Census of the United States Taken in the Year 1790: North Carolina* (Washington, D.C.: Government Printing Office, 1908)
Heads of Families . . . in the Year 1790: S.C.	*Heads of Families at the First Census of the United States Taken in the Year 1790: South Carolina* (Washington, D.C.: Government Printing Office, 1908)
JAH	*Journal of American History*
JER	*Journal of the Early Republic*
Lambert, *S.C. Loyalists*	Robert Stansbury Lambert, *South Carolina Loyalists in the American Revolution* (Columbia: University of South Carolina Press, 1987)
GHQ	*Georgia Historical Quarterly*
LP	Legislative petitions
McCrady, *S.C. in the Revolution*	Edward McCrady, *The History of South Carolina in the Revolution,* 2 vols. (New York: Macmillan, 1902)
Morrill, *Fiat Finance*	James R. Morrill, *The Practice and Politics of Fiat Finance: North Carolina in the Confederation, 1783–1789* (Chapel Hill: University of North Carolina Press, 1969)
Moss, *S.C. Patriots*	Bobby Gilmer Moss, *Roster of South Carolina Patriots in the American Revolution* (Baltimore: Genealogical Publishing Company, 1983)

Nadelhaft, *Disorders of War*

Jerome J. Nadelhaft, *The Disorders of War: The Revolution in South Carolina* (Orono: University of Maine at Orono Press, 1981)

NAW

Edward T. James et al., eds., *Notable American Women, 1607–1950: A Biographical Dictionary,* 3 vols. (Cambridge, Mass.: Belknap Press of Harvard University Press, 1971)

N.C. Census, 1784–1787

Alvaretta Kenan Register, *State Census of North Carolina, 1784–1787,* 2d ed. (Baltimore: Genealogical Publishing Company, 1973)

NCHR

North Carolina Historical Review

N.C. Recs.

William L. Saunders, Walter Clark, and Stephen B. Weeks, eds., *The Colonial and State Records of North Carolina,* 30 vols. (Raleigh, Winston, Goldsboro, and Charlotte: State Printers, 1886–1914)

Pancake, *Destructive War*

John C. Pancake, *This Destructive War: The British Campaign in the Carolinas, 1780–1782* (University: University of Alabama Press, 1985)

Rev. Recs. of Ga.

Allen D. Candler, ed., *The Revolutionary Records of the State of Georgia,* vol. 3: *Journal of the House of Assembly, From August 17, 1781, to February 26, 1784* (Atlanta: Franklin-Turner Company, 1908)

Sabine, *Loyalists of the Amer. Rev.*   Lorenzo Sabine, *Biographical Sketches of Loyalists of the American Revolution, with an Historical Essay,* 2 vols. (Boston: Little, Brown, 1864)

SCHM   *South Carolina Historical Review*

S.C. House Journals   Theodora J. Thompson et al., eds., *The State Records of South Carolina: Journals of the House of Representatives, 1783–1794,* 6 vols. (Columbia: University of South Carolina Press, 1977–85)

S.C. House Journals, 1776–1780   William Edwin Hemphill, Wylma Anne Wates, and R. Nicholas Olsberg, eds., *The State Records of South Carolina: Journals of the General Assembly and House of Representatives, 1776–1780* (Columbia: University of South Carolina Press, 1970)

S.C. Statutes   Thomas Cooper and David J. McCord, eds., *The Statutes at Large of South Carolina* (Columbia, S.C.: A. S. Johnston, 1836–41)

Siebert, *Loyalists in East Florida*   Wilbur Henry Siebert, *Loyalists in East Florida, 1774 to 1785,* 2 vols. (Deland: Florida State Historical Society, 1929)

VMHB   *Virginia Magazine of History and Biography*

Walsh, *Charleston's Sons of Liberty*	Richard Walsh, *Charleston's Sons of Liberty: A Study of the Artisans, 1763–1789* (Columbia: University of South Carolina Press, 1959)
WMQ	*William and Mary Quarterly*

Manuscript Classification Abbreviations

AD	Autograph document
ADS	Autograph document signed
D	Document
DC	Document copy
DS	Document signed

Repository Abbreviations

Ga-Ar	Georgia State Archives, Atlanta
Nc-Ar	North Carolina Division of Archives and History, Raleigh
Sc-Ar	South Carolina Division of Archives and History, Columbia
Sc-U	South Caroliniana Library, University of South Carolina, Columbia
Vi-Hi	Virginia Historical Society, Richmond
Vi-Ar	Virginia State Library and Archives, Richmond
Vi-U	Alderman Library, University of Virginia, Charlottesville
Vi-W	Swem Library, College of William and Mary, Williamsburg
Vi-WC	Colonial Williamsburg, Inc.

SOUTHERN WOMEN IN REVOLUTION, 1776–1800

INTRODUCTION

Between 1776 and 1800, women in the four southernmost American states submitted at least 780 petitions to their state legislatures.[1] Most of these petitioners asked for compensation for losses incurred during the Revolution. Soldiers' widows requested pensions and back pay. Wives of loyalist exiles sought to reverse their husbands' banishment or recover confiscated property. Others sought restitution for property the state seized or destroyed during the war years. Many petitioners included accounts of their wartime experiences when they submitted claims and grievances to their government.

This book reproduces a selection of these documents and examines them in historical context, focusing on both the stories women told and the language they employed when they petitioned their state assemblies. The Revolution, which transformed colonies into self-governing republics and subjects into citizens, was a turning point in Americans' relations with their government. For women, who continued to lack most of the rights and obligations of republican citizenship, however, the meaning of the Revolution was problematic.[2] On the one hand, colonial resistance to British imperial authority politicized many women, while the hardships of war, perhaps coupled with rising expectations for responsiveness in government, led them to petition in unprecedented numbers. On the other hand, enhanced political consciousness and women's heightened public visibility signaled neither a revolution in gender ideals nor a transformation of the formal political status of women in America. Being nei-

---

1. The exact numbers of surviving petitions, plus others mentioned in legislative records, are as follows: 242 in Virginia, 138 in North Carolina, 202 in South Carolina, and 198 in Georgia.

2. James H. Kettner, *The Development of American Citizenship, 1608–1870* (Chapel Hill: University of North Carolina Press, 1978), chaps. 1, 7; Joan R. Gundersen, "Independence, Citizenship, and the American Revolution," *Signs* 13 (1987): 60–68; Linda K. Kerber, "A Constitutional Right to Be Treated Like American Ladies: Women and the Obligations of Citizenship," in *U.S. History as Women's History: New Feminist Essays,* ed. Linda K. Kerber, Alice Kessler-Harris, and Kathryn Kish Sklar (Chapel Hill: University of North Carolina Press, 1995), 23, 27–35.

ther citizens nor subjects, most women petitioners accordingly portrayed themselves as members of a political community who, though lacking certain fundamental civil rights, nonetheless merited the consideration of their governors.

Because petitioning was the only formal political channel accessible to women and because few women petitioned the legislature before the Revolution, petitions from the revolutionary era are among the earliest surviving political statements of women in America. Collectively, these documents also constitute the largest body of women's writing about the American Revolution and its impact on civilian life. This book reproduces approximately one-eighth of the petitions that southern women submitted between 1776 and 1800. All of the documents selected pertain to war-related claims and grievances, save the petitions for emancipation, divorce, and property rights that constitute the final chapter. The war-related petitions describe the personal, economic, and intellectual effects of the Revolution and its aftermath on southern women and their families. The others demonstrate women's awareness of the libertarian ideals of the Revolution as well as their ability to invoke those ideals publicly to improve their private lives.

Petitioning the legislature was part of the constitutional tradition that came to America with its English colonizers. Medieval in origin, the right to petition was in theory accessible to all people subject to the authority of the king and Parliament. In early modern England, Parliament routinely received and considered petitions from groups and individuals of all social ranks. Before 1642, women petitioners always acted alone, but radical sectarians in the Civil War era petitioned in groups, setting an important precedent for women's collective political activism.[3]

Following English precedent, colonial legislatures began accepting and adjudicating petitions early in their history. In the colonies, as in England, all inhabitants had the right to petition, and people of all social ranks availed themselves of the opportunity to address their government. Nevertheless, petitions from groups of women were virtually unknown in America before the Revolution, and individual women submitted only a small portion of the petitions that the colonial assemblies considered.

---

3. Patricia Higgins, "The Reactions of Women, with Special Reference to Women Petitioners," in *Politics, Religion, and the English Civil War*, ed. Brian Manning (New York: St. Martin's Press, 1973), 185, 209–14, 222.

Between 1750 and 1775, for instance, women accounted for only 11 of 239 petitions heard by North Carolina's provincial assembly, while they filed only 21 of the 690 petitions received by South Carolina's lower house.[4]

Before and after the Revolution, those who petitioned their assemblies followed a standard procedure that put them in contact with their communities' governing bodies and the men who ran them. Prospective supplicants prepared their petitions either on their own or with the assistance of relatives, friends, or clerks, and then presented them to the county court for certification. If the justices approved, or certified, a petition, they then forwarded it to their county's legislative representative, who, in turn, presented it to the full assembly. Once a petition received its first reading before the assembly, it was remanded to a committee for further consideration. The committee later reported to the legislators, who usually granted or rejected the petition based on its recommendation.[5]

When women submitted their petitions, they ventured into an alien and overwhelmingly masculine environment. Although white men of all social ranks traditionally gathered when the courts convened to socialize and do business, evidence from contemporary diaries and journals suggests that women rarely attended the county courts unless they were involved in a case under consideration.[6] When women came to court, they sat not with their men in the main body of the chamber but in galleries

---

4. Raymond C. Bailey, *Popular Influence upon Public Policy: Petitioning in Eighteenth-Century Virginia* (Westport, Conn.: Greenwood Press, 1979), 26–27; Linda K. Kerber, *Women of the Republic: Ideology and Intellect in Revolutionary America* (Chapel Hill: University of North Carolina Press, 1980), 41.

For North Carolina's colonial petitions, see *N.C. Recs.*, vols. 4–21. For South Carolina, see South Carolina legislative journals, microfilm, Sc-Ar.

5. For a detailed description of the petitioning process in a representative colony and state, see Bailey, *Popular Influence*, 27–30.

6. James Gordon, "Journal of Colonel James Gordon . . . ," *WMQ*, 1st ser., 11 (1902–3): 103–6, 196, 224; Diary of Sarah Fouace Nourse, 1781–83, Nourse Family Papers, Vi-U, 5, 8, 19, 21, 23, 28, 30, 32, 35, 42, 44, 46, 49; Hunter Dickinson Farish, ed., *The Journal and Letters of Philip Vickers Fithian: A Plantation Tutor of the Old Dominion* (Williamsburg, Va.: Colonial Williamsburg, 1957), 74, 87, 116, 127; Charles Woodmason, *The Carolina Backcountry on the Eve of the Revolution*, ed. Richard J. Hooker (Chapel Hill: University of North Carolina Press, 1953), 96–970. On court day generally, see Charles S. Sydnor, *Gentlemen Freeholders* (Chapel Hill: University

far from the central space where male judges and jurors deliberated. Similarly, legislative sessions were open to "any discreet man," but women do not appear to have frequented the general assemblies' meetings, either before or after the Revolution.[7]

When prospective petitioners of either sex approached the courts and legislatures, they sought the favor of men more powerful than themselves. Deferential appeals to the authority, wisdom, and benevolence of the legislators betokened the real disparity of power between the authors of petitions and their recipients. Some petitioners who emphasized their own vulnerability and dependence may have exaggerated for effect but, as one historian notes, "the rhetoric of humility is a necessary part of the petition as a genre, whether or not humility is felt in fact."[8] Petitioners ranged from obsequious to assertive, but nearly all employed the formulaic declarations of humility and subservience that the genre presupposed.

Although the right to petition thus assumed an inequality between those who submitted petitions and the officials who considered them, eighteenth-century Americans gradually adapted the practice of petitioning to their changing ideas about the relationship between government and its constituents. For one thing, the volume of petitions that the assemblies received grew markedly over the course of the eighteenth century, suggesting that people increasingly looked to colonial and later state authorities to resolve complex issues or to supersede ineffective local governments. More important still, petitions signed by groups of men became common by the closing decades of the colonial era, and this trend became even more pronounced during and after the Revolution. Unlike individual petitions, which normally sought to resolve one person's problems, group petitions aimed to effect policy changes, usually by the enactment of new legislation. Petitions bearing the signatures of large numbers of people demonstrated widespread support for a particular measure and, despite their typically deferential tone, implied that the

---

of North Carolina Press, 1952), 64, 79; and Rhys Isaac, *The Transformation of Virginia, 1740–1790* (Chapel Hill: University of North Carolina Press, 1982), 88–94.

7. Johann David Schoepf, *Travels in the Confederation, 1783–1784*, ed. and trans. Alfred J. Morrison (New York: Bergman, 1968), 63–64; A. G. Roeber, "Authority, Law, and Custom: The Rituals of Court Day in Tidewater Virginia, 1720 to 1750," *WMQ*, 3d ser., 38 (1980): 34, 47–48.

8. Kerber, *Women of the Republic*, 85.

opinions of ordinary men should influence or even control the legislature's deliberations.[9]

The Revolution, which profoundly changed the relationship between government and its constituents, was a watershed in the history of petitioning in America. As white male property owners became conscious of their new status as citizens of a republic, they became both more assertive and less likely to rely exclusively on humble petitions to influence their government. As revolutionary Americans embraced the notion of actual representation—the idea that an individual legislator represented the particular interests of those who elected him and not those of the larger polity—men increasingly used legislative instructions, electoral politics, and other more egalitarian mechanisms to express their views and redress collective grievances.[10] At the same time, many of those who continued to petition the assembly were more demanding than their colonial predecessors. In the formal prefaces with which they introduced their requests, some postrevolutionary republicans rhetorically transformed the "petition" of a subordinate into the "memorial" of a near equal. Occasionally, they invoked libertarian political theories to remind legislators of their accountability to their constituents. Armed with increased expectations of a sympathetic hearing from their democratized legislatures, some even called for an array of economic reforms that would foster equality of opportunity among white men by benefiting small property owners.[11]

Another important development that occurred during the revolutionary years was the entry of growing numbers of women into the public sphere to petition their state assemblies. Affected acutely by the war, which was especially brutal in the southern states, individuals had more reasons than ever before to interact with their government. The states

---

9. Alison G. Olson, "Eighteenth-Century Colonial Legislatures and Their Constituents," *JAH* 79 (1992): 550–57; Richard L. Bushman, *King and People in Provincial Massachusetts* (Chapel Hill: University of North Carolina Press, 1985), 46–47.

10. Bailey, *Popular Influence*, 167–73; Gordon S. Wood, *The Creation of the American Republic, 1776–1787* (Chapel Hill: University of North Carolina Press, 1969), 189–91, 370–72; Edmund S. Morgan, *Inventing the People: The Rise of Popular Sovereignty in England and America* (New York: W. W. Norton, 1988), 213.

11. Ruth Bogin, "Petitioning and the New Moral Economy of Post-Revolutionary America," *WMQ*, 3d ser., 45 (1988): 393–97, 402–20.

paid soldiers' wages and enlistment bounties, provided pensions to their widows, purchased military supplies from civilians, and enacted laws that punished those who refused to swear allegiance to the new revolutionary governments. During and after the Revolution, loyalists petitioned for relief from the penal statutes, while southerners of all political stripes sought to settle their public accounts. When men left their homes as soldiers or as exiles, their wives or widows stepped in to represent their families in their relations with the state regimes. When postrevolutionary governments appeared receptive to reform, wives also petitioned for divorce and for property rights within marriage.

Though it verged on anachronism when employed by free white men, petitioning aptly reflected the subordinate status of women in postrevolutionary America. Petitioning, which assumed a disparity of power between those who requested favor and those who evaluated such requests, was the only formal political activity open to women, who— even if they were unmarried and owned property in their own right— could not vote, hold office, serve on juries, or bear arms in the local militia. Although the laws of some states explicitly recognized white women as "citizens," they could not participate in the activities and rituals that contemporaries identified with citizenship in its most meaningful form. Yet white women were not chattel, and law and custom ideally entitled them to protection and equitable treatment from the men who governed them.[12] Petitioning afforded women a voice with which they could seek the aid and protection of public men while demonstrating their continued deference to male authority.

The language and the logic of women's petitions reflected the political status of their authors, who were neither fully empowered citizens of the republic nor its abject dependents. As petitioners, women demonstrated both the extent and the limits of their political experience and consciousness. On the one hand, the fact that they petitioned at all—and that they did so in increasing numbers—suggests that women in the revolutionary era did not regard themselves as utterly ignorant and ineffectual. Yet women's political consciousness was more individual than

---

12. Southern courts, however, were reluctant to punish men who physically abused their female dependents. See Victoria E. Bynum, *Unruly Women: The Politics of Social and Sexual Control in the Old South* (Chapel Hill: University of North Carolina Press, 1992), 70–72, 77.

collective. Group petitions, which signaled the spread of a majoritarian political culture and rising levels of political sophistication, were comparatively uncommon among women in revolutionary America.

As this brief analysis suggests, the petitions in this volume provide a point of departure for discussing women's political culture in eighteenth-century America. In the southern states at least, women's political culture was more reactive than proactive, more personal than participatory; its public expressions were occasional, not ongoing, as befit an era in which women were neither excluded completely from the public sphere nor allowed full access to it. Although women displayed varying degrees of knowledge of and interest in legal and political matters, every woman who petitioned the legislature claimed membership in a community beyond her household. More than most petitioners, women were subordinate members of the political communities they inhabited, but they expected a fair hearing from their superiors in exchange for their manifest deference.

Besides providing insights into women's political consciousness, the documents in this volume are important as sources of social history. The right to petition, like women's political disabilities, cut across class lines, and women of all social ranks—from affluent white widows to illiterate farmers' wives to enslaved African Americans—solicited the favor of the state legislatures in the decades following American independence. Many of their petitions include extended narratives, designed to persuade the legislators of the petitioner's worthiness and the validity of her claim. For twentieth-century readers such narratives provide rare firsthand accounts of the lives of nonelite southern women before 1800. Some recreate the wartime ordeals of women and their families as well as their attempts to cope with economic and emotional losses once the war was over. As farmers and artisans, taxpayers and participants in partisan warfare, civilians played a crucial role in America's war for independence. These documents examine the civilian history of the Revolution and its aftermath, focusing on women's experiences.

This collection includes petitions that were typical in the stories they told and in their manner of presentation as well as those that were exceptional in form or content. All of the documents selected, however, concern either war-related grievances or issues—such as divorce, married women's property rights, and the manumission of slaves—which became salient at least partly due to the influence of the libertarian ideals of the Revolution.[13] Politically, the petitioners represented in this volume ranged from unrepentant Tories to committed Whigs, but others were apathetic or politically circumspect. These women petitioners included members of some of the region's most prominent families as well as middling folk, propertyless whites, free blacks, and even an occasional slave. Geographically, they represented backcountry settlements, plantation districts, inland towns, and coastal trading communities.

Although this study examines the revolutionary experience of southern women generally, it focuses particularly on those who petitioned the North Carolina and South Carolina assemblies between 1776 and 1800. The documents reproduced here in full come from the Carolinas exclusively, though the interpretive essays that introduce each chapter also draw on women's petitions from the other southern states. Virginia was unique among the four southern states in its relative absence of civil strife, freedom from occupying armies, and paucity of major military engagements between 1776 and the final British offensive that ended at Yorktown in 1781. Consequently, the wartime experiences of Virginia women and the petitions they filed differed significantly from those of their counterparts to the south.[14] Both politically and militarily, Georgia's revolutionary experience was more similar to that of the Carolinas. Many of Georgia's early legislative records are not extant, however, and no petitions have survived from the revolutionary era.[15]

---

13. For overviews of these issues, respectively, see Kerber, *Women of the Republic*, chap. 6; Marylynn Salmon, *Women and the Law of Property in Early America* (Chapel Hill: University of North Carolina Press, 1986), 190–93; David Brion Davis, *The Problem of Slavery in the Age of Revolution, 1770–1823* (Ithaca, N.Y.: Cornell University Press, 1975), 169–84, 196–212.

14. On Virginia, see generally, John E. Selby, *The Revolution in Virginia, 1775–1783* (Williamsburg, Va.: Colonial Williamsburg, 1988).

Virginia women filed nearly half of their 138 war-related petitions before 1780; most of these petitions related to civilian losses during early military engagements in Norfolk and other coastal communities. By contrast, all but nine war-related petitions North Carolina women filed dated to 1780 or later, as did all but one of those presented by women in South Carolina. Between 1776 and 1800, Virginia women presented only 13 petitions for relief from the anti-Tory laws, compared to 15 in North Carolina, 86 in South Carolina, and at least 49 in Georgia.

15. The surviving legislative journals, which cover the years 1780–90, 1796–97, and 1799–1800, give the names of petitioners for each legislative session, and the contents of petitions sometimes can be deduced from the assembly's minutes. On

Drawing primarily on evidence from the Carolinas, this book argues that southern women affected and were affected by the struggle for American independence. Chapters 1 and 2 focus on the personal and financial losses that Whig women and their families sustained as a result of their support for the Revolution. The first, entitled "Families at War," summarizes the history of the war in the southern states and, drawing on newspapers and private correspondence, shows that women were active participants in the American struggle for independence. The second chapter, "The Cost of Liberty," contends that the war's economic legacy lasted well into the 1790s, as civilians continued to seek compensation for property lost or destroyed in wartime and as the widows and orphans of southern soldiers sought back pay, land warrants, and debt relief from their governments.

Chapter 3, "The Loyalist Legacy," explores the wartime experiences of the wives and daughters of Tory exiles and their struggles to preserve their families and their property in the postwar era. Wives of Tories petitioned for their husbands' repatriation or to recover their confiscated estates. In some cases, the confiscation statutes created seemingly interminable legal disputes that involved women in protracted efforts to regain lost property. In the process, many became politically conscious, learning to deal with government officials and procedures and sometimes articulating political expectations and identities distinct from those of their discredited male relatives.

Chapters 4 and 5 examine some of the Revolution's less tangible consequences, focusing on women's changing perceptions of their relationship to government. Chapter 4, entitled "Women, Allegiance, and Citizenship," examines the language of women petitioners, most of whom accepted and internalized their political disabilities, rarely identifying themselves as citizens or claiming to possess a citizen's rights, though some professed allegiance to the Revolution or publicly took pride in their contributions to it. Chapter 5, "The Limits of Revolution," surveys the Revolution's ambiguous legacy in the areas of race and gender relations through the petitions of slaves, free blacks, working women, and wives seeking divorces or separate estates. Previously unthinkable appeals from politically marginal people, these petitions had no colonial

---

Georgia, see Kenneth Coleman, *The American Revolution in Georgia, 1763–1789* (Athens: University of Georgia Press, 1958).

precedent. Revolutionary ideology inspired such people to express their discontent. The limited impact of libertarian ideals on entrenched inequalities of gender and race led the assemblies often to refuse their brave requests.

Both literally and figuratively, the petitions in this volume were products of collaborative efforts. Petitioners benefited from the insights of relatives and friends in composing their appeals, while some employed clerks to render their tales in the appropriate written form. Even women who prepared their petitions without the advice or aid of others were influenced by the cultural context in which they wrote. Petitions, like most other historical documents, tell modern readers as much about society's expectations for their authors as about the authors themselves.[16] These documents offer insights into the gender conventions of eighteenth-century southerners and into the prescribed rules for women's participation in the public sphere. They also tell the stories of varied individuals and suggest the ways in which the Revolution affected their outlooks and lives.

---

16. See the especially pertinent discussion in Natalie Zemon Davis, *Fiction in the Archives: Pardon Tales and Their Tellers in Sixteenth-Century France* (Stanford, Calif.: Stanford University Press, 1987), 4–5, 15–23.

Chapter 1

FAMILIES AT WAR

In September 1776, Anne Terrel of Virginia, wife of a Continental soldier, urged her countrywomen to embrace the hardships that war would
inflict on them and their families. In a letter published in the *Virginia
Gazette*, Terrel admitted her own reluctance to part with "the tenderest
of husbands," but she warned her readers that sacrifices were necessary
to defeat the British, who were "conspiring with our slaves to cut our
throats [and] instigating the savage Indians to fall on our frontiers" and
murder "whole families . . . without regard to age or sex." Left to face such
vicious enemies, families also would suffer as a result of the loss of men's
labor, but Terrel encouraged wives to "support ourselves under the absence of our husbands" and emphasized the crucial contributions that
women, as civilians, might render "so glorious a cause." While they might
not be "well able to help [men] fight," she suggested, women could devote themselves to "another branch of American politics, which comes
more immediately under our province, namely, in frugality and industry."
Women could tend crops, make homespun fabric, and secure the homefront, their patriotism fortifying the courage of their "dear husbands
[who] are nobly struggling in the army for [American] freedom."[1]
     Terrel correctly foresaw women's inevitable participation in a war
that scattered families, destroyed property, and disrupted everyday life,
just as she predicted that their labor and perseverance would be essential both to their families' welfare and to the patriot cause. Whether they
were Whig, Tory, or neutral, southern women affected and were affected
by the War of Independence, despite their civilian status. Mistresses of
plantations, farms, and households produced goods that were essential to
the war effort. Other women took over family businesses that furnished

---

1. *Virginia Gazette* (Dixon and Hunter), 21 Sept. 1776.

provisions to patriot forces. Still others served the military more directly as nurses, cooks, or laundresses—many of whom traveled with the armies—and a few acted as spies.[2] Some, like Anne Terrel, used their pens for partisan purposes. Most tried desperately to preserve their homes and families from wartime devastation and, failing that, sought relief from or compensation for their hardships by petitioning their state assemblies.

In the southern states, the War of Independence had three distinct phases, each of which posed new challenges for civilians in the region. The first, which lasted from late 1775 through 1776, featured early British attempts to muster support among slaves, Indians, and local loyalists, but resulted in a series of patriot victories and the subsequent withdrawal of British forces from the region. The second, which lasted more than two years, was a period of relative peace during which civilians nonetheless suffered hardships born of inflation, high taxes, and the departure of men to fight in the northern states or, in the case of some Tories, to begin their years of exile. During the war's third phase, by contrast, its heaviest fighting occurred in the southern states. From the British invasion of Georgia in late 1778 until Cornwallis's surrender at Yorktown nearly three years later, the region would be the site of some of the Revolution's bloodiest battles.

In 1775, following the April confrontations between Massachusetts militia and British regulars at Lexington and Concord, southern Whigs began to prepare for the possible spread of armed conflict to their region. That spring, patriots in Charleston and Savannah removed the gunpowder from their provincial magazines to prevent its use by troops in the service of their colonial governors. Although Virginia's governor, the earl of Dunmore, frustrated the Whig attempt to seize the contents of the magazine at Williamsburg, by June mounting tensions led him to abandon the town for the safe haven of a British warship. Governors Josiah Martin of North Carolina and William Campbell of South Carolina would likewise leave their posts, taking refuge on nearby naval vessels in the next few months. Sir James Wright, their counterpart in Georgia, would flee Savannah the following February.

---

2. For a general overview of women's activities, see Mary Beth Norton, *Liberty's Daughters: The Revolutionary Experience of American Women, 1750–1800* (Boston: Little, Brown, 1980), chaps. 6–7.

In the coming months, British troops and displaced royal officials challenged the rebellious Whigs, cultivating the support of dissidents, whom they believed to be numerous in the southern colonies. Lord Dunmore's attempts to rally such support produced the war's first significant military engagements outside New England and, more important, raised the specter of race war in the minds of white southerners. In the fall of 1775, Dunmore organized into militia companies Virginia's small community of white loyalists, most of whom were British merchants who resided in and around the port of Norfolk. After a series of raids on Whig-owned plantations in the tidewater area, on 7 November 1775 Dunmore issued a proclamation declaring martial law in the colony and calling on every loyal Virginian to come forward to support the royal cause. Perhaps acting on the initiative of slaves who earlier offered their support in exchange for freedom, Dunmore also promised emancipation to all who fled Whig masters to join the king's forces. Dunmore's proclamation, to which hundreds of slaves responded, set a precedent for British exploitation of racial divisions to further their military objectives. It also alienated many conservative slaveholders, who previously were reluctant to disavow the authority of the king and his representatives in America.[3]

By December 1775, Virginia militia were marching toward Norfolk, Dunmore's headquarters and the center of Tory activity. On 9 December, the patriot militia defeated a combined force of loyalists and British regulars at the Battle of Great Bridge. Following this engagement, troops from Virginia and North Carolina occupied the town of Norfolk, while Dunmore, accompanied by loyalist families who feared the reprisals of the victorious Whigs, fled to the safety of the British ships in Norfolk harbor. Within a few weeks, however, the governor and his companions needed supplies, and the Whig commanders refused them access to the town to get them. Dunmore decided to destroy Norfolk in retaliation, and, on New Year's Day 1776, he ordered the navy to bombard the town and sent some men ashore to burn warehouses and other buildings. Whig militia, in turn, set fire to the homes of Norfolk's leading Tories. Most of

---

3. John E. Selby, *The Revolution in Virginia, 1775–1783* (Williamsburg, Va.: Colonial Williamsburg,1988), 64–68; Sylvia R. Frey, *Water from the Rock: Black Resistance in a Revolutionary Age* (Princeton: Princeton University Press, 1991), 53–61, 78–80; Benjamin Quarles, *The Negro in the American Revolution* (Chapel Hill: University of North Carolina Press, 1961), 19–32.

Norfolk perished in the fires, which lasted three days, while Dunmore and his troops withdrew to nearby Gwynn Island, where they remained until patriot forces dislodged them six months later.[4]

For several days in early January 1776, the inhabitants of coastal Virginia witnessed firsthand the horrors of war. Although elite families could flee to inland plantations to escape the expected violence, most townspeople remained in their homes, having nowhere to go and no horses or carriages to transport them to safety. Those who remained behind risked physical danger as well as the destruction of their homes and other property. On the first day of the British attack, Mary Webley of Norfolk "while suckling her Child . . . had her Leg Broken by a Cannon Ball from the Liverpool Man of War." She and her family lost their house and "all their Effects" during the bombardment. Sarah Hutchings, who lived outside of town, saw her husband captured and her house destroyed in the "general conflagration." Others reported that soldiers commandeered food, supplies, and buildings, often damaging the property of civilians.[5]

During and after the siege of coastal Virginia, the Whig militia depended on civilians to supply them with food and lodging and they relied on women, in particular, to tend sick or wounded soldiers. A Virginia militia captain brought one of his men to the home of Margaret Rawlings, who nursed the soldier for sixteen days before he recovered from "the Flux." Maria Carter Armistead boarded prisoners at her house in Williamsburg, where one officer died under her care. Other women later would take up nursing on a more formal basis. As early as July 1776, the newly established Continental Hospital in Williamsburg solicited "some Nurses to attend the sick." Poorly paid, overworked, and usually inexperienced, women served as nurses throughout the war in the hospitals that Congress created to care for diseased and wounded soldiers.[6]

---

4. Selby, *Revolution in Virginia*, 69–74, 80–84, 124–26; Merrill Jensen, *The Founding of a Nation: The History of the American Revolution, 1763–1776* (New York: Oxford University Press, 1968), 643–45.

5. Petition of Mary Webley, 1776, LP, Norfolk City, Vi-Ar; Petition of Sarah Hutchings, 1786, LP, Norfolk Co., Vi-Ar.

6. Petition of Margaret Rawlings, 1 Dec. 1777, LP, Misc., Vi-Ar; E[lizabeth] Feilde to Maria Carter Armistead, 7 Feb. 1776, Armistead-Cocke Papers, Swem Library, Vi-W; Linda K. Kerber, *Women of the Republic: Intellect and Ideology in Revolutionary America* (Chapel Hill: University of North Carolina Press, 1980), 58–61; Holly A. Mayer, *Belonging to the Army: Camp Followers and Community during the American Revolution* (Columbia: University of South Carolina Press, 1996), 221–23.

Norfolk was the most destructive engagement of the war's opening phase, but early confrontations between Whig patriots and their foes also occurred in other southern locales, where Whig forces generally prevailed, as they had in coastal Virginia. In South Carolina, Whig attempts to subdue resistance in the backcountry culminated in the Snow Campaign of December 1775, when patriot militia defeated a Tory force and captured its leaders.[7] In North Carolina, Governor Josiah Martin gathered a force of some sixteen hundred loyalists, only to see them routed by a much smaller party of Whig militia on 27 February 1776 at Moore's Creek Bridge near Wilmington.[8] A week later, from aboard a nearby warship, British troops launched an ill-fated attempt to reclaim Savannah, Georgia's colonial capital.[9]

In June 1776, with the Whig provisional governments increasingly secure and Congress inching toward a formal declaration of independence, the British launched their most ambitious early offensive against the southern colonies, which they still regarded as potential hotbeds of loyalist sentiment. After destroying a pro-British encampment of runaway slaves on Sullivan's Island in December 1775, South Carolina's lowcountry Whigs began fortifying the island, which stood at the entrance to Charleston harbor. By May, the British decided to attack the nearly completed fort in an attempt to capture Charleston, the largest city and busiest port in the southern colonies. The British fleet, carrying some twenty-five hundred troops, reached Charleston harbor in early June. For weeks both sides prepared for the expected battle, which began on 28 June, when the British naval commander, Sir Peter Parker, ordered his fleet to bombard the fort on Sullivan's Island. After nearly eleven hours of shelling, however, both the fort and the city remained in the hands of their Whig defenders.[10]

The successful defense of Charleston ended the fighting in the coastal areas, but southern Whigs continued their efforts to secure the allegiance of the backcountry, an area whose residents included both Indians who resented the colonists' encroachment on their lands and many

---

7. Lambert, *S.C. Loyalists*, 35–46.

8. DeMond, *Loyalists in N.C.*, 88–96.

9. Kenneth Coleman, *The American Revolution in Georgia, 1763–1789* (Athens: University of Georgia Press, 1958), 68–70.

10. McCrady, *S.C. in the Revolution*, 1:137–46, 153–62; Frey, *Water from the Rock*, 64–65.

white settlers who were either hostile or indifferent to the revolutionary cause.[11] The war's first phase ended in the backcountry in late 1776, when Whig militia from Virginia and the Carolinas annihilated the Cherokee Indians, who in July had initiated an all-out war against the white frontier settlements. The Cherokees acted on their own, without British support or encouragement, but they were increasingly aided by backcountry loyalists, who used the opportunity to attack their Whig neighbors. Tory involvement in the Cherokee war discredited the loyalists in the eyes of many backcountry people, who believed that the British encouraged the Indians to terrorize their settlements. On the other hand, the Whigs' swift and decisive suppression of the Cherokees enhanced the credibility of their new state governments, which appeared both willing and able to restore order in the backcountry and protect its white inhabitants.[12]

The war's first phase, which ended with the capitulation of the Cherokees in December 1776, gave civilians a small sampling of the hardships they would suffer during the coming years. Families saw their homes demolished by British bombs or damaged by soldiers who appropriated them for use as barracks. Whig troops who lodged for seven months in the Norfolk County, Virginia, home of Charles and Lydia Mayle damaged the house and other property, while Elizabeth Elliott, a Norfolk County widow, blamed the destruction of her warehouse on the "negligence" of the militia quartered in it. Henry Laurens, a prominent South Carolina Whig, found it "melancholy to see the abuse of so many good houses in [Charleston], which are now made barracks for the country militia," who had come to defend the city from the anticipated British attack. Laurens sadly reported that the soldiers "strip the paper-hangings, chop wood upon parlour floors, and do a thousand such improper acts."[13]

---

11. A. Roger Ekirch, "Whig Authority and Public Order in Backcountry North Carolina, 1776–1783," in *An Uncivil War: The Southern Backcountry during the American Revolution*, ed. Ronald Hoffman et al. (Charlottesville: University Press of Virginia, 1985), 108–13; Jeffrey J. Crow, "Liberty Men and Loyalists: Disorder and Disaffection in the North Carolina Backcountry," in ibid., 127–28; Ronald Hoffman, "The 'Disaffected' in the Revolutionary South," in *The American Revolution: Exploration in the History of American Radicalism*, ed. Alfred F. Young (DeKalb: Northern Illinois University Press, 1976), 273–316.

12. Rachel N. Klein, *Unification of a Slave State: The Rise of the Planter Class in the South Carolina Backcountry, 1760–1808* (Chapel Hill: University of North Carolina Press, 1990), 91–95; James H. O'Donnell III, *Southern Indians in the American Revolution* (Knoxville: University of Tennessee Press, 1973), 34–53.

13. Henry Laurens to Martha Laurens, 29 Feb. 1776, in *The Papers of Henry Lau-*

Casualties, though light in comparison to those of later years, often devastated the families who suffered them. In 1775, John and Anne Armstrong and their children had moved to a five hundred–acre farm on the South Carolina frontier. The following year, the Cherokees attacked their settlement, killing John, destroying their farm, and leaving Anne the sole provider for her large family (Doc. 13). While Anne Armstrong could try to rebuild her plundered homestead, other widows and their families were left virtually indigent. Margaret Irvine was the mother of four young children "& Pregnent with the fifth" when her husband died "much in Debted" a few months after his enlistment.[14] When Robert Black became one of only twelve patriots to die during the defense of Charleston, his wife, Elizabeth, found herself and her five children destitute and with no means of subsistence (Doc. 1). As early as 1776, widows like Black and Irvine were petitioning their state legislatures for relief, just as many more would do in the years that followed.

The war's opening phase also revealed the extent to which the Revolution would divide southerners into Whigs and Tories, beginning a process of dislocation and dispossession among the latter which in some cases would disrupt their lives for decades. From 1775 through 1777, the Whig governments in every state gradually implemented a series of resolutions and statutes that defined loyalism as a crime that merited specific punishments. All states required suspected Tories to swear an oath declaring their allegiance to the state and abjuring royal authority, and most provided for the imprisonment or execution of those who actively aided the Crown or opposed the new revolutionary governments. The states also imposed economic penalties on those who refused to take the oath of allegiance. Virginia and North Carolina confiscated the estates of non-jurors, while Georgia loyalists forfeited one-half of their property to the state. South Carolina banished those who eschewed the oath but allowed them to sell off their assets and take the proceeds into exile after satisfying their creditors. By 1778, all four southern states had formally banished their most conspicuous Tory residents, many of whom had taken up arms for the king during the war's early engagements.[15]

---

rens, ed. George C. Rogers Jr. et al. (Columbia: University of South Carolina Press, 1968–), 11:129–32; Petition of Elizabeth Elliott, 1777, LP, Norfolk Co., Vi-Ar; Petition of Lydia Mayle, 1777, ibid.

14. Petition of Margaret Irvine, 10 Nov. 1777, LP, York Co., Vi-Ar.

15. On anti-Tory legislation in the southern states, see Selby, *Revolution in Virginia,* 75–76, 149–50, 155–56, 234–35; DeMond, *Loyalists in N.C.,* 153–56; Lam-

Even the earliest attempts to penalize Tory opponents of the Revolution separated families for long periods and, in some cases, forever. Thomas Rutherfurd, a North Carolina Tory, was imprisoned in Philadelphia following his capture at Moore's Creek Bridge in February 1776. He remained there until 1780, when he died trying to return to his wife, Jean, in North Carolina. Tory Samuel Williams and his four sons fled North Carolina after the Battle of Moore's Creek Bridge, going first to Georgia and then to East Florida, while Williams's wife and seven remaining children resettled in Savannah. The family never reunited even after the war was over. Samuel Williams was dead by 1787, and there is no evidence about the postwar residence of his widow and their daughters. Of the Williamses' surviving sons, all of whom fought for the British, one moved to Canada, another to London, and two settled in the Bahamas.[16]

Others narrowly escaped the sad fates of the Williams and Rutherfurd families. Mary Lewellin nearly lost her husband, who was tried and convicted under North Carolina's Treason Act in 1777. John Lewellin spent several months in an Edenton jail awaiting an execution that never happened, despite the assembly's refusal to grant him formal clemency (Doc. 2). Widower John Champneys, a Charleston merchant, almost lost two families by refusing to swear allegiance to the Revolution. In the custody of state authorities when his only child died in the fall of 1776, Champneys left for England as an exile a few months later. In 1780, he returned to Charleston and remarried during the British occupation of the city.[17] His second wife gave birth to a child, but the British surrender soon forced him into exile again, separated from his wife and child, at least for the time being (Doc. 15).

Early attempts to enforce the Tory laws also revealed potential difficulties in distinguishing Tories from Whigs and the extent to which punitive laws might ensnare those who may have been innocent of counterrevolutionary activities. Thomas Gilchrist of Halifax County, North Carolina, was not a Tory, though he refused to swear allegiance to the

bert, *S.C. Loyalists*, 59–63; Heard Robertson, ed., "Georgia's Banishment and Expulsion Act of September 16, 1777," *GHQ* 55 (1971): 274–82.

16. Petition of Jean Rutherfurd, 5 May 1782, GASR, Apr.–May 1782, Nc-Ar; Carole Watterson Troxler, *The Loyalist Experience in North Carolina* (Raleigh: North Carolina Division of Archives and History, 1976), 38.

17. Lambert, *S.C. Loyalists*, 59–60, 188, 256.

state in hopes of reclaiming property that a Tory business associate carried off to British Bermuda. Gilchrist believed that renouncing his allegiance to the Crown would prejudice the Bermuda authorities against him, but his decision to go to Bermuda to plead his case and his refusal to take the patriot oath led officials in North Carolina to banish him from the state and confiscate the portion of his estate that was within its borders. Gilchrist relied on his wife, who remained in Halifax, to explain his predicament to North Carolina's revolutionary government (Doc. 3).

With many men in the military or in exile, Whig and Tory women alike struggled to protect their families and their property from wartime depredations. During the war's second phase, though partisan raids and skirmishes occasionally endangered southern women and their families, the hardships most endured were primarily economic.[18] British naval blockades, which disrupted trade, gave rise to scarcities of cloth and other imported articles. In eastern North Carolina, wartime shortages led many families to set up looms in their houses, where women, according to one observer, made "cotton and woolen clothes to dress [their] entire family." Women in rural South Carolina used thorns for pins, while one Charleston woman reported that she "used to darn my stockings with the ravellings of another, and . . . flossed out our old Silk Gowns to spin together with Cotton to knit our gloves." Virginian Sarah Nourse spent the war years patching her family's old clothes, receiving a long-awaited parcel of new goods from Europe only after the British surrender. Many women must have shared her preoccupation with mending, aware that cloth would be hard to come by until peace made possible the resumption of transatlantic commerce.[19]

---

18. For some examples of military encounters involving southern civilians during this period, see Petition of William Gipson, 1832, in *The Revolution Remembered: Eyewitness Accounts of the War of Independence,* ed. John C. Dann (Chicago: University of Chicago Press, 1980), 187, 189; Petition of Samuel Riggs, 1833, in ibid., 306; DeMond, *Loyalists in N.C.,* 102–7; O'Donnell, *Southern Indians,* 76–79; Coleman, *American Revolution in Georgia,* 100–109.

19. John S. Ezell, ed., *The New Democracy in America: Travels of Francisco de Miranda in the United States, 1783–1784* (Norman: University of Oklahoma Press, 1963), 8; Louisa Susannah Wells, *The Journal of a Voyage from Charlestown to London* (New York: New York Times and Arno Press, 1968), 2; Sarah Fouace Nourse diary, 1781–83, Nourse Family Papers, Vi-U, esp. 29, 41.

On the southern wartime economy, in general, see Selby, *Revolution in Virginia,*

Southern patriots appealed to women to work in their homes and on their farms to produce commodities that could aid the American cause. In the fall of 1776, the *Virginia Gazette* informed its readers that women in Chester County, Pennsylvania, were "determined to put in the crop themselves" should their "husbands, brothers, and lovers, be detained abroad in the defence of the liberties of these states" and deemed the Pennsylvanians a "very laudable example . . . highly worthy of imitation" by the women of Virginia. A year later, the proprietors of a new paper mill near Hillsborough, North Carolina, called on the women of their state to save rags, fabric scraps, and "old Handkerchief[s], no longer fit to cover their snowy Breasts" to be used as raw materials for this "necessary Manufacture."[20]

By the late 1770s, southern families also suffered the ill effects of inflation, which soared as state governments issued paper money to finance the war, while calling on civilians to pay increasingly higher taxes. Wartime taxes and inflation were especially onerous for soldiers' families, whose economic fortunes often declined severely when men left home for military service. At best such families exchanged the labor of their men for soldiers' wages paid in nearly worthless paper currency. At worst soldiers neither received their pay nor survived their enlistment to return to their families.[21] Aware of the hardships their families suffered, soldiers occasionally protested their lack of wages, even to the point of mutiny (Doc. 5). On the homefront some soldiers' wives found themselves unable to pay their taxes (Doc. 7), while the families of men who died in service tried desperately to reclaim their arrears in pay and perhaps secure additional relief from their state or local governments (Doc. 4).

Wartime inflation posed special problems for widows and orphans who lived on fixed incomes from estates or government pensions. When Elizabeth Crowley's husband died fighting the western Indians in 1774,

---

175–83, 229–33; Nadelhaft, *Disorders of War,* 49–50; Walsh, *Charleston's Sons of Liberty,* 77–81.

20. *Virginia Gazette* (Purdie), 6 Sept. 1776; *North Carolina Gazette,* 14 Nov. 1777.

21. On the payment and nonpayment of soldiers' wages, see Charles S. Royster, *A Revolutionary People at War: The Continental Army and the American Character, 1775–1783* (Chapel Hill: University of North Carolina Press, 1979), 295–308; James Kirby Martin, ed., *Ordinary Courage: The Revolutionary War Adventures of Joseph Plumb Martin* (St. James, N.Y.: Brandywine Press, 1993), 131, 159–64.

Virginia's House of Burgesses awarded her a pension of ten pounds "towards the Releif of her Self and her numerous Family of small Children." During the Revolution, however, Crowley found that the "extraordinary and unexpected Depreciation of the Money" rendered this allowance "quite inadequate to that benevolent and charitable Purpose."[22] At least one North Carolina widow protested that inflation would diminish the inheritance of her fatherless children by enabling debtors to her late husband's estate to repay what they owed in depreciated paper money (Doc. 6). A group of men in Brunswick County, Virginia, echoed her concern, informing their legislators that orphans who "had been comfortably provided for by their Deceased Parents, are now reduced to that State of Indigence and Poverty as to depend solely . . . on the charitable Assistance of their Friends and Relations."[23]

As the war entered its final phase, beginning with the fall of Savannah in December 1778, economic considerations became secondary for many southerners, who now witnessed a full-scale British invasion of their region. Savannah suffered destruction, first from the British assault and then from an abortive Franco-American attempt to regain the Georgia capital. When the bombing was over, the British retained Savannah, and the town "offered a desolate view," its streets "cut into deep holes by the shells, and the houses were riddled by the rain of cannon balls," according to one observer. Meanwhile, British forces, supported by some Indians and by thousands of runaway slaves, entered Georgia's interior and reinstated the state's old royal government.[24]

Hoping to repeat their success in South Carolina, in early 1780 British detachments from Georgia, New York, and Virginia converged outside of Charleston, where land and naval forces surrounded the city to trap Gen. Benjamin Lincoln and his army of some six thousand Continentals and militia. Under pressure from Charleston's civilian leaders to defend the city, Lincoln's forces fought for six weeks before surrendering.

---

22. Petition of Elizabeth Crowley, 23 Nov. 1780, LP, Henry Co., Vi-Ar.

23. Petition of Sundry Inhabitants of the County of Brunswick, 11 Nov. 1780, LP, Brunswick Co., Vi-Ar.

24. Coleman, *American Revolution in Georgia,* 120–27; Elizabeth Lichtenstein Johnston, *Recollections of a Georgia Loyalist* (New York and London: M. F. Mansfield and Company, 1901), 58–60, 63. On African-American participation in the war in Georgia, see Frey, *Water from the Rock,* 86–107.

On 9 May, the British initiated a massive bombardment, and the people of Charleston experienced a "dreadful night" of "cannon-balls whizzing and shells hissing continually . . . ammunition chests and temporary magazines blowing up; great guns bursting, and wounded men groaning along the lines." After the shelling, Lincoln surrendered both his army and the city it had defended, and every white adult man in Charleston became a British prisoner. Gen. Henry Clinton, the British commander, installed a military government in Charleston and then dispatched troops under Lord Charles Cornwallis to secure the interior of South Carolina.[25]

Although British attempts to subdue the Carolinas began auspiciously with the occupation of Charleston and Cornwallis's victory at Camden a few months later, in the coming months the fortunes of the British regulars and their Tory allies declined precipitously. Gen. Nathanael Greene, who assumed command of the American forces in the southern theater in December 1780, led Cornwallis's army on an arduous trek through the Carolinas before engaging them in a costly battle at Guilford Court House, North Carolina, in March 1781. Cornwallis retreated to Wilmington before marching northward into Virginia, where, in the war's last major offensive, American and French forces eventually trapped him on Yorktown's peninsula. Meanwhile, Whig and Tory militia fought a series of large and small engagements in the Carolina backcountry, where in late 1780 and early 1781 Whig guerilla bands won important victories at Kings Mountain and Cowpens, respectively. Civilians were particularly vulnerable to violence in the backcountry, where Tory and Whig militia waged what amounted to a brutal civil war.[26]

Once the British invaded the southern states, Whig leaders called on the white men of the region to enlist in the military to protect their homes and families. Seeking recruits to fight in Georgia to avert the enemy's advance into South Carolina in 1779, one Carolinian asked his countrymen, "where will we find secure retreats for our wives, our children, our negroes, and our moveable property" in the event of a British invasion? An-

25. Robert Middlekauff, *The Glorious Cause: The American Revolution, 1763–1789* (New York: Oxford University Press, 1982), 438–49; and Pancake, *Destructive War*, chap. 4. For a contemporary account of the siege of Charleston, see William Moultrie, *Memoirs of the American Revolution*, 2 vols. (New York: David Longworth, 1902), 2:65–92.

26. Pancake, *Destructive War*, chaps. 5–8.

other South Carolinian invoked "the awful voice of your Country—with the supplicating Voice of a Mother, Wife, Child, or Sister" to inspire patriotic men to answer the call to arms.[27]

In fact, men could not shield their families from the war and its consequences, particularly during its final and most destructive phase. Civilians lost livestock, crops, and sometimes their homes to armies who commandeered property, often without regard for the politics of its owners (Docs. 18, 20). Perhaps most unsettling for white southerners, however, was loss of thousands of slaves who, though their owners preferred to believe they were captured by the British, more commonly seized their freedom by joining the king's forces as they traversed the region. Other enslaved people emancipated themselves when their owners fled and left them behind in their haste to escape the approaching enemy.[28]

Mobility, however, was not always a matter of choice for African Americans. Troops raided plantations belonging to their foes, capturing slaves, whom they compelled to work for the army in menial occupations. American officers also distributed captured slaves as bounties among their poorly paid troops (Doc. 9). Soldiers from many states participated in the southern campaign, and those who received slaves as bounties generally put them to work on their own farms and plantations. Consequently, such transactions often destroyed slave families and communities by uprooting black captives, who found themselves forcibly removed by their new masters from their prerevolutionary homes (Doc. 19).

White southerners rarely suffered the brutal and purposeful disruptions of family life which were commonplace among African Americans, but military engagements and loyalty oaths, like the anti-Tory laws enacted earlier, increased both mobility and mortality among white families and sometimes scattered their members. Take, for instance, the case of the Sarah Jones, whose family included several prominent Georgia Whigs. When the British captured Savannah, they took Jones's husband prisoner, and he remained in custody until the war was over. The Joneses' eldest son died during the siege of Savannah, and two of Sarah's brothers, who were also soldiers, perished shortly thereafter (Doc. 11). Like many Georgia Whigs who sought refuge in South Carolina, Sarah Jones,

27. *State Gazette of South Carolina*, 20 Jan. 1779, 24 Mar. 1779.
28. Frey, *Water from the Rock*, 85–89, 113–19, 156–93; Mary Beth Norton, *Liberty's Daughter's*, 209–12.

her daughter and son-in-law, Sarah and John Glen, and their children, fled to Charleston, where they remained during the British occupation (Doc. 10). In 1782, John Glen was among those banished from South Carolina as a result of his capitulation to British rule, and he had been among those previously banished from Georgia for his unwillingness to swear allegiance to the restored royal government. Only in 1784 did the South Carolina legislature rescind Glen's sentence, thus enabling all the surviving members of Sarah Jones's circle to resume their lives in Georgia, where Sarah Glen already was petitioning for restitution for property her family lost there during the war.[29]

The 1778 exodus of Georgia Whigs like the Glens and the Joneses foreshadowed the wartime perambulations of others in the region. When the British attacked Charleston, some of that city's more affluent Whigs withdrew to their plantations upriver, just as Whigs in North Carolina and Virginia later would move inland in hopes of escaping the advancing enemy. Refugees from North Carolina's Cape Fear region flocked to New Bern, the colonial capital, and to other smaller communities, while residents of tidewater Virginia moved inland the following year in anticipation of what would be the war's final offensive. In January 1781, St. George and Frances Tucker and their newborn child left Williamsburg for Matoax, their plantation near Petersburg. Two months later, when St. George returned to his military post, Frances made her way to another family plantation some sixty miles distant. Frances Tucker and her infant spent the next six months at various family estates, journeying as far west as Roanoke. That same year the Amblers of Yorktown fled first to Richmond and then to rural Louisa County, an isolated spot that young Betsey Ambler "def[ied] the British or even the d[e]vel himself to find."[30]

---

29. *Rev. Recs. of Ga.*, 3:549. The petition Glen filed in Georgia in February 1784 is not extant. The legislative record mentions this petition without describing its contents.

30. Caroline Gilman, ed., *Letters of Eliza Wilkinson, during the Invasion and Possession of Charleston, SC, by the British in the Revolutionary War* (1839; reprint, New York: New York Times and Arno Press, 1969), 13–17; Alonzo Thomas Dill, *Governor Tryon and His Palace* (Chapel Hill: University of North Carolina Press, 1955), 204–5; Selby, *Revolution in Virginia*, 204–8, 221–23; Frances Bland Randolph Tucker to St. George Tucker, 2 Mar., 9 June, 7 July, 14 July, 7 Sept. 1781, Tucker-Coleman Papers, Vi-W; Elizabeth Ambler to Mildred Smith [1781], Elizabeth Jacquelin Ambler Papers, Vi-WC.

Wartime migrations made food and lodging scarce in some southern communities. When James Iredell stayed in New Bern in 1781, he spent the "monstrous" sum £160 a day for his room and board as a result of inflation and overcrowding. When his sister-in-law, Jean Johnson Blair, moved her extended family from Edenton to the inland town of Windsor, she had to squeeze twenty white people and several slaves into a "very indifferent" house. In Windsor, Blair was responsible for "a large family" who had "not anything to eat but salt meat and hoe cake and no convenience to dress them." In Virginia, the members of the Ambler family settled for a "frugal supper of Bonny Clauber honey."[31]

The wartime odysseys of some southern women took them to distant and unfamiliar places. In the war's early years, Tory families had fled to England or the British West Indies or to occupied New York City, which, from 1776 on, was the largest community of loyalist refugees in America.[32] Whig women also left their homes to reunite with captured loved ones or to escape hostile armies after the British invasion. Ann Fullerton spent five years trying to secure the release of her surgeon husband, taken prisoner in New York in 1776, only to have him die when his release was pending. Mary Sansum's search for her husband, whom the British captured at Camden, took her on a perilous journey north to Philadelphia in 1781 (Doc. 16). Mary Cochran, whose husband, Robert, spent nearly a year in a British prison in Florida after the fall of Charleston, also went to Philadelphia to await the exchange of prisoners that would enable him to rejoin his family in South Carolina.[33]

Whether they remained at home or sought safety elsewhere, civilians risked hazardous encounters with the soldiers who roamed the region. Eliza Wilkinson and her sisters-in-law left Charleston when the British invasion seemed imminent, hoping to take refuge at a nearby plantation. Shortly after their arrival, however, British troops stormed the plantation

---

31. Dill, *Governor Tryon and His Palace,* 204–5; Jean Johnson Blair to Hannah Johnson Iredell, 10 May, 19 May, 24 May 1781, Charles Johnson Collection, Nc-Ar; Jean Johnson Blair to James Iredell, 11 May, 15 May 1781, ibid.; Elizabeth Ambler to Mildred Smith [1781], Elizabeth Jacquelin Ambler Papers, Vi-WC.

32. Mary Beth Norton, *The British-Americans: The Loyalist Exiles in England, 1774–1789* (Boston: Little, Brown, 1972), 32–34; Middlekauff, *Glorious Cause,* 544–46.

33. Petition of Ann [Fullerton] McKnight, 5 Dec. 1800, LP, Misc., Vi-Ar; Mary Cochran to Charles Burnham Cochran, 27 Mar. 1781, 16 July 1782, Cochran Family Papers, Sc-Hi.

house, plundered its contents, and insulted Wilkinson and the others. The soldiers returned the following day, taking more household goods, along with clothes, jewelry, and shoe buckles belonging to its inmates. The women also weathered the visits of Tory bandits and American soldiers before abandoning the house for a safer location.[34]

Widow Mary Willing Byrd, who spent the war years with her eight children at Westover plantation in tidewater Virginia, tried to offend neither Whigs nor Tories, only to be mistreated by soldiers on both sides. In February 1781, American troops, who suspected Byrd of aiding the British, came to her house before daybreak, awakened her and her daughters, and "made prisoners of [the] whole family." Byrd complained of "the *savage* treatment" inflicted on her family by the soldiers, who entered her house with their swords drawn but apparently did not damage the house or injure its inhabitants. A few months later, when the invading British forces took up residence at Westover, Byrd was less fortunate. When these troops departed, forty-nine slaves and several horses left with them.[35]

Other civilians suffered violence and humiliation at the hands of the British and Tory partisans. During a brief attack on southeastern Virginia in May 1779, four British soldiers plundered the Stragn residence in Nansemond County, kidnapping three "young Ladies," whom they forced to board their nearby ships. When Cornwallis arrived in Duplin County in eastern North Carolina in April 1781, his army seized slaves and crops and forced local women "to deliver them the Rings off their fingers and the Buckles out of their Shoes." At several houses Cornwallis's men "Ramsacked every Chest & Trunk, took away all the Beding etc. all the appeareal even the Baby Cloathes." They also "Choaked" and intimidated the children they encountered "in order to make them confess if their Father had not hid his money and to tell where it was."[36]

Terror and destruction similarly accompanied the British invasion of South Carolina. "Windows, china-ware, looking-glasses and pictures, were dashed to pieces. Not only the larger domestic animals were cruelly and wantonly shot down, but . . . nothing within their reach, however

34. Gilman, ed., *Letters of Eliza Wilkinson*, 27–67.

35. "The Affair of Westover," in *The Papers of Thomas Jefferson*, ed. Julian P. Boyd et al. (Princeton: Princeton University Press, 1950–), 5:671–705.

36. *Virginia Gazette* (Dixon and Nicolson), 15 May 1779, William Dickson to Robert Dickson, 30 Nov. 1784, William Dickson Papers, Nc-Ar.

small and insignificant, was suffered to live," one South Carolinian later recalled, asserting that "the destructions and depredations committed by the British were so enormous, that . . . they who live at a distance would scarce believe what could be attested by hundreds of eyewitnesses."[37]

The most violent confrontations between soldiers and civilians occurred in the backcountry, where Whigs persecuted local Tories during the war's first phase and Tories got their revenge later when the British returned to the region. In the war's final phase, Whig militia continued to harass their Tory neighbors, as the two sides engaged in a brutal partisan war. But scholars and contemporaries agree that the Whigs were less ruthless than their opponents, whose cruelty alienated even many backcountry people who previously had been hostile or indifferent to the revolutionary cause.[38]

After the British victories at Savannah and Charleston, Tories and British regulars terrorized the backcountry's civilian population, murdering, plundering, taking prisoners, and causing chaos in many communities (Doc. 14). Tory marauders turned families out of their homes in winter, leaving them without food and shelter. As South Carolina's governor informed his state's delegates to the Continental Congress in 1780, loyalist militia, under the command of Lt. Col. Banastre Tarleton, "hanged many of our people . . . [and] they have also burnt a prodigious number of houses, and turned a vast many women, formerly of affluent and easy fortunes, with their children, almost naked into the woods." Worse still, Tory militia tortured the families of their Whig counterparts to obtain information and forced local Whigs to witness the summary execution of their relatives and neighbors. In the backcountry, where guerilla warfare predominated, civilians also sometimes unexpectedly found themselves in the middle of armed confrontations. One North Carolina woman graciously agreed to share her meager stock of food with some hungry American soldiers, only to have her house become the site of a minor skirmish. The enemy approached the house, and the battle

---

37. David Ramsay, *The History of the Revolution in South Carolina*, 2 vols. (Trenton, N.J.: Isaac Collins, 1785), 2:34.

38. Pancake, *Destructive War*, chap. 5; Klein, *Unification of a Slave State*, 95–104; Nadelhaft, *Disorders of War*, 55–68; Crow, "Liberty Men and Loyalists," 139–45; Ekirch, "Whig Authority and Public Order," 107–16; Robert M. Weir, "'The Violent Spirit,' the Reestablishment of Order, and the Continuity of Leadership in Post-Revolutionary South Carolina," in Hoffman et al., eds., *Uncivil War*, 72–77.

ensued, one Whig militiaman later recalled, "while the woman was frying our hominy."[39]

Stories of Tory atrocities made their way eastward, where they evoked fear and outrage among expectant Whigs. Jean Blair heard that British troops at Hillsborough broke into the homes of civilians, where they "tied" parents and forced them to watch as they "abused" their daughters. Another resident of eastern North Carolina learned that bands of robbers accompanied Tarleton's army, plundering the houses and farms of the "Distressed Inhabitants" of the region.[40]

In the backcountry, perhaps more than anywhere else, women were among the perpetrators, as well as the victims, of wartime violence. According to some reports, women were prominent in the ranks of Tory robbers, riding "the best Horses and Side Saddles, and Drest in the finest and best cloaths that could be taken from the inhabitants as the [British] army marched through the country." Conversely, one South Carolinian observed that the Whig women of his state "talk as familiarly of sheding blood & destroying the Tories as the men do." Women who accompanied the army of Gen. Nathanael Greene may have joined the soldiers in burning Tory houses near Gum Swamp, South Carolina. The legendary Nancy Hart of Wilkes County, Georgia, shot one Tory, wounded another, and held their three associates at bay in her house until some Whig men arrived to hang the intruders. Another Whig woman heroically assisted her son-in-law in fighting off a party of 150 Tories who attempted to destroy a cache of ammunition at Ninety-Six, South Carolina.[41]

The final years of the War of Independence were a time of unprecedented danger and dislocation for southern women and their families. Death, the most obvious consequence of any war, weighed heavily on many families, some of whom were especially unfortunate in their losses. By 1780, when her younger son returned from Georgia with "but little hopes of his Life," Virginian Dorothy Long already had lost her husband

---

39. Moultrie, *Memoirs*, 2:239; Petition of John Taylor, 1832, in Dann, ed., *Revolution Remembered*, 208–9.

40. Jean Johnson Blair to Hannah Johnson Iredell, 10 May 1781, Charles Johnson Collection, Nc-Ar; William Dickson to Robert Dickson, 30 Nov. 1784, William Dickson Papers, Nc-Ar.

41. William Dickson to Robert Dickson, 30 Nov. 1784, William Dickson Papers, Nc-Ar; Aedanus Burke to Arthur Middleton, 25 Jan. 1782, quoted in Nadelhaft, *Disorders of War*, 75; Middlekauff, *Glorious Cause*, 539; "Hart, Nancy," in *NAW*,

and elder son "in the Service of their Contary." The war deprived Mary
Ohara of a husband and two sons, all of whom died in battle, leaving her
with two small children and "nothing . . . to support [them] on." Mary
Mullen's husband was "Killed in the servis of his Cuntry in the Battle at
Stonow," while her eldest son, "the support of the Family," returned from
action badly wounded and unable to walk without crutches. At least one
South Carolina woman lost two successive husbands in the war, as did
Rebeckah Nicholls of Georgia. After the death of her first husband, a
Whig militiaman, Rebeckah married the Tory Nicholls, who was "Kill'd
by the Liberty People" shortly thereafter.[42]

The trials of war brought emotional and economic hardship to southerners of all social ranks. John Spevis, a poor soldier from North Carolina
whose knee was shattered by a musket ball in battle, worried that his injury rendered him "unable by any means to support his wife & Child."[43]
He, like the widows of poor soldiers, sought a government pension for
his subsistence (Docs. 8, 12, 17). At a much higher social level, Frances
Seayers, the wife of a "gentleman" who rose to the rank of lieutenant
colonel in the Virginia militia, claimed to be "the most disconsolate and
almost the most indigent of widows" after he fell in battle. The death of
John Seayers deprived his family of the "very comfortable subsistence"
he had earned and left his widow unable to fulfill "his benevolent and
truly Paternal designs" for educating their sons. Frances Seayers declared
that John's heroic death "was as fatal to his family, as it was Glorious to
himself."[44] Her observation reflected a combination of pride and regret
that many of her contemporaries must have shared as they began to rebuild their troubled lives.

In the coming decades, many historians and Fourth of July orators
would glorify the military triumphs of the War of Independence, equating patriotism with battlefield exploits and ignoring civilians' participation in the Revolution and the sacrifices that many had made on behalf of

2:150–51; Petition of Josiah Culbertson, 1832, in Dann, ed., *Revolution Remembered*, 175–76.

42. Petition of Dorothy Long, 10 Nov. 1780, LP, Misc., Vi-Ar; Petition of Mary
Ohara, 2 Dec. 1780, ibid.; Petition of Mary Mullen, 16 Apr. 1782, GASR, Apr.–
May 1782, Nc-Ar; *S.C. House Journals, 1783–1784*, 484; *Rev. Recs. of Ga.*, 3:209.

43. Petition of John Spevis, 24 Apr. 1782, GASR, Apr.–May 1782, Nc-Ar.

44. Petitions of Frances Seayers, 1779, 17 Dec. 1799, LP, Misc., Vi-Ar.

the patriot cause.[45] A few, however, more truthfully remembered the Revolution as an event that affected and was affected by Americans from every walk of life. In his 1802 *Memoirs,* Gen. William Moultrie of South Carolina especially praised the "patriotic fair . . . for their heroism and virtue in such dreadful and dangerous times," adding that "their conduct during the war contributed much to the independence of America." David Ramsay, a prominent South Carolina physician and early Whig historian, believed that "there was scarcely an inhabitant of the State, however obscure in character or remote in situation . . . , who did not partake of the general distress" of the revolutionary years. Like Moultrie, Ramsay reserved special praise for the Whig women of his state, who "conducted themselves with more than spartan magnanimity . . . [and] like guardian Angels, preserved their husbands from falling in the hour of temptation, when interest and convenience had almost gotten the better of honour and patriotism."[46]

DOCUMENT 1

Elizabeth Black

Robert and Elizabeth Black were probably among the great wave of settlers who poured into the South Carolina backcountry from northward points after 1750. Robert's death from wounds received in the Whigs' successful defense of Charleston in 1776 left his family destitute, and on 9 October 1776 Elizabeth asked the state legislature for funds to help her return to her family in Pennsylvania. The legislature granted her four hundred pounds to go there "or to any other northern State in which she . . . shall think the health of her family may be established."[1]

---

45. Royster, *Revolutionary People at War,* 364–68; Cynthia A. Kierner, "Genteel Balls and Republican Parades: Gender and Early Southern Civic Rituals, 1677–1824," *VMHB* 104 (1996): 185–210.

46. Moultrie, *Memoirs,* 2:357; David Ramsay, *History of South Carolina, from Its First Settlement in 1670 to the Year 1808* (1808; reprint, Newberry, S.C.: W. J. Duffie, 1858), 1:266; Ramsay, *History of the Revolution in South Carolina,* 2:123–24.

1. *S.C. House Journals, 1776–1780,* 134–35; Klein, *Unification of a Slave State,* 13–14.

That the Petitioner's late husband, Robert Black, was late a soldier in the Second Regiment in the service of this State and was in the gallant defence of Fort Moultrie on Sullivan's Island on the 28th day of June last, grievously and mortally wounded, and died on the 11th day of July next after.

That the Petitioner, besides a daughter married, hath one daughter fifteen years old, another twelve years, a son of a very sickly habit of body about eight years, a daughter about six and another son about four years old.

That she hath no friends or relations in this State from whom she can expect the least assistance for the support of herself and this family, and that she is in very poor and indigent circumstances.

That the Petitioner having lately made application to his Excellency the President and Honourable the Privy Council,[2] his Excellency was pleased, with the advice of that Board, to order fifty pounds to be paid her, and that she should be intitled to receive the pay of her husband until the sitting of this House.

That the Petitioner is very desirous of returning from this State, in which herself and children have been very sickly, to her native state, friends and relations, in Pennsylvania, but is unable to bear the expence of such a journey.

The Petitioner therefore humbly prays that this Honourable House will take the premises into consideration and grant her such relief as to them in their wisdom shall seem meet.

(Petition quoted in William Edwin Hemphill, Wylma Anne Wates, and R. Nicholas Olsberg, eds., *The State Records of South Carolina: Journals of the General Assembly and House of Representatives, 1776–1780* [Columbia: University of South Carolina Press, 1970], 134–35)

DOCUMENT 2

Mary Lewellin

John Lewellin led a secret society of more than ninety Tory conspirators in eastern North Carolina. Initially motivated by a desire to prevent the disestablishment of the Anglican Church under the

---

2. Under the March 1776 constitution, South Carolina's executive was known as the president, while the upper house of the legislature—composed of the president,

state's new constitution, Lewellin eventually plotted to overthrow the Whig regime, murder its leaders, and foment a slave rebellion. Tried and convicted of treason, he awaited execution when his wife, Mary, petitioned for clemency on 15 November 1777. Governor Richard Caswell supported her petition, but the assembly did not. Nevertheless, perhaps as a result of several other petitions on his behalf, Lewellin escaped execution and returned to his home in Martin County.[3]

The Petition of Mary Lewellen,[4] humbly Beseeching, that your Excellency will be pleased to extend your abundant humanity toward your Petitioners unfortunate Husband, who stands condemned to die at Edenton, on Tuesday the thirtieth of this present Instant, for the Crime of High Treason:[5] Your Petitioner does not presume at an endeavour to lessen his guilt, but appealing to your Excellency's Clemency, and tender merciful Disposition, most humbly begs to be indulged while she fondly refers to the honesty and integrity, of the life and Character, of her Husband, before his entering into this detested conspiracy, as well as to remind your Excellency that should he fall under his present sentence (which heaven avert) the Confiscation of his estate being, a positive Consequence,[6] your disconsolate Petitioner and her Children[7] will

---

vice president, and eleven other members chosen by the lower house—was called the Legislative Council. Black's use of the term *Privy Council* reflects colonial usage (McCrady, *S.C. in the Revolution*, 1:111, 114–15).

3. Jeffrey J. Crow, "Tory Plots and Anglican Loyalty: The Llewelyn Conspiracy of 1777," *NCHR* 55 (1978): 4–10, 14–15; Troxler, *Loyalist Experience in North Carolina*, 12–17.

4. Addressed to "his Excellency Richard Caswell Esquire Governor and Commander in Chief in and over the State of North Carolina," who, in turn, forwarded it to the assembly.

5. Charged with "maliciously and advisedly endeavor[ing] to excite a great number of People to resist the Government," Lewellin was judged guilty of high treason on 16 September 1777 (Crow, "Tory Plots," 14).

6. A May 1777 statute mandated that those "adjudged guilty of High-Treason, . . . shall suffer Death without the Benefit of Clergy, and his or her Estate shall be forfeited to the State," though the courts "shall and may order and appropriate so much of the Traitor's Estate, as . . . may appear sufficient, for the Support of his or her Family" (*N.C. Recs.*, 24:10).

7. Two sons and five daughters. At least one of the former also took part in the conspiracy (*N.C. Census, 1784–1787*, 90; Crow, "Tory Plots," 7).

not only have to combat shame, and Disgrace, but also the keenest poverty.

Oh Sir to Heart[s] [full?] and burst asunder and overwhelmed [by] sorrow how much harder to be born mus[t] be the Burthen of woe when aided and agravated by Extremity of poverty.

Yet could the Confiscation take place, and the life of the unhappy misguided Criminal be spared; could he be permitted to return once more to the Arms of his affected wife and Children, the Forfeiture of his small fortune[8] would be an offering too inconsiderable to cost one Tear one Sigh.

With a Heart too full for further utterance your Petitioner bowed down with sorrow prostrates herself before your Excellency and in Silence pleads for mercy.

(DS, Nc-Ar)

DOCUMENT 3

Martha Gilchrist

Martha Jones Gilchrist (1743–1801) was a member of one of North Carolina's leading Whig families, but her husband's attempt to retrieve property from British Bermuda led to his banishment by state authorities. On 14 August 1778, Martha Gilchrist successfully petitioned the legislature on his behalf. Thomas Gilchrist returned to his home in Halifax shortly thereafter.[9]

The petition of Martha Gilchrist Humbly sheweth

That your petitioner is a Native of Virginia, a Daughter of Mr. Robert Jones, (some time since Attorney General of the State of North Carolina)[10] and the Wife of Mr. Thomas Gilchrist, who formerly lived at Suf-

---

8. In fact, Lewellin was a substantial planter whose estate in 1779 was valued at £12,026. The first federal census indicates that he owned twenty slaves in 1790 (Crow, "Tory Plots," 4).

9. *Dict. of N.C. Biog.*, 2:298, 3:326; Will of Martha Gilchrist, 1801, Halifax County Will Book, no. 3, 348, Nc-Ar.

10. Born in Surry County, Virginia, Robert Jones (1718–66) moved to Northampton County, North Carolina, in the early 1750s. From 1754 to 1761, he was a

folk in Virginia, but for some Years previous to the passing of the Treason
Act, at and near Halifax, in this State. Your petitioners said Husband having been in partnership in Trade with his Brother John Gilchrist of Norfolk, for several Years, the partnership at length expired, and the said
Thomas Gilchrist went to Scotland,[11] leaving almost all his Estate in the
hands of his said Brother John. Your petitioners Husband having trans-
acted his Business in Scotland, returned to Virginia, with a View to take
possession of his Estate, and spend the Remainder of his Days in America, all his Connections, as well as Your petitioner's, being in Virginia and
North Carolina. But during his absence, his Brother John Gilchrist had
unfortunately shot himself, and John Campbell of Norfolk had obtained administration on his Estate,—who was either unable or unwill-
ing to account with Thomas Gilchrist, your petitioners Husband,—and
the Courts of Law being then shut in Virginia, he could not compell
Mr. Campbell to do him Justice; wherefore he retired, with your petitioner and four Daughters, and four or five Negroes, all the Estate he
could command, to Halifax Town; and this happened a little before the
passing of the act for shutting up the port of Boston.[12] Hostilities then
commencing between Great Britain and the United States, Lord Dunmore with the British Troops, and General Howe, with the Troops of Virginia, destroyed a great part of the Estate of John Gilchrist by Fire, and
Ld Dunmore, by his Emissaries decoyed most of his Negroes on board
the Fleet, and John Campbell the administrator went off to Bermudas,
with the Remainder. Thus, from Circumstances sufficiently easy, if not
affluent, were your petitioners Husband and his Family reduced to the
gloomy prospect of poverty & Dependance. Your petitioners said Husband continued at Halifax until the passing of the Treason Act, during all

---

member of the colonial assembly, and he served as attorney general for all but two
years between 1756 and 1766 (*Dict. of N.C. Biog.*, 3:326).

11. Gilchrist went to Scotland in 1773 and returned to America the following year.
The North Carolina Treason Act, which required all royal officials and merchants
"who have traded immediately to Great-Britain or Ireland, within ten years past" to
swear an oath of allegiance to the state, was enacted in May 1777 (*N.C. Recs.*, 24:11).

12. Gilchrist's chronology here is faulty. Parliament passed the Boston Port Act on
31 March 1774, but Virginia's royally appointed county courts ceased functioning only
after the election of local committees, the first of which was formed in Alexandria on
28 May (H. J. Eckenrode, *The Revolution in Virginia* [Boston: Houghton Mifflin,
1916], 43–45).

which time he conducted himself so as to gain the good will of his Acquaintance, and never, directly or indirectly by Word or Deed, interfered in or obstructed the Measures of the United States; on the contrary he chearfully acquiesced in the Determinations of Congress, and agreeable to their Recommendation hired a Soldier to serve in the Continental Army.[13] But when that fatal Act passed, he was reduced to the greatest Dilemma, as his Fortune here was not sufficient to maintain a Wife and four Children, born to Affluence, and if he should take the Oath of Allegiance, he would in all probability be barred from a Recovery of any thing in Bermudas, as Campbell, his Brothers Administrator was a violent Tory, and would undoubtedly make use of that circumstance as an Argument to defeat his Claim. Under these Circumstances your petitioners said Husband was induced to leave the State, with Intention to go the Bermudas, if haply he might recover something out of the Wreck of John Gilchrist's Estate, declaring at the same time that he meant to return as soon as possible, & become a Citizen of the State of North Carolina if he could obtain permission.

Your petitioner further sheweth that her said Husband, since his Departure, hearing of the Resolution of Congress recommending to the United States to allow even such persons as had taken arms against them to return, flattered himself that he, whose conduct had never been inimical, should be again restored to his Family and Friends, and accordingly sailed for Georgia, arrived there and was admitted a Citizen; and now anxiously waits the permission of Your Honourable Body to embrace his disconsolate Wife and Helpless Children.

As the Case of Mr. Gilchrist has been attended with Circumstances uncommon and peculiarly hard, as he never while here, or since his Departure, murmured at or obstructed the American Measures; and as Mercy is the most amiable Attribute even of the Allmighty; Your Petitioner prays and conjures you that you will not banish her and her helpless Infants, who are Americans like you, from their Country, their Relations, their Friends and Connections; but humbly hopes that you will allow her Husband to return and bless his Family.

(ADS, Nc-Ar)

---

13. A common practice among affluent men in every state, especially by 1777, when the initial enthusiasm for war had waned (Royster, *Revolutionary People at War*, 65–66, 267).

DOCUMENT 4
Kathrine Smith

When James Smith died of wounds sustained in battle at Stono on 20 June 1779, his mother was left bereaved and destitute. On 29 January 1780, widow Kathrine Smith petitioned the South Carolina legislature for her son's back pay and for a modest pension. The legislature referred the petition to a committee, but Smith's case remained unresolved when the British occupied Charleston in May 1780. In 1783, she renewed her request, submitting two similar petitions, which the assembly ordered returned to the Charleston members, who probably advised her to seek poor relief from local authorities.[14]

That the Petitioner is old, infirm, and in poor and low circumstances, not in any manner capable of getting a subsistence. That her only son, upon whom all her hopes depended, was killed in the service of his Country, and there are arrears of pay due him from the Second Regiment. And therefore praying that her deplorable situation may be taken into consideration and such relief granted as, in the wisdom of the House, shall seem most meet.

(Petition quoted in William Edwin Hemphill et al., eds., *State Records of South Carolina: Journals of the General Assembly and House of Representatives, 1776–1780* [Columbia: University of South Carolina Press, 1970], 249)

DOCUMENT 5
Ann Glover

Ann Glover and her husband, Samuel, resided in the Halifax District of North Carolina. Samuel served in Capt. Charles Allen's com-

*pany of the Second North Carolina Continental Regiment until his
execution on 23 February 1780.*[15] *In April or May of the same year,
Ann Glover submitted her petition, accompanied by a statement
signed by four men, recommending her to the legislators as "an Object of Charity." The assembly, nevertheless, tabled Glover's petition
and did not act on it in this or subsequent sessions.*

The Humble Memorial & Peti[ti]on of Ann Glover, widow of Samuel
Glover late a Soldier in t[his] State enlisted himself some time in the sec-
ond Regiment raised here, Humbly Sheweth, That your Petitioners late
Husband well and faithfully discharged his Duty as a Soldier and Friend
to the Cause of American Freedom and Independance, & marched to the
Northward under the Command of Col. Robert Howe,[16] who if he was
here would bear honest & hon[ora]ble Testimony that your Memorialists
deceased Husband was deemed by him and every other Officer in that
Battalion a good Soldier and never was accused of being intentionally
Guilty of a Breach of the Laws Martial or Civil. Your Petitioner begs leave
to inform your Honors that her late husband continued in the Service of
the United States of America upwards of three Years & then returned by
Orders of his Commanding Officers to the Southward at which time he
had above twelve Months pay due for his Services as a Soldier & which
he ought to have received and would have applied for the sole support of
himself, his wife your Petitioner & two helpless orphan Children. That
many of the poor Soldiers then on their March under the Command of
General Hogan possessed of the same attachment & affection to their
Famalies as those in Command but willing to endure all the Dangers &
Hardships of War began their March for the Defence of the State of
South Carolina, could they have obtained thei[r] Promised but Small allowance dearly earned for the Support of their distressed Families in
their absence, but as they were sure of suffering for want of that Subsistance, which was cruelly & unjustly witheld from them, a General Clamor
arose among the common Soldiers & they called for their Stipend al-

---

15. [Hay et al.], *N.C. Soldiers*, 61, 339–40.
16. In December 1775, Col. Robert Howe marched the Second North Carolina
Regiment northward to assist Virginians in the defense of Norfolk (Boatner, *Ency. of
Amer. Rev.*, 521–22).

lowed by Congress,[17] but it was not give[n] them altho their just due. Give your poor Petitioner Leave to apologize for her unhappy Hus[ban]ds Conduct & in Behalf of her helpless Self as well as in Favor o[f] [h]is poor Children on this Occasion and ask you what must the Fee[lin]g of the Man be who had fought at Brandewine, at Germantown & at Stony Point[18] & did his Duty; and when on another March in Defence of his Country, with Poverty staring him full in the Face he was denied his Pay?

His Brother Soldiers incensed by the same Injuries & had gone through the same Services & would have again bled with him for his Country whenever called forth in their Service looked up to him as an Older Soldier, who then was a Serjeant raised by his Merit from the Common Rank, and stood forth in his own and their Behalf & unhappily for him demanded their pay and refused to obey the Command of his Superior Officer and would not march untill they had Justice done them. The honest Labourer is worthy of his Hire. Allegiance to our Country and Obedience to those in Authority, but the Spirit of a Man will shrink from his Duty when his Services are not paid and Injustice oppresses him and his Family. For this he fell an Unhappy Victim to hard, but perhaps necessary Law of his Country. The Letter penned by himself the day before he was shott[19] doth not breath forth a word of Complaint against his Cruel Sentance, Altho he had not received any pay for upwards of fifteen Months. He writes to your humble Petitioner with the spirit of a Christian. This Letter is the last adieu he bid to his now suffering widow & she wishes it may be read in public Assembly & then returned to her by some of the Members who will take it with them when they return to New Bern, and [sh]ow it in the case of Major Pasteur.[20] Your humble Peti-

---

17. In November 1779, Brig. Gen. James Hogun left Pennsylvania with his North Carolina Continentals, leading them on a three-month journey southward to help defend South Carolina. On arriving in Wilmington, Hogun's troops refused to continue their march unless they were paid (Hugh F. Rankin, *The North Carolina Continentals* [Chapel Hill: University of North Carolina Press, 1971], 218–19).

18. The Battles of Brandywine and Germantown, both in Pennsylvania, occurred on 11 September 1777 and 4 October 1777, respectively. The engagement at Stony Point, in southern New York, took place on 16 July 1779.

19. Not found.

20. Probably Dr. William Pasteur, assistant quartermaster general for the North Carolina troops. Pasteur's business was based in New Bern (*N.C. Recs.*, 14:149, 174–75, 846; *Dict. of N.C. Biog.*, 5:28).

tioner, distressed with the Recollections of the fatal Catastrophe will not trouble your Honors any longer upon the Subject, but humbly request you will extend your usual Benevolences & Charity to her & her two Children, & make her some Yearly allowance for their Support.

(DS, Nc-Ar)

DOCUMENT 6

Martha McGee Bell

Martha McFarlane McGee (1735–1820) was a nurse, a midwife, and the wealthiest widow in Randolph County when she married William Bell in 1779. On 28 January 1781, she petitioned the North Carolina legislature as executrix of her first husband's estate on behalf of his heirs. The assembly did not act on her petition, but Bell remained a committed Whig, acting as an informer and guide to Gen. Henry Lee during his stay in piedmont North Carolina.[21]

Whereas Colo. John McGee formerly of Guilford County did, before the Commencement of these Times, Oblige a Number of Persons by Lending them Sums of money in Specie, and Since is dead, & Left Several Orphan Children[22] Poss[ess]ed at that Time, of a Considerable Share of Property, But the Difficulty of times and the Great Depretiation of the Currency,[23] will not admitt of any Part of the Said Property to be Collected, as People would Wish to Pay their debts with Paper Curr[enc]y; Now as Some of S[ai]d Orphan Children, Would Wish to have their Parts in their own hands, I would Sincearly Pray that your Honours would Make Some Provision for all Such Orphans and that Equity & Justice might be done in Regard of the Collection of former debts due. There is

---

21. *Dict. of N.C. Biog.*, 1:132.

22. Col. John McGee died in 1773, leaving two children from a previous marriage as well as three sons and two daughters born to Martha and him (ibid.).

23. North Carolina's paper currency had depreciated to a rate of approximately 200:1 by 1781 (Morrill, *Fiat Finance*, 19).

also a number of those People Who are Indebted; is Remov'd and about to remove out of this State, and without, Your Honours will take these things into Consideration, all such Orphans Must Suffer. I Leave the Event to yours Honours—and am with Great Esteem yours &c.

(ADS, Nc-Ar)

DOCUMENT 7

Ann Christenbury

This petitioner was the wife of North Carolina militiaman Nicholas C. Christenbury of Mecklenburg County who, along with some eight hundred other wounded Americans, was taken prisoner when Cornwallis defeated Gen. Horatio Gates at Camden in August 1780. Ann Christenbury received the tax relief she requested in her petition of 1 February 1781. She survived her husband, Nicholas, who returned to his home and family and died in Mecklenburg County in 1814.[24]

The Humble Petition of Ann Christenbury

Sheweth that your Petitioner had the misfortune to have Her Husband taken in the unfortunate defeat of Genl. Gates of the 16th of August last and is still in Captivity, which renders it exceedingly inconvenient to your Petitioner to pay Her Taxes for the present Year together with the charge of Five small Children. Your Petitioner Humbly hopes your Honorable Body will take Her distressed situation into your consideration and grant Her such redress as you in your wisdom shall think meet.

And your Petitioner as in duty Bound shall ever pray.

(ADS, Nc-Ar)

---

24. *Heads of Families . . . in the Year 1790: N.C.,* 160; Will of Nicholas C. Christenbury, 27 Apr. 1813, Mecklenburg County Will Book A, 221, Nc-Ar; Howard H. Peckham, *The Toll of Independence: Engagements and Battle Casualties of the American Revolution* (Chicago: University of Chicago Press, 1974), 74.

Document 8
Elizabeth Forbes

Elizabeth Forbes, a resident of Guilford County, North Carolina,
was the widow of militia colonel Arthur Forbes, who died of wounds
sustained in battle at Guilford Court House. On 6 May 1782, the as-
sembly considered Forbes's petition for economic assistance, which
she submitted with a supporting letter from a county official. The
legislature granted her relief in the form of "twenty five barrels of
Corn out of the Specifick Tax for the County of Guilford for the year
1782, and the like Quantity out of the Tax for 1783." [25]

The Petition of Elizabeth Forbus humbly Sheweth
That your Petitioner formerly with the help of a Loving and Industrious Husband lived without being under the necessity of troubling your
Honourable Body with either Petition or Remonstrance but my circumstances are so at present that I must trouble your Honourable Body with
a small account of my distressed condition. It is well known by all the
Friends of America in this County that your Petitioner's Husband from
the commencement of this unnatural war has distinguished himself as a
true friend to the American Cause, and that he was always ready and willing to go when called, in difence of his Country, and being in Service on
the fifteenth of March in the year 1781 at the Battle of Guilford Court
House where he recieved a mortal wound of which he afterward died.
And your Petitioner being left with a helpless family of Small children [26]
is at this time in great distress. Your petitioner therefore humbly prays
that your Honours would take her distressed condition into consideration
and grant her such relief as your H[o]nour's think she stands in need of
and your Petitioner as in duty bound shall ever pray &c.

(D, Nc-Ar)

25. [Hay et al.], *N.C. Soldiers*, 35, 380; Committee report on the petition of
Elizabeth Forbes, 1782, GASR, Apr.–May 1782, Nc-Ar.

26. Elizabeth and Arthur Forbes had six children—two sons and four daughters—
all of whom were unmarried and living under their mother's "command and direction
and government" (Will of Arthur Forbes, 2 July 1780, Guilford County Will Book A,
115, Nc-Ar).

DOCUMENT 9

Anne Lord

> *Widow Anne Gadson Lord was one of many civilians who sought to recover property state troops commandeered during the southern campaign. The wife of Andrew Lord, who served in the South Carolina militia but later swore allegiance to the Crown, Anne remained in Charleston after the war, despite her husband's deathbed request that she "embark for Great Britain" with their children so as to "give them a virtuous and good Education." On 22 January 1783, Anne Lord submitted her claims, which the legislature partially approved the following year, awarding her £6,160 sterling as compensation for her lost slaves.[27]*

The petition of Anne Lord, widow of Andrew Lord deceased Setting forth

That the Said deceased died the 12th May 1781 and bequeathed his Estate at the Congaree to herself and children,[28] that on the 18th May 1781, as she is informed, 74 Negroes was taken away by Order of General Sumpter and distributed among the State Troops[29] and after the reduction of the Fort at Congaree,[30] was taken away from the plantation aforesaid 22 head of horses, 100 head of Cattle and upwards of 100 head of Sheep besides other Considerable property, all which Losses she be-

---

27. Moss, *S.C. Patriots,* 581; Clemens, *Marriage Recs.,* 166; Will of Andrew Lord, 11 May 1781, Charleston County Will Book, 1783–86, typescript, 21:647–50, Sc-Ar; *Heads of Families . . . in the Year 1790: S.C.,* 23, 43; *S.C. House Journals, 1783–1784,* 309, 443, 458, 504, 509, 549, 550.

28. That estate consisted of a plantation in the Camden District with a slave population of 120 in 1790. Anne Lord and her two sons and four daughters appear to have been absentee owners, residing in a Charleston house staffed by an additional 14 slaves (*Heads of Families . . . in the Year 1790: S.C.,* 23, 43).

29. In April 1781, Sumter sought to recruit six regiments by promising each enlistee as many as four slaves (Quarles, *Negro in the American Revolution,* 108–9). He presumably distributed Lord's slaves among these new recruits.

30. Tory forces at Fort Granby, located on the Congaree River at the site of present-day Columbia, surrendered to Col. Henry Lee on 15 May 1781 (Pancake, *Destructive War,* 200–201).

lieves to be Sustained through the State Troops Commanded by General Sumpter, And prays Such relief as you in your Wisdom shall see meet.

(Petition quoted in South Carolina Senate Journals, 8 Feb. 1783, Sc-Ar)

DOCUMENT 10

Sarah Glen

> *Col. John Glen of Savannah, a prominent Whig, was one of 114 men Georgia's restored royal government formally banished and dispossessed of their estates. Glen fled with his family to South Carolina, where he fought on the side of the Whigs. His decision to stay in Charleston during the British occupation, however, led the South Carolina government to regard him as a Tory and accordingly to banish him when the British evacuated the city in 1782. On 23 January 1783, Glen asked the assembly to rescind his sentence, and two days later his wife, Sarah Jones Glen, submitted this separate petition on his behalf. The assembly granted the Glens' petitions in the next legislative session.* [31]

The Petition of Sarah Glen Humbly Sheweth—

That your Petitioner is the Wife of John Glen whose person has been banished & Estate Confiscated by an Act of Assembly of this State. The distress in which She is involved by this Measure is truely Calamatous. She has Six small Children to maintain, and her Husband on leaving his Country left her nothing to maintain them with. This great misfortune She regrets the more when she looks back on the Conduct of her husband and his Zeal and Attachment to the American Cause. On the British invading Georgia in 1778 he fought and defended Savanah; instead of Staying by his property he abandoned it. This retreat was so Sudden that your Petitioner lost her wearing apparel. He settled in this Town afterwards and the times were such, that it was with difficulty he Supported his family. He risked his life in the assault on Savanah, helped to defend Charles Town during the Siege and fell with it into the Enemys hands. This event

---

31. Davis, *Ga. Citizens and Soldiers,* 12, 21, 68, 75, 78; *S.C. House Journals, 1783–1784,* 552.

found him without a Shilling. The impossibility of his quiting the Town or following any kind of business while a prisoner of War, is well known. He had your Petitioner and five Children to Support and there was no alternative but to take the Enemies protection. The proclamation of Govr. Rutledges[32] he cou'd not Possibly have Obeyed for he & Two friends were bound in recognizances of £16,000 Sterling which the British usurpers in Georgia obliged him to enter into on a Charge of high Treason.[33] Your Petitioner can assure this Hon[ora]ble house that after the reduction of Charles Town, such was his attachment & affection to the Cause of his Country, & his aversion to the Enemy that he even Secluded himself from all Society or Acquaintance with British Officers or the Tories; who in their turn regarded him as their Enemy. This can easily be proved.

Your Petitioner makes this appeal to the Hon[ora]ble members of the legislature requesting that her husband and father of her Children may be restored to her. There is no other resource for their Support and Education, but the labour and Industry of Mr. Glen; shou'd She be deprived of that, She is utterly unequal to the task; And they must turn out an incumbrances to the Community in Stead of being of Service to it.

And your Pet[itione]r as in Duty bound will pray.

(DS, Sc-Ar)

DOCUMENT 11

Sarah Jones

Sarah Davis Jones was the mother of Sarah Glen and the wife of Noble Wimberly Jones (1723–1805), a prominent Georgia Whig. After the fall of Savannah in 1778, the Joneses fled to South Carolina. Unlike his son-in-law John Glen, however, Jones was taken prisoner when the British occupied Charleston and spent the following year as a captive in St. Augustine. In 1782, he returned to

---

32. Rutledge's proclamation of 27 September 1781 offered full pardon to most Tories who surrendered themselves and thereafter served six months as privates in the state militia (McCrady, *S.C. in the Revolution,* 2:521–24).

33. As stipulated in "An Act to attain of High Treason the several Persons herein named," 7 June 1780 (Davis, *Ga. Citizens and Soldiers,* 67–70).

Georgia to serve in the state assembly, while Sarah Jones remained
in Charleston with her daughter's family. Both mother and daugh-
ter petitioned the South Carolina assembly on 25 January 1783.[34]

The Petition of Sarah Jones Humbly Sheweth—
That your Petitioner is the Wife of Doctor Jones of Georgia, and their
Daughter being the Wife of John Glen, She takes the liberty of appealing
to the Justice and humanity of this Hon[ora]ble House with regard to the
banishment of her Son in Law, Who has left a Wife and Six Small Children; and no kind of property to Support them. In this misfortune Doctor Jones and your Petitioner is deeply interested; for the affection which
they bear to their Child & Grand Children will never allow them to be-
hold their Suffering distress, while anything is left. The whole burthen of
supporting them must therefore fall on Doctor Jones, who has been already been ruined by the Enemies invasion of Georgia, by his long Captivity in the hands of the British and by his attention to Publick business,
in total Neglect of his own. Your Pet[itione]r has had too much affliction
besides. She has had her Eldest Son killed in the defence of Savanah, One
brother lost in the Service in Georgia And a Second died of a fever he received in the defence of Charles Town.

She trusts this distress may be some what alleviated by restoring her
Son in Law to his Country and family, and by giving him a hearing. And
She is in Duty bound will pray &c.

(DS, Sc-Ar)

DOCUMENT 12

Sarah Galloway

This petitioner appears in neither the North Carolina state cen-
sus nor in the federal census of 1790, and her husband cannot be
identified from the Continental Army rosters. In 1783, however, the
Wayne County court certified her, as a soldier's widow, as a suitable
"Object of Charity." As a result, on 30 April 1784, Sarah Galloway
petitioned the state assembly for relief. The assembly granted her

34. *Dict. of Ga. Biog.*, 1:553–54; Claghorn, *Women Patriots*, 115.

petition, awarding her a stipend of £15 for each of the next three years.[35]

The Memorial of Sarah Galloway humbly sheweth—That your Memorialist is a poor distressed Widdow with four helpless Children the oldest not more than nine years old, left without food & raiment sufficient for there support, whose Husband joined the Continental Army for twelve months and before the expiration of said time died in Camp, and your Memorialist not being able through Sickness as well as poverty to support the said Family, humbly prays that you in your great Wisdom would provide ways & means to keep them from suffering. And your Memorialist is in duty bound shall ever pray &c. &c.

(DS [by mark], Nc-Ar)

DOCUMENT 13

Anne Armstrong

Widow Anne Armstrong resided in South Carolina's Ninety-Six District near the present-day border between Laurens and Greenwood Counties. Her successful petition, submitted on 23 February 1784, underlines the significance of racial conflicts on the southern frontier and shows how war brought grief and hardship to many southern families.

Setting forth

That John Armstrong, Your Petitioners late Husband, having in the year 1775 Purchased of Joshua Pettit, a Certain tract of 500 acres of Land, Situate on Saluda river, about two Miles below the fork of the same—which Richard Pearis late of this State, purchased of the Cherokee Indians.[36]

---

35. Committee report on the petition of Sarah Galloway, 5 May 1784, GASR, Apr.–June 1784, Nc-Ar.

36. Richard Pearis, a veteran of Indian trade and diplomacy, in 1775 became the proprietor of twelve square miles of Cherokee land in the valley of the upper Saluda River, a portion of which he then sold to Joshua Pettit. During the Revolution, Pearis fought for the Crown and recruited backcountry men for the Tory militia, while Pettit

That your Petetioners late husband, being in possession of said tract of five hundred acres of land, and living thereon with his Numerous family of Small Children, in the year 1776, being the time when the said Cherokee Indians broke out in an Open war with this State—At which time your Petetioners late Husband Unfortunatly fell into their hands, was taken Captive to their Towns, and Most inhumanly Butcher'd by the Aforesaid Savages who also took the whole of his Stock, and every other Necessary Support of life, leaving your Petitioner in these distressing Circumstances, to Struggle for a support for her helpless Ofspring, through the Calamities occationed by the late war—and with the greatest difficulty have Supported them hitherto. Your Petetioner therefore Prays, that the said five hundred Acres of land, Purchased by her late husband, May be Vested in your Petetioner & her Children, free from any other Claim, Or grant your Petetioner such other relief as your Honourable house shall think Proper.

(Petition quoted in Theodora J. Thompson and Rosa S. Lumpkin, eds., *The State Records of South Carolina: Journals of the House of Representatives, 1783–1784* [Columbia: University of South Carolina Press, 1977], 486)

DOCUMENT 14
Sarah Rounsevall

Sarah Rounsevall was a committed Whig who provided supplies for North Carolina's troops on at least one occasion. On her husband's capture by Tory militia, she tried to fulfill his responsibilities as tax collector in Rowan County. The chaos and destruction of the backcountry's partisan warfare, however, complicated her task as well as her later efforts to settle accounts with the state government. On 11 December 1786, Rounsevall petitioned the legislature for some £8,000 in 1780 currency, the equivalent of roughly £250 in current money. Although she had misplaced some of her vouchers, the assembly granted her petition.[37]

served in the state forces (Lambert, *S.C. Loyalists*, 43, 69, 106–7, 268; Clark, *Loyalists*, 3:431–34, 492–500; Moss, *S.C. Patriots*, 769, 827).

37. Claghorn, *Women Patriots*, 429; Committee report on the petition of Sarah Rounsevall, 15 Dec. 1786, GASR, Nov. 1786–Jan. 1787, Nc-Ar. On partisan raids in

The Memorial of Sarah Rounsavel adm[inis]t[ri]x of Jonah Rounsavel de[cease]d who was Sheriff of Rowan County in the year 1779 &
part of the year 1780 who was taken Prisoner on the 21st day of June 1780
& died at Camden in a few months after in the same Year as prisoner
afores[ai]d. your memorialist & her son proceeded to make the Collection of Taxes for that year to the utmost of their power but in Vain so as
to compleat the same but Trust it is Nearly compleat Notwithstanding the
Troubles that then prevaded the Country. Your memorialist Begs leave to
Suggest to the Hon[ora]ble the Genl. assembly that they woud in their
wisdom appoint a Committee Composd of their Body to Examine & En-
quire in to the Premises & Grant such relief to your Memorialist as your
wisdom & Justice shall think proper & your memorialist as in duty Bound
shall ever pray &c &c.

(DS [by mark], Nc-Ar)

DOCUMENT 15

Mary Champneys

*After fleeing to East Florida in 1782, Tory John Champneys
spent the next seven years trying to secure formal readmission to
South Carolina. On 28 February 1787, Mary Harvey Champneys
obtained the assembly's permission for him to return to the state
for six months to settle his affairs. John Champneys arrived in
Charleston, but he never left, requesting and receiving formal relief
from the penal statutes in 1789.*[38]

Rowan County and throughout the backcountry in 1780–81, see Crow, "Liberty Men
and Loyalists," 139–46, 157–69; and Ekirch, "Whig Authority and Public Order,"
107–8.

38. Lambert, *S.C. Loyalists*, 59–60, 188, 256; Robert W. Barnwell Jr., "The Migration of Loyalists from South Carolina," in *Proceedings of the South Carolina Historical Association: 1937* (Columbia: South Carolina Historical Association, 1937),
35; Siebert, *Loyalists in East Florida*, 2:12–14, 28n; *S.C. House Journals, 1785–
1786*, 118, 153, 235–36; *S.C. House Journals, 1787–1788*, 161, 177; *S.C. House Journals, 1789–1790*, 247.

The Petition of Mary Champneys, Humbly Sheweth—

That Your Petitioners husband John Champneys was by a Resolution of Your Honourable House, some time past among others ordered to depart this State being under the Act of Banishment that in consequence thereof he was obliged through the short notice he had, to leave behind him Your Petitioner and only Child whose ill state of health would not permit them to Venture to Sea neither does it at preasent. Your Petitioner therefore humbly prays her husband may be allowed to Return to this State for twelve Months to Remove his Family to Eaurope and endeavour to dispose of the small Property left Your Petitioner and settle his affairs Finally—Your Petitioner is encourag'd to m[ake app]lication to Your Honorable House as her [h]usband never [ms. torn] injurd any of the Good People of the State but on the Contray [a]s[siste]d many of the distressed as Several Members of Your Honorable House can testify as his Return will be agreeable to Nine tenths of the Good Citizans of the State who know him as will appear by the annexd Petitians which unfortunately could not be presented to the Legislature last Sessian owing to a Resolve of the Honorable Senate[39]—Your Petitioner there fore Implores Your Honorable House will so far extend their Mercy as to Grant the Prayer of her Petitian and she as in duty Bound Will ever pray.

(ADS, Sc-Ar)

DOCUMENT 16

Mary Sansum

Mary Sansum, the wife of a Charleston tavernkeeper, probably ran the family business after 1779, when her husband, John, enlisted in the state militia and served as forage master general. After John died in 1785, Mary tried in vain to collect what she believed the state owed him. On 9 October 1788, Sansum petitioned the assem-

---

39. Supporting petitions not found. On 8 February 1786, the House resolved that no petitions "of a private nature" would be received after 18 February; the Senate disagreed but, on 10 February, resolved to stop hearing private petitions as of 1 March (*S.C. House Journals, 1785–1786*, 383, 391).

*bly for compensation, but the legislature rejected her claims, pre-
sumably for lack of documentation.*[40]

The petition of Mary Sansum Widow of the late John Sansum deceased Humbly sheweth—

That your petitioner is the Executrix of the Estate of her late Husband John Sansum, who during the late War, was in the service of this
State as Forage Master General, that at the time of his Death, his Accounts with the State was not finally liquidated, by the Auditor General,
but that in some short time thereafter, your Petitioner call'd at the Office
of the Auditor General, and found the Accounts liquidated and carryed
into the Treasury for payment, that your petitioner then received Indents
to the full Amount of the demand rendered in by her late Husband, as
likewise the Interest arising thereon she has regularly received, until last
year, your petitioner was then informed by the Treasurers, that they
could not pay her any further Interest, as the Auditor General had found
out since his Books were brot. up, a charge of £159,625 depreciated Currency which was advanc'd your petitioners late Husband, which he had
not accounted for, and that unless your petitioner cou'd produce vouchers for the appropriation of those Sums, she must refund the Indents and
Interest received.

Your petitioner wou'd beg leave to observe that in the year 1781 her
late Husband, was among several other Citizens, sent to St. Augustine a
prisoner by the British, and left most of his Books and papers with your
petitioner, (excepting one of his Forage Books, which the British troops
took from him at Camden, when he was taken a prisoner, just before the
fall of Charleston, and destroyed it) that your petitioner was among others, in the Month of October 1781 order by the British Commandant to
depart from Charleston to Philadelphia, where her late Husband there
was, that your petitioner with some other families hired a Vessel to convey them to that place, that after having all their baggage on board, and
was ready to sail, a most violent storm came on, which stove the Vessel,
then lying at the Wharf, in such a manner, as demolished the most of
your petitioners baggage, in which was the Books and papers of nearly

40. *State Gazette of South Carolina,* 2 Sept. 1778; Moss, *S.C. Patriots,* 844; Will of
John Sansum, 10 Sept. 1784, Charleston County Will Book, 1783–86, typescript,
21:520–23, Sc-Ar.

the whole transactions of the Forage department, which put it out of the power of her late Husband to furnish the whole of the necessary vouchers—Your petitioner would beg leave to observe, that she is ready to attest to the authenticity of the above and to bring proof of the facts, That your petitioners only support for herself and three Children, was on the Interest arising on those Indents, that since she has been deprived of that resourse, she has been compell'd to apply for the Childrens support, to the bounty of the South Carolina Society,[41] this being the Case, and as the vouchers were lost by the casualties of War, Your petitioner humbly solicits your honorable House, that you wou'd be pleased to direct the Auditor General to audit the Account, upon the principle of the Vouchers lost, and that the Treasurers be likewise directly to pay your petitioner the Interest on the Indents as usual, and your Petitioner as in duty bound will pray.

(ADS, Sc-Ar [Accounts Audited, no. 6754, roll 130, frames 422–24])

DOCUMENT 17

Jeane Tols

Jeane Tols, the widow of a South Carolina militia captain, does not appear in the 1790 census. On 6 February 1789, she petitioned the legislature for economic assistance and received her husband's arrears in pay with interest for the period between August 1779 and his death in 1781.[42]

The Petition of Jeane Tols Widdow of Olivpher Tols in the County of Newberry—Humbly Sheweth

That your Petetioner's Husband was a prisenor 14 Months after the fall of Charleston, after which time he was killed in the year 1781 and

---

41. Founded in 1739, the South Carolina Society was a gentlemen's benevolent association that distributed alms and ran charity schools in Charleston (Carl Bridenbaugh, *Cities in Revolt: Urban Life in America, 1743–1776* [New York: Alfred A. Knopf, 1955], 127, 374).

42. Moss, *S.C. Patriots*, 935; *S.C. House Journals, 1789–1790*, 210, 257–58.

your Petetionar depending on Some of the Officers whose Duty it was to have Returned the Same to the Publick by which Means it was Neglected your Petetionar Therefore Humbly prays your Honorable House to take her Case into your Serious Consideration and grant her Such Relief as Your Honours Shall think fit and in Duty bound will Ever Pray.

(DS [by mark], Sc-Ar [Accounts Audited, no. 7872–A, roll 147, frames 440–41])

DOCUMENT 18

Mary Taggart

> *In early 1780, Gen. Benjamin Lincoln ordered William Taggart to burn his house and outbuildings at Hampstead, a rural area outside Charleston, to prevent their use by the approaching enemy. Taggart died in 1783, and his widow spent the next eighteen years seeking restitution from various state and federal authorities. This petition of 5 December 1793 was the first of four that Mary Taggart submitted to the South Carolina assembly, which ruled initially that her account was "one that should be . . . discharged by the Union." In 1801, however, the state legislature finally satisfied her claim.*[43]

The humble petition of Mary Taggart Sheweth,

That in the month of March in the year 1780 the husband of yr. petitioner being then possessed of a house at Hampstead, received a letter from Genl. Lincoln then commanding in Charleston recommending the removal of his property out of said house & to have the house and other buildings appraised, as the approach of the enemy near the lines made it probable that the said house and buildings would be burnt. In consequence of this letter Yr. petitioner's husband on the 6th of March in the same year had the same valued & the appraisement amounted to the sum of One hundred thousand continental dollars equal to four hundred &

---

43. Will of William Taggart, 12 Dec. 1783, Charleston County Will Book, 1783–86, typescript, 20:355–56, Sc-Ar; *S.C. House Journals, 1792–1794*, 445; Petitions of Mary Taggart, 2 Dec. 1794, 9 Dec. 1796, 25 Nov. 1800, LP, Sc-Ar; Senate resolution on the petition of Mary Taggart, 18 Dec. 1801, Legislative Papers, Sc-Ar.

forty two pounds Six shillings Sterling[44]—Your petitioner further states that the said house, buildings & fences were burned by order of General Lincoln & Governor Rutledge[45]—Your Petitioner rendered in her accounts for the above losses in the Year 1783 to the Auditor General who examined & found them correct. They have also been laid before the Comm[issione]rs of Public accounts who referred them to Simeon Theus Esqr. Commissioner from this State to settle with the United States— The Commissioner has certified that her acco[un]t against the United States would not be allowed as it had not been paid by this State[46]—Thus the payment of yr. petitioner's demand hath been delayed, which has prevented her from satisfying those to whom she's indebted—Your Petitioner therefore prays your honorable house to take her case into consideration and order that her Said demand with interest thereon be paid. And Your Petitioner will ever pray.

(ADS, Sc-Ar)

DOCUMENT 19

Joanna Boylstone

During the Revolution, Joanna Boylstone lived with her husband, son, and a slave woman named Rachel in upcountry South Carolina. By 1790, Joanna and her son, George, lived alone, and by 1800 they had disappeared from the state census. Joanna and George Boylstone filed this petition on 12 December 1793. Al-

---

44. Copies of Lincoln's letter of 1 March 1780 and of the sworn assessment of three freeholders, dated 6 March 1780, accompanied this petition but are filed with that of 25 November 1800 (LP, Sc-Ar).

45. John Rutledge was president of South Carolina (1776–78) under the first state constitution and served as governor (1779–81) under the second (*DAB*, 8:258–59).

46. In 1783, the state government appointed commissioners to review and settle claims against Congress and the state government. A congressionally appointed commissioner arrived in South Carolina the following year to liquidate outstanding Continental debts (E. James Ferguson, *The Power of the Purse: A History of American Public Finance, 1776–1790* [Chapel Hill: University of North Carolina Press, 1961], 182–85).

though the state Senate recommended compensating them for the
loss of their slave, the House did not concur, and the petition was
rejected.[47]

The Petition of Joannah Boylstone & George Boylstone Administrators of the Estate of Wm. Boylstone late of Fairfield County Deceased humbly sheweth.

That Wm. Boylstone Deceased was during the late war & ever since till the time of Death a decrepid & infirm old man being about seventy five Years of Age at the time of his death. That during the war from his great age & decrepitude he was incapable either of bearing Arms or going abroad to look to his common affairs of Business. That in the year our Lord 1781 he was owner of a certain Negro Wench named Rachel, of about Seventy five pounds value. That the s[ai]d Wench being sent out on business of her Master in the said year, was forcibly taken & carried off, by an armed party of Troops under the command of Genl Sumter,[48] without the Knowledge of her Master & Owner who supposed her to have ran away or been stolen. That the Deceased was ignorant what had become of s[ai]d Negro till the begining of the Year 1790 when he was informed & found she was in the possession of Major John Davidson of North Carolina,[49] but knew not by what authority or Claim he held her—That s[ai]d Deceased in March 1790 instituted a Suit in the Superior Court of Salisbury District in said State against said Davidson to recover said property—That a Trial was had in September 1791 when it appeared in Evidence that said Negro had been taken by a party of Troops under the Command of Col. Henry Hampton of Sumter's Brigade in the service of this State & had been paid to one Thomas Williams a soldier in said Brigade[50] for £86 Sterling in full of his pay as a Soldier in said Brigade. That by an Act of the General Assembly of this State, persons who have been

---

47. *Heads of Families . . . in the Year 1790: S.C.*, 22.

48. On the seizure of slaves by Sumter's troops, see n. 29.

49. Maj. John Davidson of Mecklenburg County, North Carolina, served as an officer in the state militia for the entire war (*Dict. of N.C. Biog.*, 2:24–25).

50. Hampton was a captain in the Sixth Regiment in 1779, and in 1781 he was lieutenant colonel in the light dragoons under Gen. Thomas Sumter. Thomas Williams served in Capt. Samuel Martin's Company in the brigade Sumter commanded (Moss, *S.C. Patriots*, 409, 998).

deprived of their property as aforesaid can have no remedy in Law against the persons who took the same but must apply to the Legislature of this State for relief.[51]

That the Legislature of No. Carolina have passed in 1788 an act, confirming the act of this State & the Title of their Citizens to such Negroes as were delivered over to them in payment of their Citizens who has served this State in said Brigade. And that under the said act of North Carolina & the act of this State a Verdict & Judgment were given for the Defendant John Davidson, whereby the said Wm. Boylstone lost his said Negro & had to pay a considerable sum for Costs—As by the record of the said Court & a Copey of said Act of No. Carolina accompanying this Petition[52] may appear—That the said John Boylstone has lately died & left an aged Widow (one of your Petitioners) & Child in very indigent Circumstances without recieving any satisfaction for his said Negro taken & appropriated as aforesaid in payment of one of the just Debts of this State & they are without remedy except from the justice of the General Assembly.

That they concieve their claim on the State cannot be considered within the Resolves of the Legislature which required Accounts to be delivered in to the Auditors before a certain time for liquidation inasmuch as their Claim would not come properly before the Auditor but by order of the Assembly on special Application inasmuch as he was never impowered to issue Indents in such Cases but only where property had been sold to the public or impressed for public use & proper vouchers given—That in this case they had no vouchers & knew nothing of the Transaction until it was disclosed by evidence in a Court of Law which was some years after the Auditor's Office was closed against All accounts. That they hope the doors of this house will not be shut against so just a Claim for a Negro which has been appropriated as herein Stated. That they concieve they have a just & legal claim on this State for their sd. Ne-

---

51. "An Act to Procure Recruits and Prevent Desertion," 1784, *S.C. Statutes,* 4:514.

52. A copy of the transcript of the Salisbury court as well as George Boylstone's affidavit, identifying the slave in question as his property, accompany the petition. The pertinent North Carolina statute was the 1786 "Act to confirm the Rights and Titles of Several Citizens of this State in certain Negroes therein defined, and preventing unjust and vexatious Law Suits" (*N.C. Recs.,* 24:954).

gro so appropriated to its use in discharge of their Debts. That they are ready to make the facts appear satisfactorily to the House which are herein Stated in such manner as they shall direct—They therefore pray the Honble House of Senate to take their case into Consideration & grant that they may stand in the place of the said Th[oma]s Williams would have done had he not recieved the said Negro & recieve such Indent as would have been granted to him or that they may be paid in money the value of said Negro with the Interest thereon & such Costs as the said Deceased sustained by reason of the taking of such property from him—Or that this Honorable House will grant such relief as they in their wisdom Shall think proper & will do justice to the aged & poor Widow & the Orphan of the Deceased William Boylstone And Your Petitioners as in Duty bound will pray.

(ADS [by George Boylstone only], Sc-Ar)

DOCUMENT 20

Elizabeth Deveaux

Jacob and Elizabeth Barnwell Deveaux (b. 1749) maintained a plantation near Beaufort and a townhouse in Charleston, where Jacob conducted his mercantile business. As a result of his capitulation to British rule in 1780, Jacob Deveaux lost his estate under the anti-Tory statutes, but in 1784 the assembly rescinded his sentence. Jacob never attempted to obtain restitution for the property Elizabeth later claimed to have lost during the war. He died sometime after 1788 but before 10 December 1794, when the assembly heard her petition, which it tabled.[53]

The Humble Petition of Elizabeth Deveaux Sheweth—

That, some Time in the Year one thousand seven hundred & eighty two, when the city of Charleston was a British Garrison, Some Americans, unknown, took a Boat & three Negroes, The Property of Your Petitioner, coming from Wando Plantation to the City, with a few Necessaries

---

53. Stephen B. Barnwell, *The Story of an American Family* (Marquette: n.p., 1969), 56; *S.C. House Journals, 1783–1784*, 58, 552.

for Family use, & carried them to General Marrion's Camp at Watboo Bridge,[54] Where They were sold upon a Supposition of having Violated Governor Mathew's Proclamation.[55] Whereby your Petitioner has been depriv'd of any satisfaction or compensation for the Same, To the great Injury of her & a large Family[56] in distress—Your Petitioner therefore humbly prays such Relief as in your Humanity, you will please to grant & your Petitioner as in duty bound will ever Pray.

(ADS, Sc-Ar)

---

54. Watboo (or Wadboo) Bridge crossed the Fair Forest Swamp, off the western branch of the Cooper River, about twenty-five miles from Charleston.

55. On 17 August 1782, South Carolina governor John Mathews (1782–84) warned that, if the departing British and their Tory allies carried off slaves belonging to "citizens" of the state, his government would prevent British creditors from collecting debts there. Mathews issued this warning in a letter to the British commander, not as a formal proclamation (McCrady, *S.C. in the Revolution*, 2:658–60).

56. Between 1770 and 1789, Deveaux gave birth to seven children who survived to maturity. All but two appear to have been married by 1794 (Barnwell, *Story of an American Family*, 56).

Chapter 2

THE COST OF LIBERTY

For more than twenty years after Jonathan Barrett died aboard a British prison ship, his family paid both the economic and emotional costs of American liberty. Left "in poor and indigent circumstances, and by the product of her own labour to support two unhappy Orphans," Jonathan's widow, Amy, petitioned the Virginia legislature three times before securing a modest pension in 1792. By then, according to Amy Barrett, she was "old and infirm, and the utmost efforts of her industry [were] barely adequate to her own maintenance." In 1800, when her pension was due to expire, Barrett submitted another petition, requesting its renewal. For the fourth time in twenty-two years, she recounted the sad story of her husband's imprisonment and death aboard the *Jersey*, a vessel already notorious for the disease, starvation, and wanton brutality its inmates suffered.[1]

Amy Barrett's story was probably unique, but many women must have shared her frustration and, perhaps, a sense of achievement, as they navigated their claims through a complex array of administrative channels in the postrevolutionary decades. In 1778, the Virginia state legislature responded to Barrett's first petition by instructing her to submit her case to the county courts, which, in turn, referred it back to the assembly. State legislators in Virginia and elsewhere instructed other petitioners to

---

1. Petitions of Amy Barrett, 3 Nov. 1778, 13 Oct. 1792, 13 Dec. 1800, LP, Princess Anne Co., Vi-Ar; Petition of Amy Barrett, 1784, LP, Misc., Vi-Ar.

Philip Freneau, a prisoner aboard the *Jersey*, immortalized the ship in poetry, and efforts to erect a memorial to its inmates—of whom some eleven thousand died during their incarceration—began as early as 1792. See Albert Greene, *Recollections of the Jersey Prison Ship from the Manuscript of Captain Thomas Dring*, ed. Lawrence H. Leder (New York: Corinth Books, 1961), vi–viii.

pursue their claims at the national level.[2] Many spent years attempting to resolve outstanding debts and other war-related grievances, extending the economic legacy of the Revolution well into the 1790s.

The war and its attendant hardships created situations that brought women into the public sphere and at times forced them to interact with their government. Because petitioning was the only formal political channel accessible to women during this period, war-related claims and grievances fueled the growth of women's petitioning in the postrevolutionary era. In the Carolinas, women sent 349 petitions to their state legislatures alone between 1776 and 1800, compared to only thirty-two in the entire preceding quarter-century. Approximately 60 percent of these 349 petitions dealt with war-related matters. The fact that roughly 40 percent did not, however, shows that women increasingly called on the legislatures to act on other types of issues, which suggests that the Revolution was a watershed in the evolution of their perceived relationship to government.

During and after the Revolution, women's war-related petitions fell into four main categories. First, soldiers' widows—or sometimes their mothers or children—petitioned to recover their arrears in pay or to obtain the annuities that the government provided to the families of men who died in service. Second, women, and civilians generally, petitioned to obtain compensation for goods and services they provided to the government and its troops in wartime. Third, the wives of Tories, whose experience will be examined in a separate chapter, sought the repatriation of their banished spouses and the return of all or part of their confiscated estates. Finally, Whig petitioners also tried to resolve problems and grievances arising from the state's confiscation and sale of loyalist property. Some who held prerevolutionary liens against confiscated properties petitioned to protect their interests, while others who bought such properties requested more time to satisfy their debt to the state or the cancellation of a transaction whose outstanding balance they could not pay (Doc. 9).

---

2. On women's petitioning at the national level during this period, see George C. Chalou, "Women in the American Revolution: Vignettes or Profiles," in *Clio Was a Woman: Studies in the History of American Women*, ed. Mabel C. Deutrich and Virginia C. Purdy (Washington: Howard University Press, 1980), 73–90; and Constance B. Schulz, "Daughters of Liberty: The History of Women in the Revolutionary War Pension Records," *Prologue* 3 (1984): 139–53.

Although the issues surrounding the seizure and disposition of loyalist estates were unique to this period, the other petitions women filed during the revolutionary era had colonial precedents. Widows of soldiers who died in the French and Indian War had requested and received pensions from their colonial assemblies, as did the widows of North Carolina troops who died fighting the Regulator insurgents at the Battle of Alamance in 1771.[3] Colonial women also petitioned to obtain compensation for goods and services that they or their spouses furnished to their provincial governments. For instance, in 1760 Martha Miller petitioned to recover the funds her late husband expended procuring carpenters and building materials for South Carolina's new "state house," and in 1766 Jean Holmes requested compensation for provisioning the colonial troops at Fort Loudoun.[4]

The volume of petitions women submitted beginning in 1776, however, had no colonial parallel. In the last half-century of the colonial era, Americans filed legislative petitions in growing numbers, increasingly turning to their assemblies to resolve both individual and community grievances.[5] Nevertheless, the rising rate of colonial petitioning was no match for the explosive growth that occurred during and after the Revolution. Between 1715 and 1720, South Carolinians submitted an annual average of 10.8 petitions to their assembly, and they filed an average of 27.6 petitions a year in the last quarter-century of the colonial era. In the 1780s, however, South Carolina's state assembly received an average of 122.2 petitions each year and as many as 571 in a single legislative session. In North Carolina, the growth of postrevolutionary petitioning was even more striking. North Carolinians had averaged fewer than ten petitions a

---

3. Petition of Elizabeth Chappel, 7 Dec. 1759, GASR, Nov. 1759–Jan. 1760, Nc-Ar; Petition of Mary Adamson, 4 May 1761, S.C. legislative journals, microfilm, Sc-Ar; Petition of Mary Morrison, 22 Apr. 1761, ibid.; Petition of Susanah Regan, 24 Nov. 1761, in *N.C. Recs.*, 6:493, 497; Petition of Faithy Smith, 20 Nov. 1771, GASR, (Colonial), box 5, Nc-Ar; Petition of Ann Bryan, 28 Nov. 1771, ibid.; Petition of Anne Ferguson, Dec. 1771, ibid.; Petition of Elizabeth Harper, Dec. 1771, ibid.

4. Petition of Martha Miller, 20 Apr. 1760, S.C. legislative journals, microfilm, Sc-Ar; Petition of Jean Holmes, 26 Nov. 1766, ibid. See also, Petition of Elizabeth Mercier, 28 Feb. 1755, ibid.; Petition of Lydia Mortimer, 9 May 1761, ibid.; Petition of John and Mary Kesson, 9 Sept. 1769, ibid.

5. Statistics on colonial petitioning can be found in Alison G. Olson, "Eighteenth-Century Colonial Legislatures and Their Constituents," *JAH* 79 (1992): 554–59.

year between 1750 and 1775, but that figure increased more than tenfold in the decade following the British surrender.

During and after the Revolution, the number of petitions that women filed increased both absolutely and as a proportion of the total submitted. In the 1780s, North Carolina women accounted for 6.5 percent of the petitions the legislature received, nearly 2 percent more than the share they filed in the late colonial era. In South Carolina, the portion of petitions submitted by women ranged from 3 percent before the Revolution to 12.5 percent between 1776 and 1780. Women accounted for less than 1 percent of Georgia's colonial petitions, but they presented more than 11 percent of those submitted during the turbulent 1780s. In all three states, women's petitioning declined somewhat after 1790, but it continued to exceed its prewar levels in 1800.

The volume of petitions and the pervasiveness of war's impact made for a diverse group of women petitioners who in some ways represented a cross-section of the region's white female population. Petitioners included women of all social ranks. Frances Brewton Pinckney, who petitioned for tax relief in 1783, belonged to one of Charleston's leading families. Annabella Moultrie was a slaveholding heiress and the niece of both a Whig general and the Tory lieutenant governor of British East Florida (Doc. 4). Mary Pratt was a patriotic working woman who lost her position as housekeeper at Charleston's statehouse during the British occupation (Doc. 1). Further down the social scale, other petitioners described themselves as "poor," "infirm," or "distressed," while Rachel Sharp, who was illiterate, solicited economic relief from the legislature on the grounds that she was "a Poor person . . . born with such natural Defects as render her incapable of doing any kind of Manual Labor."[6]

Petitioners also varied widely in the sums they requested. While Sharp requested a pittance to sustain herself until the county commissioners of the poor attended to her case, Ann Summerall sought payment for a slave that state troops allegedly took from her plantation (Doc. 13). Even more ambitious were the sisters Hannah and Margaret Ash, both widows of South Carolina Whigs, who requested some five thousand pounds to compensate for the inheritance they lost as a result of the confiscation and resale of the estate of their Tory father (Doc. 22).

---

6. Petition of Rachel Sharp, 1 Dec. 1797, LP, Sc-Ar; Petition of Frances Brewton Pinckney, 22 Feb. 1783, ibid.

Women's petitions also revealed varying levels of worldly experience and financial knowledge. Unlike the loyalist women who followed their husbands into exile and whose petitions to the British government reflected minimal knowledge of nondomestic matters, many women who remained at home in wartime knew what property their families owned, what compensation soldiers received, and what the government paid for produce.[7] Widow Elizabeth Petrie recounted the intricate details of her family's business transactions with future Tories before the Revolution and cogently asserted that the confiscation of loyalist estates unfairly compromised her own financial interests (Doc. 15). Sarah Howley of Georgia described how inflation had ravaged the fund that her husband left for her maintenance.[8] Others reported the specific losses their families suffered as a result of the war in a deferential but generally dispassionate manner (Doc. 17).

Some of the most effusively deferential supplicants used the conventional language of feminine innocence and dependence to mask genuine understanding of their family's economic circumstances and interests. Mary Davidson, widow of Gen. William Davidson, was shrewd enough to bargain with both state and national authorities after the adoption of the Constitution to assure herself of getting the largest possible sum for her husband's back pay, though she described herself as a "helpless woman" when she petitioned the North Carolina assembly (Doc. 21). Even more striking was the case of Alice Robison, who in 1792 carefully explained to the North Carolina legislature that her husband, Benjamin, bought two hundred acres in Anson County from the commissioners of confiscated estates, intending to use his earnings as an auctioneer of confiscated property to pay what he owed for the land. Unfortunately, the state never paid Benjamin for his services as auctioneer, and, as a result, his debt remained unpaid when he died in 1791. Alice Robison, who described herself as "a helpless widow, with two helpless children," showed detailed knowledge of this transaction and its consequences in requesting its can-

---

7. On the women exiles and their petitions, see Mary Beth Norton, "Eighteenth-Century American Women in War and Peace: The Case of the Loyalists," *WMQ*, 3d ser., 33 (1976): 389–92.

8. Petition of Sarah Howley, 15 Feb. 1785, in "Journal of the House of Assembly of Georgia, Session Jan. 21, 1784 to Aug. 15, 1786," Works Progress Administration typescript, 1938, 233.

cellation. In stating her case, however, she explicitly invoked the conventional stereotypes of male power and female dependence, appealing to the assembly "with a dependent eye, as to the Patrons and Protectors of the Widow, and the fatherless."[9]

While widow Robison's language was unusually maudlin, she shared two characteristics with most other petitioners that distinguished them as a group from many of their contemporaries. First, because the common-law doctrine of coverture effectively erased a wife's legal existence and empowered her husband to represent her in all legal and economic matters, the overwhelming majority of petitioners were widows, single women, or wives of Tory exiles. In keeping with the logic of coverture, they were women who entered the public sphere to state their cases because they had no husbands to do it for them.[10] Second, at a time when most white women in the southern states were probably incapable of even signing their names, the vast majority of women petitioners were literate at least to that extent.[11] Moreover, roughly half penned the entire text of the documents they submitted for the legislators' consideration.

Women and men who petitioned the assemblies represented only a small fraction of those who had unresolved business with the government. During and after the Revolution, the unprecedented volume of public business led both the states and the Continental Congress to establish rudimentary bureaucracies to handle routine cases without direct legislative involvement. At both the state and national levels, securing payment of public debts usually required three separate transactions:

9. Petition of Alice Robison, 28 Dec. 1791, GASR, Dec. 1791–Jan. 1792, Nc-Ar.

10. On coverture, see Linda K. Kerber, *Women of the Republic: Intellect and Ideology in Revolutionary America* (Chapel Hill: University of North Carolina Press, 1980), chap. 5.

11. Kenneth A. Lockridge estimated the literacy rate of eighteenth-century Virginia women at approximately 50 percent. By equating literacy with the ability to sign one's name, however, Lockridge may have overestimated women's capabilities. Qualitative evidence suggests improvements in white women's literacy throughout America after the Revolution, largely as a result of republican ideology. See Lockridge, *Literacy in Colonial New England: An Inquiry into the Social Context of Literacy in the Early Modern West* (New York: W. W. Norton, 1974), esp. 11–12, 92, 97, 127; E. Jennifer Monaghan, "Literacy Instruction and Gender in Early New England," *American Quarterly* 40 (1988): 18–41; Mary Beth Norton, "Communication," *WMQ*, 3d ser., 48 (1991): 639–45; Kerber, *Women of the Republic*, 164–65, 191–93.

verifying the claim, obtaining funded certificates to satisfy the debt, and having the certificates retired or paid. In most cases, all three steps would have been effected without legislative intervention.

In the 1780s, states struggled to systematize, fund, and retire their revolutionary debts. While northern states had raised loans and taxes to pay the bulk of their wartime expenses, southerners had relied primarily on a combination of paper currency and certificates to finance their war effort. As the war dragged on and as currency depreciated to near worthlessness, state governments increasingly issued certificates in place of or in exchange for the discredited paper money. Representing the government's promise to pay its creditors, often with interest, certificates accounted for most of the public debt by the time the war was over. States issued certificates to soldiers for wages, pensions, and enlistment bounties. Civilians received them as payment for supplies and loans, liens on confiscated property, and compensation for damages inflicted by state troops.[12]

In the revolutionary era, North Carolina was representative of the southern states in its handling of public accounts. Beginning in 1778, the assembly authorized various military officials to issue certificates for the purchase or impressment of supplies for the state's militia and Continental regiments. Poor bookkeeping and lack of central control over the issuing of these certificates, however, gave rise to confusion and fraud. In 1780, the assembly therefore appointed a board of auditors to review and validate all outstanding claims against the state. In 1781, the legislature established seven district boards of auditors that convened at various locations in North Carolina to evaluate claims and issue new interest-bearing certificates to deserving creditors, in so doing bringing a degree of order and uniformity to the state's certificate debt.[13]

While government creditors submitted their claims to auditors appointed expressly for that purpose, the assembly directed disabled veterans and soldiers' widows and orphans to apply initially for pensions through their county courts. In 1784, a North Carolina statute stipulated that all prospective pension recipients "shall apply directly to the court of the county in which he or they reside" to have their "distresses" certified.

12. See, generally, B. U. Ratchford, *American State Debts* (Durham, N.C.: Duke University Press, 1941), 30–45.

13. Morrill, *Fiat Finance*, 16–21, 27–29.

The certified application, in turn, would be forwarded to the state legislature, which would grant the claimant "an allowance adequate to their relief for one year, which allowance shall be continued for the next succeeding year, and so long as the court shall certify" the pensioner's continued need for it. The speaker of the assembly countersigned the court certificate, which the law deemed "a sufficient voucher to any sheriff, collector, or treasurer paying the same in the settlement of their public accounts."[14]

Although pensioners sometimes received their annual allowance in the form of produce, more often they, like other government creditors, were issued government certificates. In the 1780s, holders of such certificates could redeem them in several ways, as the states employed a variety of strategies to retire their public debts. States accepted certificates as payment for the purchase of confiscated property and western lands as well as for certain taxes. Ultimately, however, most states devalued their certificates, like their currency, and in so doing repudiated a portion of their debts.[15]

Auditors and other state officials settled thousands of public accounts in the immediate postwar era, while hundreds of claimants whose cases remained unresolved petitioned the legislature for special consideration. As the documents in this chapter show, each petition pertaining to the settlement of public accounts represents either the petitioner's failure to follow the prescribed guidelines for recovering public debts or the state bureaucracy's inability to meet the petitioner's needs. In some instances, petitioners lacked documentation sufficient to persuade the auditors of the validity of their claims. In other cases, however, petitioners were unable to travel to the towns where the auditors convened, or they simply lacked accurate information about how and when to file their claims.

In desperation or perhaps hoping that elected officials would be more solicitous of their interests, many petitioners turned to the legislature as a last resort after failing to attain satisfaction elsewhere (Doc. 11). Virginian Catharine Helvistine, a soldier's widow who sought to recover his back pay after the war was over, complained that "the Auditors and others concerned in adjustm[en]t of public accts. pretend that their Powers are incompetent to the Settlement of [her] claim, notwithstanding the

14. *N.C. Recs.*, 24:568–69.
15. Ratchford, *American State Debts*, 68–70; Morrill, *Fiat Finance*, 35–48.

justice thereof." In 1786, she successfully appealed to the state assembly to authorize payment of her husband's arrears. Similarly, in 1789, unable to collect from the auditors what the state owed her for flour and salt supplied to the Continental forces, Janet Burges requested and received compensation from the North Carolina legislature.[16] Other petitioners appealed to the legislatures to correct administrative errors. Some accused the auditor's office of misplacing the documents necessary to substantiate their claims against the state (Doc. 3). Others reported that government officials, having approved their accounts, delayed payment or mistakenly sent it to someone other than its proper recipient (Docs. 12, 18).

The creation of a two-tiered federal system of government compounded the administrative obstacles that some petitioners encountered in the postrevolutionary decades. During the war, both the states and the Continental Congress had raised troops and purchased supplies, leaving creditors to apply for compensation from the appropriate authorities when the war was over. But distinctions between state and Continental debts could be obscure and sometimes changeable. For instance, in the war's early years, the national government paid the officers and troops of the Continental Army, but Congress shifted that responsibility to the states in 1780. Consequently, when the widow of a Continental soldier who died in battle at Germantown in 1777 applied to the North Carolina assembly for his back pay fourteen years later, the legislators informed her that her claim was "a continental debt, for the payment whereof, ample provision is made by Congress." Officials also dispensed state and Continental certificates indiscriminately when they purchased or impressed supplies from civilians. A farmer therefore could find himself selling produce to Continental officers who paid in state certificates, which remained obligations of the state regardless of their disbursement for Continental purposes.[17]

---

16. Petition of Catharine Helvistine, 20 Dec. 1786, LP, Misc., Vi-Ar; Petition of Janet Burges, 14 Dec. 1789, GASR, Nov.–Dec. 1789, Nc-Ar.

17. E. James Ferguson, *The Power of the Purse: A History of American Public Finance, 1776–1790* (Chapel Hill: University of North Carolina Press, 1961), 50–51, 62–63, 179, 181–82; Petition of Elizabeth Doughlas, 10 Nov. 1791, GASR, Dec. 1791–Jan. 1792, Nc-Ar; Committee report on the petition of Elizabeth Doughlas, ibid.

Some government officials may have exploited the ambiguities inherent in the federal system to evade the payment of public debts. In 1791, Mary Fuller applied to the Virginia assembly for arrears in pay due her late husband, William, who had served as a sergeant with the Virginia Continentals. The assembly deemed Fuller's petition "reasonable" but instructed her to refer her claim to the national Congress. Three years later, however, Fuller reported to the assembly that "Application has been attempted conformably to the petitioners instructions . . . [but] the said proceedings which have terminated in a total frustration . . . [h]er claims being considered as by no means chargeable to the Union." Ann McKnight, whose husband died in 1781, spent years appealing to the national government for compensation. She believed that "the false suggestion of some officers in the Warr Office that her [captured] husband had been exchanged" delayed their consideration of her case until the statute of limitations prevented her from obtaining a government pension. In 1800, she turned to the Virginia legislature, asking that "the time which she hath suffered to elapse from an ignorance of whom to make the demand and the mistaken information communicated by the Warr Office, will not be considered as influencing the equity of her claim."[18]

South Carolinian Mary Taggart spent eighteen years submitting her case to a succession of state and federal authorities, each of whom attempted to avoid paying her well-documented claims. As we have seen, Gen. Benjamin Lincoln had ordered the Taggarts to burn their house and outbuildings in March 1780, when the British were advancing toward Charleston. The Taggarts complied and retained a copy of Lincoln's order as well as a sworn affidavit verifying the value of the affected property, which Mary Taggart presented when she sought compensation. In 1783, South Carolina's auditor general approved Taggart's claim but forwarded it to the commissioner charged with settling Congress's outstanding debts in South Carolina. The commissioner, in turn, rejected Taggart's claim, which she then submitted to the state legislature for consideration. In 1793, the legislature ruled that "the Charge is one that should be & have been discharged by the Union." Taggart doggedly petitioned the state assembly again in 1794 and 1796, and she also attempted without success to submit her claim to Congress. Finally, in 1800, she ad-

---

18. Petition of Mary Fuller, 24 Nov. 1794, LP, Misc., Vi-Ar; Petition of Ann McKnight, 5 Dec. 1800, ibid.

mitted to the state assembly that she was now "uncertain . . . from what department of Government she was to expect compensation." Without explanation the assembly paid her claim in full, thus reversing its previous ruling.[19]

Although the legislatures granted the requests of many supplicants, petitioning was a complex process fraught with potential obstacles. Literacy or access to a literate person was a precondition for filing a formal petition, as was the ability to convey the petition to the county seat for the required certification by the courts prior to submission to the assembly for consideration. Ideally, the prospective petitioner also would know when the legislature was due to meet, so as to have sufficient time to deliver the certified petition to her local representative before he left for the state capital. Most important, the legislative committees that considered petitions insisted that those who filed them follow the legally prescribed procedures for the settlement of public accounts. They, like state auditors and other officials, also expected petitioners to present documentation to substantiate their claims.

Soldiers' relatives probably had the greatest difficulty securing the proof necessary to persuade the legislators to act in their behalf. In order to receive a soldier's arrears in pay, for instance, his heir needed to prove not only that the state was indebted to the soldier in question but also that the soldier was deceased and therefore unable to collect the debt himself. Many soldiers' widows, especially the wives of men who died in battle, could recover neither the vouchers and certificates that verified their monetary claims nor the official papers that proved their spouse's enlistment (Doc. 7). Others, whose husbands or sons never returned from the war, could not specify when and where these men had died, nor, for that matter, could they prove conclusively that they were in fact dead. Accordingly, Ann Meadows of North Carolina informed the legislature that "from the best information [she] could ever hear," she believed that her only son had died at the Battle of Camden. Even an officer under whom he served could say only that he "ha[d] reason to believe" that James Meadows died in service (Docs. 5, 6). When Ann Dowell petitioned to obtain her son's arrears in pay, she likewise observed that "it is generally

---

19. *S.C. House Journals, 1792–1794,* 445; Petitions of Mary Taggart, 2 Dec. 1794, 9 Dec. 1796, 25 Nov. 1800, LP, Sc-Ar; Senate resolution on the petition of Mary Taggart, 18 Dec. 1801, Legislative Papers, Sc-Ar.

supposed he died" in an army hospital. The legislators rejected both Dowell's and Meadows's petitions for lack of evidence.[20]

Other petitioners, some of whom had sufficient evidence to authenticate their claims, maintained that their ignorance of the laws and procedures for seeking restitution discouraged them from recovering what the government rightly owed them. As late as 1793, the widow of a Virginia militiaman who died in service more than a decade earlier informed the legislature that she had only "lately been told that in such Cases the laws of the land has made some provision to assist in supporting the bringing up of the orphans of those who died or were killed in the service of their Country." That same year, Elizabeth Alley, another Virginia widow, requested a government pension, explaining that she was "till only lately entirely Ignorant of that provision" that granted pensions to soldiers' widows. Mary White, whose late husband, David, cleaned and repaired arms for the Virginia forces, knew the state government owed her money, but she could not decide which state officials should evaluate her claim. White possessed "an audited Specie Warrant for thirty six pounds four shillings and a penny, granted to her late Husband . . . [but] being poor, and distressed, with a large family, and ignorant of what method was to be pursued to obtain payment of the said Warrant," she petitioned the governor, who referred her to the assembly, which rejected her claim.[21]

Some women appear to have been genuinely unfamiliar with the relatively impersonal procedures for reclaiming public debts, but other petitioners may have feigned ignorance to win the sympathy of the men who passed judgment on their requests. Mary Magdalen Burger was the widow of Michael Burger, a soldier who served for several years in the Second South Carolina Continental Regiment. Although Burger was taken prisoner at some point during his service, he returned to his family unharmed when the war was over and died a few years later. After he died, however, his widow applied to the state legislature for relief on the grounds that she was "aged and infirm, without any means of Support, by which she is reduced to great distress." At a time of general economic distress, when states teetered on the brink of financial ruin, Mary Magdalen

20. Petition of Ann Dowell, 15 Nov. 1788, LP, Misc., Vi-Ar.
21. Petition of Mary Edwards, 22 Oct. 1793, LP, Louisa Co., Vi-Ar; Petition of Elizabeth Alley, 30 Oct. 1793, LP, Henrico Co., Vi-Ar; Petition of Mary White, 21 Nov. 1788, LP, Norfolk Co., Vi-Ar.

Burger probably knew that only the widows of men who died or were disabled during their terms of enlistment could expect to receive government pensions. Although the assembly postponed indefinitely consideration of her request, by ignoring the law and presumably persuading the courts that she was truly needy, Burger did her best to make the system work for her benefit.[22]

Despite the precarious financial circumstances in which they lived, some women delayed seeking to settle their public accounts. Between 1791 and 1795, more than half of North Carolina's women petitioners were still submitting war-related claims, as did nearly three-quarters of their counterparts in South Carolina. In some cases, women may have delayed petitioning because they were not aware of prescribed procedures and deadlines for the settlement of public debts (Doc. 16). In others, pride in the ability to support their own families or intimidation in the face of impersonal government procedures may have deterred them from acting more quickly. Some petitioners clearly waited until they were truly desperate to seek relief or restitution. South Carolinians Margrat Clendening and Ann Dabney waited thirteen years to seek payment of debts that the state had contracted with their husbands in 1779. By then, one woman described her situation as "Exceeding hard," while the other depended on "Relief from the County" for her subsistence (Docs. 19, 20). Mary Boush, wife of a naval officer, was widowed and left with "Six Small Children" in 1779. She spent the next eleven years "Struggling thro' life without being burthensome to her friends or her Country . . . without any Support but what proceeded from her own Industry," before successfully seeking a government pension in 1790. Mary Cornhill delayed eighteen years after the death of her husband before applying for a government pension, explaining that "her own personal strength" supported her family until she "bec[a]me much enfeebled by age and infirmities" and thus reduced "to the necessity of soliciting the public Bounty by Way of Pension for Life." "Feeling a zeal for the cause of her native Country and of course an unwillingness to ask for a favour," Elizabeth Jameson survived with the help of the "continued benevolence of the Society of Free Ma-

---

22. Petition of Mary Magdalen Burger, 12 Feb. 1788, LP, Sc-Ar; *S.C. House Journals 1787–1788*, 549–50. On the financial difficulties of state governments and their constituents during this period, see, for instance, Nadelhaft, *Disorders of War*, chap. 9.

sons" until 1797, when "her external resources failed her as well as her abilities for exertion," and she was forced "to cast herself upon the humanity of her Country."[23]

For other women, delay was not a matter of choice. While a husband lived he, not his wife, contracted and collected debts, but when he died his widow assumed these economic rights and obligations, especially if her husband chose her to administer his estate. In the 1790s, therefore, recently widowed women petitioned to recover arrears and land warrants that their husbands, often veterans of the Revolution, had neglected to collect during their lifetimes (Docs. 14, 23). Others petitioned to settle disputed accounts with the state, which in some instances involved large sums of money and government certificates (Doc. 10).

Some women, perhaps alarmed by the financial problems they inherited as they entered widowhood, appealed to the legislature to cancel their spouses' public debts. Most of these cases involved unpaid balances on land purchases, and, as the land in question was often unimproved, most petitioners proposed returning it to the state in exchange for the cancellation of their debts. In such instances, most widows simply informed the assembly that their husbands' estates were insufficient to satisfy the government's claims, though occasionally petitioners also disparaged the business judgment of their deceased spouses. In 1800, for example, one North Carolina woman asked the legislature to forgive a debt that she believed her husband had paid, though the records indicated otherwise, explaining that both he and the land commissioner with whom he dealt "in their latter days . . . were both incapable of transacting business in a proper manner."[24]

Left to their own devices, many women worked energetically to sustain their families and to win compensation for the losses they incurred during the revolutionary years. While some petitioned the authorities for relief or to recover outstanding debts, others took in sewing or boarders or worked for wages to supplement the income of their households. Widows in Charleston sent their servants through the streets selling the fruits of their domestic labors so that they might "Obtain an Honest Lively-

23. Petitions of Mary Boush, 1790, 19 Nov. 1796, LP, Norfolk City, Vi-Ar; Petition of Mary Cornhill, 25 Nov. 1795, LP, Misc., Vi-Ar; Petition of Elizabeth Jameson, 18 Dec. 1797, LP, Dinwiddie Co., Vi-Ar.
24. Petition of Elizabeth Oneal, 17 Dec. 1800, GASR, Nov.–Dec. 1800, Nc-Ar.

hood in defence of their fatherless Children" (Doc. 2). Postrevolutionary Charleston also included among its inhabitants at least sixty-seven
women who described themselves as seamstresses who "by the loss of
their husbands, friends or near relations during the war, . . . are . . .
obliged to earn Subsistence for themselves" and for their children
(Doc. 8). Aware that they had shared the costs of American liberty and
independence, these women perhaps hoped to win a portion of the fruits
of victory when they asked the state legislature to increase the tariff on
the imported apparel that flooded the Charleston market immediately
following the Treaty of Paris. The assembly rejected the seamstresses' petition, admitting that their trade policies were designed more to promote
manufacturing than to protect the livelihood of poor women.[25]

When women petitioned their legislatures, they staked their claim to
part of the public sphere, albeit a part that was less expansive than that
most white adult men increasingly claimed. Women petitioners believed
that their requests and grievances merited serious consideration, which
in most cases the legislators appear to have afforded them. Making their
way through unfamiliar bureaucracies and impersonal procedures, southern women presented and often resolved their war-related claims. Doing
so was an explicitly public act, probably the first such act for many petitioners. Southern women may have regarded their new republican governments as particularly humane and just, as they submitted petitions to
them in unprecedented numbers.

By 1800, persons seeking redress of war-related grievances were
a minority among those petitioning the legislatures. Between 1796 and
1800, only nine of the seventy-eight petitions Carolina women filed dealt
with war-related matters. The closing years of the eighteenth century
were a turning point in the evolution of women's petitioning, as creditors and debtors increasingly laid to rest their revolutionary claims and
women, instead, began to call on the legislatures to settle inheritance and
property disputes and, in some states, to enable them to jettison un-
desirable husbands or circumvent the constraints of coverture.[26] Yet, for
some families, perhaps most especially for the loyalists, the personal and
economic legacies of the Revolution endured long after 1800.

---

25. S.C. House Journals, 1789–1790, 88–89.

26. In North Carolina, four of forty-two petitions women submitted during these
years dealt with war-related issues, while only five of thirty-six did so in South Carolina. On petitions for divorces and separate estates, see chap. 5, below.

DOCUMENT 1
Mary Pratt

In 1775, Mary Pratt witnessed the Whigs' confiscation of the arms and gunpowder in Charleston's public stores and risked the loss of her position as keeper of the statehouse rather than reveal the culprits' identities to the lieutenant governor. Pratt, a staunch Whig who later furnished supplies to the patriot forces, lost her job under the restored British regime but regained it when the war was over. On 29 January 1783, she sought her back pay from the assembly, which granted her rations of meat, bread, and wood "to relieve her present distress . . . the amount thereof [to] be deducted from her Account against the Publick." Pratt appears to have resigned her post after marrying John McLean later that year.[1]

The Humble Petition of Mary Prat Sheweth

That your Petitioner was many years ago appointed Housekeeper for the State House with an allowance of Two Hundred Pounds Currency p[er] year which place she held until the Capture of Charlestown when at the intercession of Robert Williams[2] she was discharged and turned out of it to make room for another Person who was more attached to the British Government, at that time she had due to her upwards of a year and four months Salary Viz: from the first of January 1779 to the 12 of May 1780. Since the Evacuation of this Capital she has had to her great satisfaction the good fortune to be reinstated in her former post but thro' the Cruel and inhuman treatment of the British she is so much reduced in her circumstances as to be nearly in want of all the necessaries of life. She therefore begs leave to submit her case to this Honourable House humbly hoping they will take it into their most serious consideration and

1. John Drayton, *Memoirs of the American Revolution as Relating to the State of South Carolina,* 2 vols. (New York: New York Times and Arno Press, 1969), 1:223; Claghorn, *Women Patriots,* 417; Clemens, *Marriage Recs.,* 223; *S.C. House Journals, 1783–1784,* 60–61.

2. A Charleston lawyer who accepted the reimposition of British rule and held a civil commission in the restored royal government (Lambert, *S.C. Loyalists,* 187–88). See also the petition of Ann Williams in chap. 3 of the present study.

allow her, her arrears of Salary or such other releif as they in their Wisdom shall think fit. And as in Duty bound your Pet[itione]r will ever pray.

(DS, Sc-Ar)

DOCUMENT 2
Widows of Charleston

The petitioners were slaveholding widows who resided in the parish of St. Phillip and St. Michael in central Charleston. At least three were widows of revolutionary soldiers. In this petition of 5 August 1783, the women protested new regulations that hindered slaves' employment in the buying and selling of goods as well as in certain trades. Enacted to satisfy artisans who resented black competition, these regulations undermined the widows' economic interests. The assembly never formally considered their petition.[3]

The Petition of Sundry Widows, Inhabitants of Cha[rle]s Town Sheweth—

That Your Petitioners from a long and Accustomed time having been used to send their Baskets out in the Streets of Charles Town with Goods, wares, and Merchandize by their Servants, in Order to expose them for sale and Obtain an Honest Livelyhood in defence of their fatherless Children, But being deprived thereof by a Late order from the Commissioners of the Markets under the penalty of having their goods seized and sold, by Authority of an Act of the General Assembly for many Years past.[4]

And as Your Petitioners from the peculiar situation of their Habitations on Account of the High prices of Rent[5] many days not have a

---

3. *Heads of Families . . . in the Year 1790: S.C.*, 39, 42; Moss, *S.C. Patriots*, 277, 675, 792; Nadelhaft, *Disorders of War*, 98–102.

4. A 1740 statute allowed Charleston slaves "to buy or sell fruit, fish and garden stuff . . . and to purchase any thing for the use of their masters . . . in open market, under such regulations as are or shall be appointed by law" so long as they carried a written license, or "ticket," from their owner (*S.C Statutes*, 7:407–8).

5. Despite attempts to rebuild, housing was scarce and expensive following the fire of 1778 and siege of 1780 (Walsh, *Charleston's Sons of Liberty*, 107–8).

Chance to dispose of the least Article in their own Houses to provide a Maintenance for themselves and fatherless Children—They therefore pray Your Honour[6] and the Gentlemen of the House of Assembly will take their Case in the present hard times under their most Serious Consideration and grant them such Relief as they in their Wisdom shall think proper—

And your Petitioners as in duty Bound will pray.

Emelia Meurset	Catharine Duvall
Mary Legoold	Elizabeth Gilbert
Lena Callaghan	Martha Miggins
Eliz[abeth] Purse	Maria Litune
Sarah Yatess	

(DS, Sc-Ar)

DOCUMENT 3

Margaret Wall

Like many other government creditors in North Carolina, John Wall submitted his certificates to the district auditors who convened in Hillsborough in 1781. Unfortunately, the auditors mislaid his documents and refused to verify his accounts. On 29 May 1784, Wall's widow, Margaret, bearing a sworn affidavit from the Orange County court, petitioned the state assembly for restitution. The legislature referred the case back to the Hillsborough District auditors.[7]

The memorial of Margaret Wall humbly Sheweth that in the spring of the year One thousand Seven hundred and Eighty your Memorialists Husband John Wall (who then lived within the Town of Hillsborough)

---

6. The widows addressed their petition jointly to Governor Benjamin Guerard (1783–85) and to the state assembly.

7. Morrill, *Fiat Finance,* 27–28; Affidavit of Margaret Wall, 1784, GASR, Apr.–June 1784, Nc-Ar.

furnish'd articles &c to Genl. Gates's Army[8] at Several times to the amount of Nine thousand five hundred and Seventy-five pounds of the then Currency and Obtaind certificates from the freeholders who Valued the Same on Oath (to wit) Benjamin Leonard deceas'd & John Ellison one of which certificates for £490 were audited and a Specie certificate for the same amounting to Eight pounds Seventeen Shillings & 4d. One other certificate from the said Valuers for the Sum of Nine thousand and Eighty-five pounds Currency for which your Memorialist never could Obtain a certificate altho the claim was exhibited to the auditors, the auditors inform your Memorialist the certificate from the freeholders is lost your Memorialist therefore hopes your Honourable Body will take her case under consideration and refer her claim to the present district Auditors to grant Such relief in the pr[o]misses as to them shall appear Just and your Memorialist as in duty bound Shall Pray.

(ADS, Nc-Ar)

DOCUMENT 4

Annabella Moultrie

The petitioner was the niece of both South Carolina general William Moultrie and John Moultrie, the Tory lieutenant governor of East Florida. Her father, James Moultrie, died in 1765, after serving briefly as East Florida's chief justice; James's widow and two children probably returned to South Carolina shortly thereafter. On 26 February 1785, Annabella Moultrie successfully petitioned the assembly for permission to transport the slaves she had inherited from her father from East Florida to South Carolina. Two years later, she married Edward Harleston, whose estate included

---

8. On 14 June 1780, Congress appointed Maj. Gen. Horatio Gates to succeed Lincoln as commanding general of the Southern Department, but Gates did not arrive in Hillsborough, the Continental Army's rendezvous point in North Carolina, until mid-July. If Wall furnished supplies to the army in the spring of 1780, Maj. Gen. Johann DeKalb was the commander with whom he dealt (Hugh F. Rankin, *The North Carolina Continentals* [Chapel Hill: University of North Carolina Press, 1971], 239–41).

104 slaves, three plantations, and a house in Charleston, when he died in 1825.[9]

The Humble Petition of Anna Bella Moultrie Sheweth:

That your Petitioner by the Death of her Father became entitled to a Number of Negroes as Part of his Estate; that they remained sometime under the care of her Uncle in East Florida, untill she arrived at age, and that by means of the War, which continued after her arrival at Age, she was prevented from bringing the said Negroes into this State, untill Peace took Place.

Your Petitioner further Sheweth, that before the late Act for Imposing a Duty on Negroes imported into this State,[10] and shortly after the Peace took Place she went to bring the said Negroes into this State and accordingly hired a Vessel, and was at the Expen[se of] Insurance in so doing, and that on the arrival of the said Negroes, she was obliged to give Security for the Duty to the amount of near two Hundred Pounds;

That Part of said Negroes under her Father's Will, were the Property of her Brother,[11] but on a Settlement and a Division of the Estate, the same fell to her.

Your Petitioner apprehends her Case to be exactly Similar to those Persons Citizens of this State whose Negroes were in the British Dominions during the War;[12] and which prevented them from bringing them into this Country; And that nothing but the War and her said Negroes being in that Situation prevented her from bringing them here Sooner, and as the Act of Assembly imposing a Duty on Negroes evidently excepts

---

9. *Biog. Directory of S.C. House, 1719–1774*, 482; *Biog. Dict. of S.C. House, 1775–1790*, 316; John W. Moore, *Some Family Lines of James Peronneau DeSaussure and His Wife Annie Isabella Laurens* (Washington: n.p., 1958), 21–22, 26–27; Siebert, *Loyalists in East Florida*, 2:330–32.

10. "An Act for levying and collecting certain Duties and Imports therein mentioned, in aid of the Public Revenue," 1784 (*S.C. Statutes*, 4:608).

11. James Moultrie, a Tory and a major in the British army (Moore, *Some Family Lines*, 27).

12. The duty applied to all slaves brought to South Carolina from outside the United States except those "who having been the property of some citizen of America have absconded, been carried or sent off by their owner, or have been carried off by the enemy" (*S.C. Statutes*, 4:608).

Such Persons from Such Duty she Humbly Hopes she is entitled to the like Exemption, and prays this Honourable House to order the notes for such Duties to be given up and Cancelled.

And your Petitioner as in Duty bound will ever Pray.

(DS, Sc-Ar)

DOCUMENT 5

Ann Meadows

> *North Carolinian James Meadows joined the army in 1776 and died in service four years later. He left behind an indigent mother, who petitioned on 5 January 1787 for the back pay allegedly owed him. The assembly rejected her petition for lack of documentation.*

The Humble petition of Ann Madows Humbly Sheweth.

That whereas you Humble petitioner had Son Called James Madows that inlisted with Colo. Robt. Rowan [13] at the Commencement of the War and from the best information I could ever hear was killed at Camden in South Carolina your humble petitioner being a poor old Woman not being able to Mantain her self by Reason of old Age and infirmity And as her son never Raped the benefit of either pay or land allowed soldiers for their Services She humbly Serveth it may be granted her and your petitioner as in duty bound will ever pray.

(DS, Nc-Ar)

DOCUMENT 6

Ann Meadows

> *On 12 December 1789, Meadows again attempted to recover the arrears she believed the state owed to her deceased son. This peti-*

---

13. Capt. Robert Rowan commanded the First North Carolina Regiment from September 1775 through June 1776. He also represented the town of Hillsborough in the state assembly ([Hay et al.], *N.C. Soldiers*, 46, 499, 615).

*tion also failed. According to the 1790 census, Ann Meadows resided
in Fayetteville with a free white male under sixteen years of age,
possibly a boarder. She is not listed in the census for 1800.*[14]

The petition of Ann Meadows Humbly sheweth that your petitioner
is now very aged also infirm so that she is reduced to real poverty, and not
by Indolence, which will appear from the Candour of all the respectable
Inhabitants of Fayetteville. Your petitioner having one only son who Inlisted in Captain Rowans Company in the year 1776 and never returned
to assist her in her old age as will appear by the Certificate herewith presented.[15] She therefore prays your Honerable Body to take her Case into
Consideration and grant such releif as you in your Wisdom shall think
Just, and your petitioner as in duty bound shall ever pray &c &c.

(ADS, Nc-Ar)

DOCUMENT 7

Martha Mitchel

*This petitioner appears in neither the North Carolina state cen-
sus nor in the federal census of 1790, but her husband served briefly
as a private in the state's Tenth Continental Regiment. He enlisted
for a one-year stint in April 1781 but died a few months later. On
12 December 1787, Martha Mitchel requested her husband's arrears in pay, but the assembly rejected her petition because, as
Mitchel herself admitted, she could not document her claim.*[16]

The Memorial & Petition of Martha Mitchel Relict of Theophilus
Mitchel late a Soldier in the continental line of this State humbly
Sheweth.

---

14. *Heads of Families . . . in the Year 1790: N.C.*, 41.

15. Both this petition and its predecessor were accompanied by Rowan's signed
testimony that James Meadows had served in his company in 1776 and that he later
"died in the service of his country."

16. [Hay et al.], *N.C. Soldiers*, 146.

That your Memorialists Husband did not only become a Soldier but died in the Service of the United States; that in consequence of his having So died your Memorialist has never been able to draw any Money or Pay whatever for the Services of her Said Husband, for the want of the proper Furloughs or other discharges. She flatters herself that, her irreparable loss, her ignorance in the business of this Sort, together with a principle of justice will recommend her Situation to the consideration of your hon[ora]ble Body and that you will point out Some Mode by which justice may yet be done her.

(ADS, Nc-Ar)

DOCUMENT 8

Seamstresses of Charleston

> *On 26 January 1789, sixty-seven Charleston seamstresses petitioned the South Carolina legislature, requesting that the current 5 percent tariff on ready-made clothing be increased to protect their business from foreign competitors. The assembly rejected the women's petition, noting that "a greater duty would in fact amount to a heavy tax" on those who purchased clothing and, furthermore, that the recently adopted Constitution soon would transfer "jurisdiction in matter of impost" from the states to the national government.*[17]

The Petition of Sundry Seamstresses of the City of Charleston Humbly Sheweth

That by the loss of their husbands, friends or near relations during the war, they are reduced to indigent circumstances, and obliged to earn Subsistence for themselves (& some of them for their helpless offspring) by their needles, but for want of sufficient employ many have been reduced to apply to the Public for assistance.

That your Petitioners have reason to believe their want of employment is occasioned by the great importation of ready made Cloaths Such as Shirts Stocks, thin Jaccats & Breeches, Slops & millinary of every kind

---

17. *S.C. House Journals, 1789–1790*, 88–89; Walsh, *Charleston's Sons of Liberty*, 127–28.

that your Petitioners can make here, and which are exported in great quantities to this place by a Nation whose policy it is to employ their own industrious poor rather than give bread to foreigners.[18]

Your Petitioners therefore humbly pray that a much larger duty may be laid on the above articles which will have a tendency to give employment to your Petitioners or encrease the Revenue as they are bulky articles that cannot be easily smuggled and your Petitioners as in duty bound shall ever pray.

(DS, Sc-Ar)
Signed: Mary Ward, Mary Brewton, Elizabeth Badger, [?] Simmonds, Judith Thomas "with fore Children," Mary Martin, Elizabeth Gilbert[19] "with five children," Ruth Pickton "with four Children," Cathrin Sholl "with three yonger Sisters," Mary Seymour, Rebecah Morris, Hannah Wells, Elizabeth Hencock, [?] Drommond, Florida Rembert, Sarah Stocks "And her Daughter," Sarah Rieses, Susannah Cox, Catrine Maverick, Esther Johnson, Elizabeth Johnson, Sarah Hulsall, Ales Woolcoks, Maria Elliot, Mary Turpin, Martha Davis, Sarah Barnham, Sarah Yates, Mather Rembert, Elizabeth Tousiger, Martha Tousiger, Elizabeth Larouche
Signed by mark (X): Rabaca Overton, Mary Hall, Eleonard Evet, Mary McFarling, E[?] Mureh, Mary Lafaye, Mary Lyben, Martha Fickling, Mary Ducas, Mary Brown, Mary Clark, Mary Thomas, Margret Branston, [illiegible], Susanah Brimenritter, [?] Harper, Eleanor McHegney, Ann Moss, Mary Gray, Malsey Smallwood, Jane Fell, Mary Long, Susannah Cain, Charlotte Smith, Mary Franks, Martha Walker, Mary George, Margret Hellebera, [?] Childs, Susannah Doughtar, Martha Mitchell, Martha Gray, Jenney Thompson, Mary Smith

---

DOCUMENT 9

Nancy Horah

The confiscation and sale of Tory estates provided some Whigs
with a unique opportunity to increase their landholdings. In 1782,

---

18. Britain, the chief supplier of foreign imports to the United States, protected its own markets via an extensive system of trade regulations known as the Navigation Acts.

19. Gilbert, along with Sarah Yates, also signed the widows' petition of 1783 (Doc. 2).

Henry Horah, owner of a town lot in Salisbury and one hundred acres in rural Rowan County, sought to exploit that opportunity but found himself unable to pay the state the money he owed for some two hundred acres he purchased. On 2 December 1789, shortly after Henry's death, his widow, Nancy, asked the North Carolina legislature to invalidate the sale. The assembly granted her petition, noting that she and her daughter, Elizabeth, would be dependent "entirely on the charity of the County for means of subsistence" if the state enforced its claim against them.[20]

The memorial of Nancy Horah widow and relict of Henry Horah deceased on behalf of herself and her daughter Betsy Horah, humbly shewith that at the time of the first confiscation sale in the district of Salisbury, Henry Horah your memorialists late husband purchased a tract of land on the Yadkin river containing about two hundred acres for about the sum of three hundred and eighteen pounds, two thirds of which was to be paid in certificates and one third in money; of which the said Henry Horah paid the sum of one hundred and six pounds in certificates being one third of the purchase and gave his bond for the ballance. Your memorialist further sheweth that her late husband never obtained any title for the said land as he did not pay the full purchase money but the title still remains in the state. Your memorialist sheweth that she and her helpless orphan are now left in very indigent circumstances in so much that it will not be possible for her to raise the sum necessary to discharge her said deceased husbands bond to the state so as to obtain a title to the land; and she humbly concieves it is not the intention of the legislature to deprive her and her helpless orphan of all they have for she is positive the estate will not be able to pay all the price. She therefore humbly prays that your honors will direct that the said land shall remain to the State and that the Treasurer may be directed to deliver to her her said husbands bond and in this she is perfectly willing that the sum of one hundred and six pounds (the third part of the price of the land already paid) may remain to the state which she humbly concieves will be a sufficient advan-

----

20. Will of Henry Horah, 7 Apr. 1789, Rowan County Will Book E, 119, Nc-Ar; DeMond, *Loyalists N.C.*, 162, 172–74; Committee report on the petition of Nancy Horah, 14 Dec. 1789, GASR, Nov.–Dec. 1789, Nc-Ar.

tage to the public for any injuries already sustained and your Memorialist will pray &c.

(DS, Nc-Ar)

DOCUMENT 10
Jane Poindexter and Joseph Williams

Between 1781 and 1784, Robert Lanier was responsible for settling public accounts in the Salisbury District of North Carolina. Issuing creditors new certificates plus interest to fund their outstanding claims, Lanier retired the older government notes and received receipts from the state for those he collected. The executors of Lanier's estate, however, believed the government improperly credited his accounts, and on 3 December 1790 they petitioned to protest what they deemed its erroneous claims against him. The assembly did not act on this petition.[21]

The Memorial of Jane Poindexter, late Widow of Robert Lanier, and Joseph Williams[22] both of Surry County and joint Executors of the Estate of said Robert Lanier, Humbly Sheweth

That your Memorialists are in great Embarrassment about a Settling finally with the Comptroller for the said Robert Lanier deceased in regard to his having been Treasurer of Salisbury District which will more appear from the annexed receipt and Memorandum of Francis Child the present Comptroller to one of your Memorialists dated the 28th day of April last past.[23]

---

21. On Lanier, whose career also included brief stints in the provincial congress and state assembly, and as commissary for the Salisbury District, see *N.C. Recs.*, 10:166, 167, 172, 193, 525, 931, 15:704, 635–36, 16:86.

22. With Lanier, Williams represented Surry County in the provincial congress in 1775. He was also a lieutenant colonel in the state militia (ibid., 10:166, 206, 892, 15:123–24; [Hay et al.], *N.C. Soldiers*, 50).

23. Not found.

That there is several Persons by whose affidavits it can be investigated[24] that said Robert Lanier at Hillsborough Assembly in 1784 must have paid very large sums to Richard Caswell the late Comptroller[25] and even much exceeding the sum of 1,131,689⅜ Dollars of which there is an account, which is exclusive of aprobaly larger sum which he carried with him to the Comptrollers Office at the same time And also the Torn bundles sent by Spearpoint,[26] But that these sums were left by said Robert Lanier with said Richard Caswell to count and then to give said Lanier a Receipt for the same, & that such receipt never must have been issued, since no such receipt has been found among the papers of said Lanier.

That in the above sums mentioned to be paid it does not appear distinctly how much thereof was Continental and howmuch State money, since your Memorialists are not possessed of the journals of the Assembly at Hillsborough in 1784, in which as they are informed there is a distinct account howmuch of the money then burnt was received from each Treasurer.

⋅   That there is Interest unaccounted for between the State and said Robert Lanier on £1,243[,]415.16—Auditors Currency, Loan Office, Bounty Certificates &c which the present Comptroller has referred to calculate but of which your Memorialists suggests 10 P[er]Cent was allowed on some and the common Interest on the rest up to the time of being paid into the Treasury by the several Sheriffs and other Officers,

---

24. Affidavits signed by Col. John Armstrong, M. Hunt, William Thornton, Esq., and the petitioner Joseph Williams accompanied the petition (GASR, Nov.–Dec. 1790, Nc-Ar).

25. Caswell, who from 1776 through 1780 served the maximum of three consecutive terms as governor, held the post of state comptroller general from 1782 until 1785, when he resumed the governorship (*Dict. of N.C. Biog.*, 1:344).

Hillsborough was one of seven towns in which North Carolina's assembly convened between 1775 and 1792, when Raleigh became the state's permanent capital (Hugh Talmadge Lefler and Albert Ray Newsome, *North Carolina: The History of a Southern State*, 3d ed. [Chapel Hill: University of North Carolina Press, 1973], 202–3, 208–9, 218–19, 258–59).

26. Joseph Spearpoint, a veteran of the Tenth Regiment of North Carolina Continentals, appears to have helped Lanier dispose of the old certificates, which were torn and later burned to ensure their removal from circulation (*N.C. Recs.*, 16:1164, 17:246–47; Affidavit of John Armstrong, 25 Nov. 1790, GASR, Nov.–Dec. 1790, Nc-Ar; Affidavit of Joseph Williams, 27 Nov. 1790, ibid.).

which when allowed will amount to a Considerable sum in favour of Robert Lanier aforesaid.

That there is also Interest unaccounted for in the same manner which will also be in favor of the said Lanier for £6967.6.3 Auditors Specie Certificates. That there has been paid into the Comptrollers Office by one of your Memorialists for said Lanier £996.7.11 in Clothing Specie Certificates,[27] which your Memorialists have reason to believe was all received in payment of the 1782 tax, since on the Books of the said Lanier there is found frequent Credits given the Sheriffs in that year for Clothing Certificates, but that the present Comptroller has also referred till further, to receive them as vouchers for so much new Money.

That Robert Lanier as far as your Memorialists are informed has never been allowed by nor has charged the public for any Salary during the time that he Acted as Treasurer and which is supposed to have been about four years, nor any allowance for attending the General Assemblys or paying Expresses &c.

That your Memorialists humbly request that the General Assembly will take the premises into Consideration and grant such allowances for the matters herein mentioned as unsettled or not allowed, as to their goodness and Justice shall seem right, since it would be very distressing to two poor little orphans a Son & a Daughter of said Robert Lanier, who having acquired an affluent fortune, through Zeal for his Country incured the displeasure of our Enemies who especially under Earl Cornwallis wreaked their Vengeance on him in a well known most severe manner[28] and left him an entirely ruined Man, which he nevertheless bore patiently, and before his decease gathered a Confortable little Living for the support of his Family.

That should the above mentioned allowances not be made the said poor little Orphans will be left in a State of perfect Indigency which will

---

27. Specie certificates, issued by state auditors or by specific departments like the Clothier or Quartermaster, were redeemable only in specie "or the true and real value of the amount of such specie in the currency of the State" (Morrill, *Fiat Finance,* 28–29).

28. This attack on Lanier's property presumably occurred in February 1781, when Cornwallis's army pursued Gen. Nathanael Greene's retreating force to the Dan River, looting and burning civilian property along the way (Pancake, *Destructive War,* 165–71).

be amore fatal Blow to them than that of Earl Cornwallis's having now no Father to look to.

That your Memorialists once more request the General Assembly to consider the premises with Justice and compassion.

And they will as in duty bound forever pray &c.

(ADS [by either Poindexter or Williams], Nc-Ar)

Document 11

Selah Branham

> *The petitioner was a resident of Richland County in the Camden District of South Carolina, where she lived in a household composed of herself and six white males, who probably were her sons. Seeking payment of a public debt, Branham took her case first to the state auditor, then to court, and finally to the assembly, which she petitioned on 22 Janaury 1791. The legislators approved her petition and ordered her account paid.*[29]

The Petition of Selah Branham Sheweth

That the husband of your petitioner who is now deceased delivered to David McCord[30] in the Year 1780 Sixteen head of Cattle for which they received the Receipts which accompany this Petition; That the Said Receipts were presented in due time to the Auditor General who disputing the Authority of the Said McCord as commisary, refused to give her Compensation for the Said property—& That in consequence of advice from the Auditor General she prosecuted the S[ai]d McCord, but he proving his Authority was acquitted by the Court.

She now applies to your honorable house for that Relief for which she has hitherto sought in vain. In Granting This Petition you will relieve

---

29. *Heads of Families . . . in the Year 1790: S.C.*, 26; *S.C House Journals, 1791*, 325, 409.

30. McCord, like Branham, resided in the Camden District (*Heads of Families . . . in the Year 1790: S.C.*, 26).

from distress an unfortunate Woman who as in duty bound will ever pray &c.

(DS, Sc-Ar [Accounts Audited, no. 711½, roll 13, frames 23–24])

DOCUMENT 12

Mary Baxter

Mary Baxter, the widow of a South Carolina ferrykeeper who had served in the state militia, petitioned the legislature on 25 January 1791, hoping to rectify a clerical error that deprived her family of sorely needed funds. The assembly directed the state treasurer to investigate the case and to issue Baxter indents, or certificates, to satisfy her claim.[31]

The petition of Mary Baxter Relict of John Baxter Esqr. of kingstown Humbly Sheweth That Your Petitioner is left With seven small Fatherless Children which she is not able to Maintain as her Husbands Estate is likely to prove Insolvent, and that your Petitioner has £80.12s.1d. Justly Due the said Estate by the Publick which has been audited, but through Mistake in the Treasurers has been paid to Coln. John Baxter of Peedee[32] which payment has been Demanded of said Colonell John Baxter but not received, your Petitioner therefore humbly prays that the Distressed & unhapy Condition of her self and poor Children may be taken Into your serious Consideration & grant her Indents with the Usual Intrist for the above sum—and as In Duty bound will Ever Pray.

(DS, Sc-Ar [Accounts Audited, no. 367, roll 7, frames 10–11])

31. *S.C. House Journals, 1783–1784,* 173, 203–4; *S.C. House Journals, 1791,* 225; Moss, *S.C. Patriots,* 53.
32. Col. John Baxter served in Gen. Francis Marion's brigade and later commanded the Pee Dee Regiment. He was also a member of the state assembly in 1782 (McCrady, *S.C. in the Revolution,* 2:558; Moss, *S.C.Patriots,* 53).

DOCUMENT 13

Ann Summerall

> *On 29 January 1791, Ann Summerall sought compensation for a slave belonging to her late husband, Jacob, claiming that Capt. Richard Johnson had appropriated the slave as partial payment for wages owed him. In fact, Johnson was Jacob Summerall's commanding officer in the South Carolina militia, and it was highly unlikely that he would have plundered the property of his own soldiers. Ann Summerall's error must have seriously undermined the credibility of her claim. The assembly referred her petition to a committee, which did not act on it.*[33]

The Petition of Ann Summerall humbly Sheweth That your Petitioner is Widow & administratrix of Jacob Summerall deceased who died in the late War in America & that the Estate of the said Jacob Summerall was not confiscated as far as your Petitioner knows or believes.

But notwithstanding that, a negroe Fellow, the property of the said Jacob Summerall was taken & appl[i]ed towards the payment of a Captain Richard Johnson who Served at that time as a Captain in Colo. Samuel Hammonds Regiment of State Dragoons and by reason of the said Captain Johnsons receiving the said negro the State was exonerated by him from so much of his claim for Services done in the said regiment.

Neither your Petitioner nor her said husband having received any compensation for same, your Petitioner therefore most humbly prayeth that she may have such relief as to you in wisdom shall seem meet, and your Petitioner as in duty bound will ever pray.

(ADS, Sc-Ar [Accounts Audited, no. 7527–A, roll 143, frames 38–39])

DOCUMENT 14

Judith Morgan

> *In March 1786, the government of South Carolina imposed a three-month deadline for the submission of all war-related claims*

---

33. Moss, *S.C. Patriots*, 503, 908.

against it. A 1789 statute subsequently granted a one-year extension to creditors whose claims had been "lost or mislaid." Some claimants, however, continued to petition the assembly for redress after 1790. On 7 December 1791, for instance, Judith Morgan, the upcountry widow of a Continental soldier, sought his arrears in pay. The assembly heard her petition but did not act on it, probably because the deadline for the settlement of such accounts was long past.[34]

The petition of Judith Morgan humbly sheweth, that John Morgan deceased your petitioners late husband was a Soldier in the first regiment of Continental troops on the South Carolina Establishment commanded by Brig: Gen: Charles C. Pinckney;[35] and that he (your petitioners husband) neglected to render in his account against the public for duty as Armorer within the time required by law, owing to his being ignorant of such an existing law, by which neglect his account was not Audited.

Your petitioner further sheweth that she was left in very necessitous circumstances. Therefore humbly prays that she may be affor[d]ed such releif as you in your wisdom shall think proper: & your petitioner will as in duty bound ever pray &c.

(DS, Sc-Ar [Accounts Audited, no. 5344–A, roll 107, frames 551–52])

DOCUMENT 15

Elizabeth Petrie

Although she professed no political allegiance of her own, Elizabeth Petrie suffered severely from the confiscation of Tory estates. As the widow of a Charleston silversmith, who died in 1768, Petrie

---

34. Ibid., 701; *Heads of Families . . . in the Year 1790: S.C.,* 29, 30; "An Act to preclude all further Accounts due previous to the evacuation of Charleston . . . ," 1786, *S.C. Statutes,* 4:727; "An Act to authorize the Auditor General to Receive and audit . . . Claims . . . which have been lost or mislaid," 1789, in ibid., 5:105–6.

35. Morgan served initially in the Sixth South Carolina Regiment, but in February 1780 he transferred to Gen. Charles Cotesworth Pinckney's First Regiment, which saw action during the siege of Charleston (Moss, *S.C. Patriots,* 701; Boatner, *Ency. of Amer. Rev.,* 869).

derived her main income from the interest on a bond he had held from John Stuart, an eventual Tory who lost his estate through confiscation. In 1788 and 1789, Petrie unsuccessfully petitioned the assembly to recover the money she believed due her. On 13 December 1791, she renewed her petition, and the legislature recommended that she "have liberty to pursue her remedy in the Courts of Justice." [36]

The humble Petition of Elizabeth Petrie Widow of Alexander Petrie late of Charleston deceased.

Sheweth—

That the said Alexander Petrie purchased the 7th October 1767, a certain lot of land called the Orange Garden in Charleston aforesaid of Samuel Carne and paid for it and parcelled it out into Lots and a Street now known by the name of Orange Street. In the Month of December following he sold one of the said Lots Corner of Tradd and Orange Streets to John Stuart for £2800 Currency for which he obtained said Stuarts' Bond dated 1st January 1768 payable with Interest from the date for the effectual Securing the Payment of said Sum he also obtained 5th of the next Month Feby. '68, a Mortgage of said Lot signed by said John and Sarah his Wife which said Mortgage was recorded 26th of the same Month February by Fenwick Bull [37] who was the Register. After the death of the said Alexander said Bond and Mortgage were allotted to your Petitioner to secure the annual sum bequeathed to her Support—amount of her said Bond is now more than £5600 Curr[en]cy or £800 Sterling Principal and Interest which Sum your Petitioner cannot recover without your Permission to foreclose the said Mortgage as said Lot with the House thereon has been confiscated and sold as the Property of aforesaid John Stuart by the Commissioners notwithstanding the said Bond and Mortgage were previously shewn to Thomas Waring Esquire one of said

----

36. Will of Alexander Petrie, 13 Feb. 1768, Charleston County Will Book, 1767–71, typescript, 11:307–9, Sc-Ar; Sabine, *Loyalists of the Amer. Rev.*, 2:341; Petitions of Elizabeth Petrie, 20 Oct. 1788, 11 Feb. 1789, LP, Sc-Ar; *S.C. House Journals, 1791*, 408.

37. Fenwick Bull, a recent immigrant from England, became an outspoken Tory. A Whig crowd threatened to tar and feather him in 1775, and his estate was later confiscated. Bull was dead by 1785 (*S.C. House Journals, 1785–1786*, 93).

Commissioners by Edmund Petrie Your Petitioners Agent which is testified by said Edmund's Affidavit hereunto annexed.[38]

Your Petitioner therefore prays this Honble House to take the Contents of this humble Petition into their Consideration and grant her that Relief which will enable her to recover that which is justly due her and which she so much at present stands in need of.

(DS, Sc-Ar)

DOCUMENT 16

Elizabeth West

On 21 December 1791, this Craven County widow petitioned for arrears in pay owed to her late husband, who in 1782 enlisted for eighteen months as a private in the Tenth Regiment of North Carolina Continentals. The assembly rejected Elizabeth West's petition on the grounds that a recent statute "points out in a very explicit Manner the mode by which all persons who have Military Claims, unliquidated, are to be redress'd." Instead of petitioning the assembly, West should have submitted her claim to two justices of the peace and then to a specially appointed board of commissioners.[39]

The petition of Elizabeth West, Widow and relict, of James West, deceased, humbly Sheweth—that her late husband, the said deceased

---

38. Edmund Petrie, oldest of the six children of Elizabeth and Alexander Petrie, had his estate confiscated in 1782 but successfully petitioned for clemency the following year (Will of Alexander Petrie, 13 Feb. 1768, Charleston County Will Book, 1767–71, typescript, 11:307–9; *S.C. House Journals, 1783–1784*, 32–33, 42, 53).

Petrie's affidavit of 15 November 1791, which accompanied his mother's petition, stipulated that "previous to the sale of the House . . . he shewed Thomas Waring Esquire one of the Commissioners of Confiscation the Bond and Mortgage . . . and gave him particular and express Notice that the same was not paid or satisfied."

39. [Hay et al.], *N.C. Soldiers*, 177, 364; Committee report on the petition of Elizabeth West, Jan. 1792, GASR, Dec. 1791–Jan. 1792, Nc-Ar; "An Act to continue and amend an Act, entitled, An Act directing the Manner in which . . . those who had Military Accounts . . . shall obtain Certificates," 1791, North Carolina sessions laws, microfiche, 1791, chap. 3.

James West, was an eighteen Months Soldier, that he faithfully served his time under Colo. Archibald Lyttle, now also deceased; that all his Pay is still in Arrear, as your Petitioner has always understood from him, her s[ai]d Husband, in his life and verily believes to be the truth. Your Petitioner's Principal Allegation, of her husband having been a Soldier in manner afores[ai]d as Vouchers, to establish the same, she herewith presents the Deposition of Levi Kent and a furlow, under the hand of the Officers, whose Command her Husband was subject to[40]—your Petitioner is very poor, his Family of young Children numerous (towit) Five in Number—her distress so great as scarsly to be borne—As, Upon a Tribunal whose Knowledge of all Matters and things belonging to the Military Establishment, both as to the quantam of pay in Arrear—as well as, to dictate, from what Funds and by what mode, she shall receive The debt due her Husband—she throws her self entirely upon, this honourable House—for whose prosperity as in duty bound she will ever pray &c.

(ADS, Nc-Ar)

DOCUMENT 17

Sarah Armstrong

The petitioner was one of several Whig residents of her Sumter County neighborhood who, years after the restoration of peace, continued to seek restitution for slaves state troops seized during the Revolution. The South Carolina assembly heard Sarah Armstrong's petition on 30 November 1792 and awarded her compensation on the condition that she furnish the state treasurer with "sufficient proofs" to justify her claim.[41]

The Humble Petition of Sarah Armstrong Widow of Capt. Jno. Armstrong Decd. of Black River Salem—

---

40. Deposition and furlough not found. In 1782, both Levi Kent and James West enlisted in the Tenth North Carolina Regiment. Kent served in Capt. Joshua Hadley's Company; West was in the company commanded by Capt. Anthony Sharp. Neither man served under Col. Archibald Lytle, who at that time commanded the Fourth Regiment ([Hay et al.], *N.C. Soldiers*, 140, 177, 364; *Dict. of N.C. Biog.*, 4:114).

41. *S.C. House Journals, 1792–1794*, 261.

Sheweth to Your Honours, That Your Petitioners Husband was in his lifetime, Security for Saml. McCay, Now Decd. Also—the sum of 1000£ Old Currency, And Eight Negroes, the property of the S[ai]d Saml. Mc-Cay, was taken in the late War by Colo. Marshall,[42] Without Any Authority, But Afterwards, Contributed to the Use of Genl. Thos. Sumpters State Troops, At the same time, And After the same Manner, With Mr. Sylvester Dunns Negroes, And the whole of the Sd. Saml. McCays property being taken, your petitioners Husband, in his lifetime, Obtained Liberty from Your Honourable Body, by a Petition thereto which may be found by having Recourse to the Books of your Honourable Houses—to take as much of the property as would make him safe[43]—And as the property is Converted to a publick Use, Your Petitioner, therefore, humbly prays, for your Honours, to take her Case into Consideration, as She is Reduced to want, & in Distress, by being Divested of her property, to Discharge the Contract, for which your petitioners Husband was Security, And Grant her such Relief, as the Nature and Circumstance of her Case Shall Appear to your Honours to Require, And Your Petitioner As in Duty bound will ever pray.

(ADS, Sc-Ar)

DOCUMENT 18

Mary Ann Smith

This Pendleton County mother of six described herself as a "help-less widow" when she petitioned the South Carolina assembly in 1791. Mary Ann Smith sought to obtain her husband's back pay, and, when the assembly failed to respond to her request, she submitted another petition on 7 December 1792. The assembly granted

---

42. In 1780–81, Col. John Marshall served under Gen. Thomas Sumter. On Sumter's distribution of stolen slaves among his troops, see chap. 1, n. 29, above.

43. The assembly heard John Armstrong's petition on 12 February 1783. In response to Armstrong's and other similar requests, a legislative committee inquired into the conduct of Sumter's troops and in March 1785 passed resolutions aimed at settling accounts with those who sustained losses as a result of the soldiers' actions (*S.C. House Journals, 1783–1784*, 128–29; *S.C. House Journals, 1792–1794*, 185, 199).

this second petition. Mary Ann Smith remarried some time during the next decade.[44]

The Petition of Mary Ann Smith Widow and relict of Joseph Smith deceased and administrix of his Estate Sheweth

That your Petitioners Said Husband served for a considerable time in the Militia of this State during the late war as a Sarjent and a private of Horse, and died in the service.

That regular returns of his said Service were made by the officers under whom it was performed; on which returns the auditors passed an account in his favour for £51.18/ Sterling.

That she has made repeated applications for an indent on this account which some accident or some mistake of the officers in the Treasury always prevented her from obtaining. Once an indent of a Certain Joseph Smith was delivered to her, but she found it to be the property of a different person, another Joseph Smith, and returned it into the Treasury from whence she supposes it has since been taken by the true owner. The Treasurers then promised that She should have her own; but sometimes their absence, and sometimes their being engaged have prevented her from receiving it hitherto, though she made repeated applications for the purpose.

She therefore prays that your Hon[ora]b[l]e House will pass a resolution authorizing and requiring the Treasurers to issue an indent for the amount of the said account, and she will pray &c.

(DS [by mark], Sc-Ar [Accounts Audited, no. 7139, roll 137, frames 21–23])

DOCUMENT 19

Margrat Clendening

The petitioner was the widow of John Barnet, who hired out a wagon and team to South Carolina troops in 1779 and saw action in the state militia in 1780. Barnet died shortly thereafter and by

---

44. *Heads of Families . . . in the Year 1790: S.C.*, 85; *S.C. House Journals, 1791*, 332–33, 356; *S.C. House Journals, 1792–1794*, 347, 424; Petition of Mary Ann [Smith] Morris, 9 Dec. 1801, Accounts Audited, No. 137, roll 137, Sc-Ar.

1790 his widow, Margrat, had married Thomas Clendenin of York County. Although Clendenin owned a farm and five slaves, Margrat described her circumstances as "Necessatious" when she petitioned, on 11 December 1792, to recover a sum owed her first husband. The assembly rejected her petition, which she filed long after the statutory deadline for settling such claims.[45]

The petition of Margrat Clendening administorix of the Estate of John Barnet deceas'd Sheweth

That your petitionors Late husband John Barnet Had an account against this State for 90 days service with his wagon & team the year 1779 for which he Received no Satisfaction Except £500 of the then depreciated paper Currency which was handed him by the Governor.

That his account was duely Stated attested & avouchd & delivered to a member of the Legislator to be Returned to the auditors office within the time allowed by Law & Lay in his hands Several years untill the auditor Refused to Receive it.

That y[ou]r petitionor applyd to the Legislator at their Last Session but Cannot be informed what was their determination Respecting her account.[46]

Y[ou]r petitionor therefore Humbly prays that your Honourable House will take her Case under your wise Consideration & Recolect that her Case is Exceeding hard being Reduced to Necessatious Circumstances by the Ravages of the warr & the Loss of her husband Being Left with a number of Small Childrun[47] whose Support & Education depends wholey upon the Industry of your petitionor & if in your wisdom it appears Just that they Should Receive the Small pitence that their father So hardly Earned yr. petition[er] in duty bound Shall Ever pray &c. &c.

(ADS, Sc-Ar [Accounts Audited, no. 296, roll 6, frames 17–19])

---

45. Moss, *S.C. Patriots*, 47; *Heads of Families . . . in the Year 1790: S.C.*, 31; Will of Thomas Clendinen, 20 Jan. 1817, York County Will Book, 1816–39, typescript, 2:38–41, Sc-Ar; *S.C. House Journals, 1792–1794*, 203.

46. There is no evidence that the petitioner presented her case in the previous legislative session or that any earlier assembly considered her claim.

47. The 1790 census shows that the petitioner's household included eight white dependents, though some of these may have been Thomas Clendenin's children by a previous marriage (*Heads of Families . . . in the Year 1790: S.C.*, 31).

DOCUMENT 20

Ann Dabney

> *On 11 December 1792, widow Ann Dabney, whose place of residence is unknown, petitioned the South Carolina legislature for payment of a debt owed to the estate of her late husband. The assembly rejected her petition, as it did Clendening's, because she had missed the deadline for submitting war-related claims.*[48]

The Humble Petition of Ann Dabney Sheweth

That your Petitioners Husband James Dabney, Entered into the State service With his Waggon and Team, in Febry. 1779, and on the Eighth day of May Following he Purchased another Waggon and Team, and on the Thirteenth of May he Purchased another Waggon and Team all of Which Were Continued in the Publick Service Untill the first of July 1779, at Which time they all Were taken for the Use of Genl. Lincolns Army and, Your Petitioners husband died before the Law for obtaining Indents Was Passed[49] so that, your Petitioner never has obtained any thing Either for the Services or for the Waggons and Teams, and what is Still more Distressing, one of the Persons from whom my late Husband Purchased has administired on His Estate, has Sold my Negroe all my Little Stock my Houshold Furniture and Even my Bed—and Unless your Honourable House will Grant me Pay for the above I am Reduced so low that I must seek Relief from the County.

Your Petitioner therefore Hopes Your Honourable House Will take her Case into Consideration and will Grant her pay and She as in Duty Bound will ever pray.

(DS [by mark], Sc-Ar [Accounts Audited, no. 1710–A, roll 30, frames 117–20])

---

48. S.C. *House Journals, 1792–1794,* 203.

49. "An Ordinance for ascertaining and regulating the office of Receiver, Auditor and Accountant General of the Public Accounts . . . ," 1783, S.C. *Statutes,* 4:456–58.

DOCUMENT 21

Mary Davidson

> *Mary Brevard Davidson (d. 1824) was born into one of the lead-
> ing families in Rowan County, North Carolina. In 1767, she mar-
> ried William Lee Davidson, who became a prominent Whig, serving
> first in the Continental Army and then in the state militia, where he
> attained the rank of brigadier general. Mary Davidson supplied
> provisions to the army on at least two occasions. On 1 Febru-
> ary 1781, William died in battle at Cowan's Ford, leaving her with
> six children and pregnant with a seventh. She filed this undated pe-
> tition, which the assembly granted, sometime in December 1793.
> She later remarried and moved to Tennessee.*[50]

The Petition of Mary Davidson relict of General William Davidson respectfully Sheweth

That your Petitioner instead of the pay due her late Husband received from the State Seven years half pay which began to be paid her in the Beginning of the year 1786 when Money was greatly depreciated and when she received the last payment the Currency was nearly reduced to half its nominal Value.[51]

That the Agent of this State in Philadelphia claimed the Continental Certificates which had been issued to her Husband, because the State had given her the half Pay already mentioned.

That the General Assembly at their last sitting resolved that the Agent of this State should relinquish any Claim to the Certificates which had been issued to General Davidson provided his Widow should give Security to the Governor for returning the half Pay she had received. She has given the Security required and is now bound to discharge her Bond and to return much more than she received Provided the General As-

50. *Dict. of N.C. Biog.*, 2:27–28; Claghorn, *Women Patriots*, 281.

51. In 1786, twelve shillings in North Carolina state currency was worth only eight shillings in specie. The state's currency continued to depreciate in subsequent years (Morrill, *Fiat Finance*, 85–88).

sembly will not agree to discount some part of her Bond, by paying a Debt that has been dearly earned, is justly due, and has never been paid to the Heirs of her late Husband.

It must be recollected that General Davidson after the fall of Charleston entered as a Volunteer into the Service of the State when he might have retired, receiving his Pay like other Continental Officers who had no Troops to command.[52]

Your Petitioner will not repeat for she believes they are in the Memory of her Country the Services that General Davidson rendered in the years 1780 & 81. She will not affect your Feelings, by a Painful Detail of the sufferings of his Family after he fell in Battle. It may be supposed that a helpless woman with seven small Children—without one Slave, without Furniture, for she was plundered, without money must have suffered extreme misery.

Your Petitioner believes General Davidson had a Claim on the Patriotism the Honor and the Justice of his Fellow Citizens for Pay while he served the State in the Character of a Militia Officer, Such Pay he has never received and she confides that of the General Assembly of North Carolina will not extend the Strong Arm of Law to distress the Family of General Davidson while they retain the poor recompence of Pay earned at the Expence of Life from the afflicted Family of that Officer. And your Petitioner will ever pray &c.[53]

(DS, Nc-Ar)

DOCUMENT 22
Hannah Ash and Margaret Ash

These daughters of Andrew Deveaux, a South Carolina Tory, were prominent participants in their family's efforts to obtain full

---

52. North Carolina lost most of its Continental line as a result of the fall of Charleston. Thus deprived of his army command, Davidson offered his services to the state militia (*Dict. of N.C. Biog.*, 2:27).

53. On 11 January 1794, the state senate passed a resolution allowing Davidson to satisfy her debt to the state by remitting one-half of the certificates' face value (GASR, Dec. 1793–Jan. 1794, Nc-Ar).

compensation for the property he lost under the confiscation statutes. This petition, submitted on 21 November 1795 along with a similar one from their exiled father, was the first of four that Hannah Deveaux Ash (1761–1822) and Margaret Deveaux Ash presented to the assembly. The legislature did not act on this petition.[54]

The Petition of Hannah Ashe, Relict of Samuel Ashe, and Margaret Ashe Relict of the late John Ashe junr. deceased.

Most Respectfully Sheweth

That your Petitioners being Daughters of Andrew Deveaux Junr. whose Estate having been confiscated, was afterwards restored to him, by an Act of the Legislature.[55] That the Sales of his Estate amounting to upwards of five thousand pounds Sterling in Specie, being made prior to the evacuation of Charleston, and a subsequent Act having past, which authorised the Treasurers to receive indents in payment, which were at that time greatly depreciated. Your Petitioners Father designing them as a portion to his four Daughters who are married to Citizens of this State and residing therein,[56] thought it best to leave them in the Treasury, as a place of safety, until they might appreciate, by the establishing of funds for their extinguishment. they were then to be drawn out, and devided equally among his said four Daughters, who have never received any portion from him.

That as they have understood, a Resolution past the Hon[ora]ble Legislature some time since, directing the Commissioners to pay only

---

54. Stephen B. Barnwell, *The Story of an American Family* (Marquette: n.p., 1969), 54; Petition of Andrew Deveaux Sr., 21 Nov. 1795, LP, Sc-Ar; Petitions of Hannah Ash and Margaret Ash, 9 Dec. 1796, 4 Dec. 1804, 30 Nov. 1810, ibid. The 1796 petition is included in chap. 4, below.

Jacob Deveaux, husband of Elizabeth Barnwell Deveaux, whose petition appears in chap. 1, was the uncle of Andrew Deveaux Sr. and therefore great-uncle to Hannah and Margaret.

55. In February 1783, Andrew Deveaux Jr. unsuccessfully petitioned for relief from confiscation. In February 1784, however, the assembly granted the petition filed by John Deveaux on behalf of himself and five siblings, requesting the return of the estate of their exiled father (*S.C. House Journals, 1783–1784*, 81, 438).

56. The petitioners and their sisters Catherine Deveaux Lechmere Ash and Mary Deveaux Brisbane (Barnwell, *Story of an American Family*, 54).

one fifth for the Indents due by the Treasury;[57] they therefore, humbly beg leave to represent to your Hon[ora]ble House, that in this case, their Father's Estate being restored by law, and he compell'd to receive Indents for the Specie (which his Estate sold for) pound for pound; should these Indents, which by the Act that restored his Estate, were undoubtedly his, be, by the above Resolution, past long since, again reduced to one fifth, and the amercement and expences deducted, they are only to receive £852.1.9 principal, for £5146.3.2 for which the property sold, payable in Gold or Silver—by which they will be deprived of the greatest part of their patrimony, and reduced to great distress.

That by the very embarrassed situation of the affairs of their late Husbands your Petitioners can scarcely provide for themselves, and have each of them two Children to maintain and educate. That the Husbands of your Petitioners were well known to be staunch Friends to the American Revolution, that one of them, the late Samuel Ashe served in the Charleston Battalion of Artillery, during the Siege of Charleston, and being captured therein, was sometime afterwards confined on board a prison Ship, until sent to Virginia, where he was present and served at the capture of Lord Cornwallis in York Town. That he afterwards joined his Countrymen in Carolina, and served in the Legislature until the Evacuation of Charleston—which things are well known to many Members of your Hon[ora]ble House—he also lost 26 Negroes (being the greatest part of his property) by the depredations of the Enemy.[58]

Your Petitioners are therefore induced to hope, that your Hon[ora]ble House will take their present distress'd situation, into consider-

---

57. In May 1794, the legislature resolved to pay indents issued as compensation for formerly confiscated property at a rate of 1:5. This resolution was part of a general attempt to fund and retire the state debt (*S.C. House Journals, 1792–1794*, 554; "An Act to make such provision for the Debt of the State of South Carolina," 1794, *S.C. Statutes*, 5:239–40).

58. Samuel Ash married Hannah Deveaux in 1785 and died some time after December 1793, when he unsuccessfully petitioned the assembly on behalf of the heirs of Andrew Deveaux, requesting relief from the amercement imposed on Deveaux's restored estate. John Ash Jr., husband of Margaret Deveaux and kin to Samuel, who also served in the militia and participated in the defense of Charleston, died in 1795. Both men owned land in Colleton County, south of Charleston (Barnwell, *Story of an American Family*, 54; *S.C. House Journals, 1792–1794*, 365–66, 445; Moss, *S.C. Patriots*, 28; Federal Census of Population, South Carolina, 1800, roll 48, 160).

ation, and extend towards them and their Sisters that justice and Liberallity which you in your wisdom shall think fit.

And they, as in duty bound will ever pray &c.

(DS, Sc-Ar)

DOCUMENT 23

Mary Young

> *When she petitioned the North Carolina legislature on 12 De-cember 1799, Mary Young of Halifax County was a twice-widowed mother of five and the owner of nine slaves. Young sought the title to land warrants the state owed to the estate of her first husband, a captain in the Continental Army who died in service twenty-two years earlier. Because the deadline for settling such accounts was long past, the assembly concluded that "it would be improper to in-terfere in these cases at this time" and rejected her petition.*[59]

The Humble Petition of Mary Young Sheweth—

That your petitioner was formerly the Wife of Jacob Pollock who en-tered into the service of his Country when the first Continental Troops were raised in this State as a Lieutenant and was afterwards promoted to a Captain. That on his route from the Southward to join the Northern Army in June 1777, he Died. That his papers and Baggage were all lost so that your petitioner knew not how to make a claim for his services. That about two or three years ago application was made for, and a Land War-rant granted to the Heirs of the said Jacob Pollock for about 3700 acres,[60] as well as your petitioner recollects, that about twelve Months ago she sent the Land Warrant to Tennessee to have it Located, that her attorney

---

59. Federal Census of Population, North Carolina, 1800, roll 30, 356; Will of Dau-phin Young, 24 Jan. 1795, Halifax County Will Book 3, 251–52, Nc-Ar; Committee report on the petition of Mary Young, [Dec. 1799], GASR, Nov.–Dec. 1799, Nc-Ar.

60. Beginning in 1782, North Carolina paid the arrears of its Continental soldiers with certificates that were redeemable for western land, much of which was located in the future state of Tennessee. The land granted to the veterans and their heirs ul-timately totaled 2,912,198 acres (Morrill, *Fiat Finance*, 170–71).

informs her the name of the Heir is necessary to be known before the patent can be made out. That the said Jacob Pollock her former Husband has no Heirs in this country to her knowledge, and your petitioner conceiving that she ought of right to have the said Land as her property— She therefore Humbly prays your Honorable Body that you will be pleas'd to Vest the right and title to the said Land in her, she being poor, and this the only property of any Value which remained after the Debts of her said Husband Jacob Pollock being paid.

Your petitioner further sheweth, that her said Husband Jacob Pollock's Accounts, have never been adjusted with the State for his services as other Officers accounts have been, owing to the loss of his papers and Baggage as before mentioned and she not knowing in what manner to act, and as he was some time in the service of his Country, it woud be but reasonable that his accounts shou'd be settled in the same manner that other Officers accounts were. That altho the time for such settlement has long since expired,[61] yet it wou'd be hard that the Widow of an Officer who died while in the service of his Country shou'd suffer thro' her ignorance of the Laws and manner of proceeding in such cases, Your petitioner therefore hopes that your Honorable Body will also take this part of her care into your consideration, and grant her such relief as you in your Judgment may think right and just, and she as in duty bound will ever pray.

(ADS, Nc-Ar)

---

61. "An Act for Fixing the Final Settlement of Unliquidated Claims . . . ," initially established a 1788 deadline, which the legislature later extended an additional year. A 1799 law explicitly barred the submission of any claims against the state for goods and services furnished before 1 June 1784 (*N.C. Recs.*, 24:896–97, 956; Henry Potter et al., comps., *Laws of the State of North Carolina . . .* , 2 vols. [Raleigh: J. Gales, 1821], 2:894).

Chapter 3

THE LOYALIST LEGACY

On 22 February 1783, roughly two months after the British evacuation of Charleston, Susannah Smyth submitted two petitions to the South Carolina assembly. The first she filed on behalf of her husband, John, who, she explained, "did his duty faithfully as a Citizen of this State till the surrender of Charles Town" in 1780, when he "accepted of a Commission in the [Tory] Militia, being told refusal would render him obnoxious" to the area's British occupiers. Smyth assured the legislators that her husband, despite his own capitulation to British rule, had not "distressed one Individual attached to the American Cause," and she maintained that he was now "Weaned from every attachment to the British Crown, from thorough Conviction." In view of these circumstances, Smyth requested that her banished spouse be allowed to return to South Carolina and to recover his confiscated estate.[1]

Susannah Smyth's second petition sought to preserve a portion of her family's property and ensure her own subsistence in the event that the assembly did not rescind her husband's sentence. When his banishment appeared imminent, John Smyth had sold a house cheaply to his brother-in-law to shield it from confiscation, instructing him to hold the house in trust for Susannah. By 1783, however, Susannah Smyth believed that the deed to the property was flawed, and she petitioned the legislature to have it validated. "As provision was made for the families of those who were banished, and as the plantation of her husband has been Sold, and the Crops of three Years," she asked that "the house . . . and the very few house Negroes and furniture which her husband left with her will be Secured."[2]

---

1. Petitions of Susannah Smyth, 22 Feb. 1783 [2], LP, Sc-Ar. The petition quoted in this paragraph is reprinted in *S.C. House Journals, 1783–1784*, 176–77. John Smyth filed a petition on his own behalf in the next legislative session (ibid., 461).

2. Ibid., 182.

As Susannah Smyth's petitions suggest, loyalist families had to make several crucial determinations after the war was over. Would they settle elsewhere, or would they attempt to return to their American homes? Should they try to reclaim their lost estates, and, if so, how much property could they expect to recover? Would the family stay together at all costs, or would a wife spend years apart from her banished spouse, seeking his repatriation? Although the legislature quickly granted both of Smyth's petitions, for others the postwar process of recovery and resettlement was lengthy and sometimes unsuccessful.

Loyalists accounted for approximately one-fifth of the white population of the southern states, in addition to several thousand African Americans.[3] Eastern port towns with British trading interests and the Carolina backcountry were the region's main centers of Tory activity.[4] Southern loyalists came from all social ranks, though Crown officials and merchants—many of whom were natives of Britain, especially Scotland—were most likely to be Tories. Culturally, loyalists often belonged to ethnic or religious minorities whose members found protection within

---

3. On quantifying loyalism, see Paul Smith, "The American Loyalists: Notes on Their Organization and Numerical Strength," *WMQ*, 3d ser., 25 (1968): 259–77. On South Carolina specifically, see Lambert, *S.C. Loyalists*, 319–21. On black loyalists, see Sylvia R. Frey, *Water from the Rock: Black Resistance in a Revolutionary Age* (Princeton: Princeton University Press, 1991), 172, 192–94.

4. John E. Selby, *The Revolution in Virginia, 1775–1783* (Williamsburg, Va.: Colonial Williamsburg, 1988), 59–61, 219–20; Albert H. Tillson Jr., "The Maintenance of Revolutionary Consensus: Treatment of Tories in Southwestern Virginia, 1775–1783," in *Loyalists and Community in North America*, ed. Robert M. Calhoon et al. (Westport, Conn.: Greenwood Press, 1994), 45–53; Emory G. Evans, "Trouble in the Backcountry: Disaffection in Southwest Virginia during the American Revolution," in *An Uncivil War: The Southern Backcountry during the American Revolution*, ed. Ronald Hoffman et al. (Charlottesville: University Press of Virginia, 1985), 179–212; Jeffrey J. Crow, "Liberty Men and Loyalists: Disorder and Disaffection in the North Carolina Backcountry," in ibid., 125–78; Richard R. Beeman, "The Political Response to Social Conflict in the Southern Backcountry: A Comparative View of Virginia and the Carolinas during the Revolution," in ibid., 226–39; Ronald Hoffman, "The 'Disaffected' in the Revolutionary South," in *The American Revolution: Exploration in the History of American Radicalism*, ed. Alfred F. Young (DeKalb: Northern Illinois University Press, 1976), 273–316; Rachel N. Klein, *Unification of a Slave State: The Rise of the Planter Class in the South Carolina Backcountry, 1760–1808* (Chapel Hill: University of North Carolina Press, 1990), chap. 3; Kenneth Coleman, *The American Revolution in Georgia, 1763–1789* (Athens: University of Georgia Press, 1958), 75, 123–24.

the British Empire and perhaps feared the creation of a majoritarian political order. Highland Scots, backcountry Germans, and recent immi-
grants of all sorts thus dominated the ranks of white southern loyalists.[5]
Blacks and Indians, the most endangered of all minorities, also flocked to
the king's standard to fight enslavement and dispossession, respectively,
at the hands of the Whig majority.

Regarding slaves as property and native Americans as beyond the immediate jurisdiction of their governments, southern Whigs passed punitive laws that pertained exclusively to white loyalists in their respective
states. As we have seen, each southern state criminalized Toryism in an
attempt to discourage the spread of active opposition to the revolutionary cause, banishing those who refused to pledge their allegiance to the
state and confiscating the abandoned property of Tory exiles. The heads
of nearly two hundred southern loyalist families arrived in England by
the end of 1778, traveling alone or accompanied by their relatives. To
punish Tories and to raise money to support the war effort, both Virginia
and North Carolina initiated the sale of confiscated property by 1780. In
North Carolina, where loyalism was more widespread and the sales of
property more substantial, more than 100,000 acres changed hands, with
the largest land sales occurring in 1786 and 1787.[6]

In South Carolina and in Georgia, where the partial or complete reinstatement of British rule prevented the continued enforcement of anti-
Tory policies, Whig officials were left to determine the fate of their
defeated foes once the war was effectively over. In May 1782, Georgia's
restored state government banished 279 Tories by name and confiscated
their property, though by July a more lenient statute allowed 93 of the
enumerated offenders to return and reclaim their property subject to an
annual amercement. In the coming years, other Georgia Tories successfully petitioned to have their punishments reduced. Meanwhile, in 1782,
when the South Carolina legislature convened in Jacksonborough, meeting for the first time since 1780, it also established a dual system of punishment for those who actively or passively abetted the British invasion

5. William H. Nelson, *The American Tory* (Oxford: Clarendon Press, 1961),
86–92, 110–14; Lambert, *S.C. Loyalists*, 24–29, 186–87, 306–7; DeMond, *Loyalists in N.C.*, 50–57; Coleman, *American Revolution in Georgia*, 75.

6. DeMond, *Loyalists in N.C.*, 172–74, 180, 240–50; Isaac S. Harrell, *Loyalism in
Virginia: Chapters in the Economic History of the Revolution* (Durham, N.C.: Duke
University Press, 1926), 92–98; Mary Beth Norton, *The British-Americans: The Loy-
alist Exiles in England, 1774–1789* (Boston: Little, Brown, 1972), 37.

of the state during the war's final phase. South Carolina's Confiscation Act provided that those who explicitly recognized British authority—by signing congratulatory addresses to British commanders, holding civil or military commissions, or acting in any way in support of the occupying regime—would suffer banishment and the loss of their property in South Carolina. The Amercement Act punished those who attempted to remain neutral after 1780—withholding support from the American cause but not actively aiding its opponents—by imposing a punitive tax of 12 percent on the estates of these lesser offenders.[7]

The passage and enforcement of the anti-Tory laws, along with the departure of British military and civilian authorities, occasioned a mass exodus of southern loyalists, many of whom never returned to their prerevolutionary homes. After the decisive American victory at Yorktown, the British colonies of East Florida and Jamaica were the most popular destinations for southern Tories. In 1784, however, Britain ceded East Florida to Spain as part of the postwar settlement, and most of the loyalist exiles, who preferred not to live under Spanish rule, resettled again elsewhere. Some moved to Britain, but most slaveholders took their bond people to Jamaica or the Bahamas, both British plantation colonies. Others joined the substantial numbers of backcountry Tories who already had settled in eastern Canada. Nova Scotia was the main destination of the several thousand black southerners who won their freedom by supporting the Crown during the Revolution. After nearly a decade there, however, a substantial minority left to establish the colony of Sierra Leone in West Africa.[8]

Some loyalists traveled extensively in search of congenial postwar homes. In late 1782, South Carolinian James Cary, who commanded a Tory regiment during the war, sailed to Jamaica, accompanied by his wife, Mary, and about a dozen slaves, whom he soon put to work on

---

7. Coleman, *American Revolution in Georgia,* 183–87; Nadelhaft, *Disorders of War,* 77–84.

8. Frey, *Water from the Rock,* 172–82, 192–99; Norton, *British-Americans,* 32–34, 37, 235–42; DeMond, *Loyalists in N.C.,* 182–201; Carole Watterson Troxler, *The Loyalist Experience in North Carolina* (Raleigh: North Carolina Division of Archives and History, 1976), 7–11, 37–54; Coleman, *American Revolution in Georgia,* 143–46; Lambert, *S.C. Loyalists,* 259–81. One careful estimate holds that South Carolina alone yielded between nine thousand and ten thousand refugees, slightly more than half of whom were slaves who shared the fate of their Tory owners (ibid., 307).

a sugar plantation that he operated in partnership with another exile. When the partners suffered financial difficulties, James and Mary Cary moved on to Nova Scotia, where James sought to recover his wartime losses by submitting his case to the royal commission that convened there to adjudicate loyalist claims. When the commission refused him restitution, the Carys sailed to England, where they remained after James successfully appealed his case and secured a modest pension. Even more peripatetic, William and Elizabeth Johnston of Georgia moved, successively, to Florida, Scotland, and Jamaica, before settling permanently in Nova Scotia.[9]

Many women who followed their husbands into exile sorely missed their American homes. While men often found occupations and companions in the worlds of business and politics, exiled women left their extended families for unfamiliar places that, in their deteriorated financial circumstances, offered fewer opportunities for sociability. As one South Carolina man lamented, "with out sum American Friends" living nearby, exiles found it "very difficult to form any society in [England]." South Carolinian Mary Fraser likewise described England as "a foreign land, where she was made to taste, in Common with her young and unoffending Offspring, the bitter Cup of Sorrow and Affliction." After years in exile, Fraser returned to South Carolina to request a reversal of her husband's sentence, "which virtually banishes your petitioner and her Nine helpless Children." Paulina Telfair, who shared her husband's decade-long exile, came home to North Carolina after his death, "hoping to procure those blessings of life which have been denied to her elsewhere" (Doc. 24). When her husband, James, died in 1794, Mary Cary also abandoned London to live among kin in her native Virginia.[10]

Partly as a result of such homesickness, many banished loyalists hoped to return to America in the postwar era. Tories and their representatives in every state sought clemency, but South Carolinians petitioned in especially large numbers. That state's attempt to differentiate major from minor offenders and to establish a hierarchy of penalties en-

9. Robert S. Lambert, "A Loyalist Odyssey: James and Mary Cary in Exile, 1783–1804," *SCHM* 79 (1978): 167–78; Elizabeth Lichtenstein Johnston, *Recollections of a Georgia Loyalist* (New York and London: M. F. Mansfield and Company, 1901), 73–112.

10. Lambert, "Loyalist Odyssey," 180–81; Petition of Mary Fraser, 30 Nov. 1796, LP, Sc-Ar; Elias Ball to [Elias Ball], 22 Nov. 1784, quoted in Norton, *British-Americans*, 98. See also ibid., 62–72, 122–26.

couraged many of those affected by the penal laws to seek lesser punishments. At the same time, many low-country legislators, who sympathized with the loyalists but feared a popular outcry against granting them full pardons, saw the amercement as an appealing alternative to more draconian measures.[11]

In 1783 and 1784 alone, 137 banished South Carolinians or their representatives petitioned for permission to return to the state and reclaim their confiscated property. In 92 of these cases, the assembly decreased the offenders' sentences to a 12 percent amercement, while relieving 30 of them from all penalties whatsoever.[12] By 1787, only 87 South Carolinians were still officially banished and dispossessed of their estates, though many others chose to remain in exile. Meanwhile, the growing numbers of former Tories who now paid an annual amercement in lieu of more stringent penalties continued to flood the legislature with petitions to rescind even that more moderate sentence.

Among those petitioning for leniency, women were well represented. Between 1776 and 1800, South Carolina women filed 86 petitions for relief from the anti-Tory laws, and during the crucial years of 1783 and 1784 they accounted for more than a third of the petitions pertaining to loyalism which their state assembly considered. During those same years, when the women of Georgia accounted for an unprecedented 15 percent of all petitions submitted, relief from the state's recent anti-Tory statute was the objective of at least two-thirds of these petitioners.[13]

In South Carolina, where the resolution of loyalist issues appears to have taken longer than other southern states, some women continued to petition for relief from the penal statutes into the 1790s.[14] The widow and

---

11. The British occupation of Charleston weakened the low country's usual dominance in the assembly when that body met to enact the state's most significant anti-Tory legislation in 1782. See Nadelhaft, *Disorders of War,* 71–84; George C. Rogers Jr., *Evolution of a Federalist: William Loughton Smith of Charleston (1758–1812)* (Columbia: University of South Carolina Press, 1962), 104–7.

12. Lambert, *S.C. Loyalists,* 287–96.

13. In 1783–84, Georgia women submitted forty-six petitions, of which thirty-one pertained to loyalist issues. Four petitions dealt with other matters, while incomplete records prevent identification of the contents of the remaining eleven. See Journals of the Georgia House of Representatives, 1783–84, microfilm, Ga-Ar.

14. In Virginia, where there were relatively few loyalists, no women petitioned for relief from the anti-Tory statutes after 1790, while only one women did so in North Carolina. Georgia's legislative records are missing for the years 1790 through 1795, after which the women of that state filed no such petitions.

daughter of Peter Leger, a Charleston merchant, spent years trying to reverse the banishment of his Tory business partner, the only man whom they believed possessed the expertise to settle the firm's affairs "without great Loss" to themselves (Doc. 5). Mary Philp and her mother, Margaret Williams, spent more than a decade seeking to remove the amercement from a house and lot that was Mary's legacy from her father but was nonetheless amerced along with the property of her Tory husband (Doc. 25). In the closing decade of the eighteenth century, a total of thirteen South Carolina women continued to seek relief from the confiscation and amercement acts. Several of their cases remained unresolved as late as 1800.

For practical and for legal reasons, women were unusually prominent in the ranks of petitioners seeking relief from the anti-Tory statutes. Banished men ordinarily could not speak for themselves, and, though some chose male friends or relatives to plead their cases, others enlisted their wives to do so. Many women did not accompany their loyalist husbands into exile because, by remaining at home, they could shield at least a portion of their estates from confiscation. While the law provided for the confiscation of all abandoned loyalist properties, in most states the penal statutes also stipulated that a wife who did not join her husband in exile would be treated as a widow who, under the common law, retained her dower right to one-third of her spouse's property. The statutes of most states explicitly guaranteed such women widows' shares of their husbands' estates, while resident wives of South Carolina Tories could secure their dower rights by petitioning the state assembly.[15]

Wives who remained at home to protect property from confiscation were well situated, both physically and culturally, to appeal to the legislature on behalf of their banished spouses. In Georgia and South Carolina especially, many had relatively easy access to the legislature, which convened in or around the coastal cities in which loyalist families congregated. On the other hand, in a culture that customarily envisioned women as vulnerable and weak, these women who now lacked male protection must have made sympathetic supplicants. Gender, which in so many ways impeded women's access to the public sphere, may have given them an

---

15. Linda K. Kerber, *Women of the Republic: Intellect and Ideology in Revolutionary America* (Chapel Hill: University of North Carolina Press, 1980), 125–26. On the common law right of dower, see Marylynn Salmon, *Women and the Law of Property in Early America* (Chapel Hill: University of North Carolina Press, 1986), 141–47, 160–72.

advantage when they attempted to sway the legislators by portraying themselves as blameless victims deserving of their benevolence.

In fact, the treatment of women under the anti-Tory laws in the southern states and elsewhere reflected their ambiguous relationship to the public sphere in revolutionary America. When a state government subjected only men to loyalty oaths and other political tests, it presumed that women either lacked political consciousness or that their political allegiance automatically followed that of their spouses. At the same time, the preservation of the dower rights of wives who did not follow their husbands into exile derived more from the assumption that women were apolitical, and therefore blameless, than from the belief that those who remained behind differed politically from their husbands. By preserving women's dower rights, legislators attempted to protect the private interests of women and children from the consequences of men's public offenses. Yet recognizing the property rights of the wife of an exiled Tory, by presuming her political innocence, also implied that she might be a distinct political being with an allegiance separate from that of her husband.[16] As we shall see, some women claimed such a separate identity when they petitioned their legislatures. Most, however, instead played the culturally prescribed role of the wife and mother who put private concerns before public ones, the welfare of her family before the interests of the commonwealth.

The latter strategy better suited the purposes of women who petitioned on behalf of their Tory spouses. If a woman sought repatriation of a banished husband, she promoted her cause less effectively by emphasizing her own patriotism than by making his conduct appear less culpable in the eyes of state authorities. Because loyalty to the Crown was politically indefensible, most petitioners offered nonpolitical explanations for their spouses' offenses. Exploiting the prevailing gender stereotypes that deemed women apolitical and wholly preoccupied with domestic matters, most petitioners argued that their husbands merited clemency because their Toryism was less the result of a conscious political choice than of a desire to protect their families and their households. Such reasoning accorded well with the patriarchal values that continued

---

16. Kerber, *Women of the Republic*, 119–27; Linda K. Kerber, "The Paradox of Women's Citizenship in the Early Republic: The Case of Martin vs. Massachusetts, 1805," *AHR* 97 (1992): 355–62, 375; Joan R. Gundersen, "Independence, Citizenship, and the American Revolution," *Signs* 13 (1987): 68–71.

to shape relationships in families and in some communities, if not in the wider world of libertarian politics, in which republicans defined virtue as a willingness to sacrifice private interests in pursuit of the public good.[17]

Although some petitioners simply asserted that their husbands went over to the British to protect their families' physical and material well-being (Doc. 2), most attributed their spouses' Toryism to both a concern for their families and a desire to shield their neighbors from the worst abuses of British rule. Mary Cape of Charleston maintained that her husband, Brian, made his peace with the British because his family was "in want and greatly distressed," and that he later became a commissioner for sequestered estates both to support his "large family" and to "prevent cruelties from being inflicted on his [Whig] Friends" during the British occupation (Doc. 14). According to their wives, John and Theodore Gaillard, members of a prominent low-country clan, each took a British militia commission to "please his Parishioners and protect a numerous Family" (Doc. 12).

In some cases, neighbors came forward to support a woman's explanation of her husband's wartime conduct. Mary Brown, who sought leniency for her banished husband, Archibald, maintained that he accepted a British militia commission chiefly to prevent the appointment of "one Blackman a Cattle-driver . . . of very illiberal Principles" and demonstrated her neighbors' support for his decision by presenting their petition on his behalf (Doc. 10). When Sarah Capers requested a reversal of the penalties imposed on her husband, Gabriel, men from four low-country parishes presented a separate petition that attested to his services as a benevolent mediator between his Whig neighbors and the British regime after 1780 (Doc. 11).

Other petitioners exploited the racial tensions inherent in southern society, suggesting that their husbands' efforts to protect slave property and preserve white supremacy might compensate for their political errors in the eyes of state authorities. Petitioner Mary Inglis recounted her

---

17. On patriarchy, see Jay Fliegelman, *Prodigals and Pilgrims: The American Revolution against Patriarchal Authority* (Cambridge: Cambridge University Press, 1982), esp. chap. 5; Carole Pateman, "The Fraternal Social Contract," in Pateman, *The Disorder of Women* (London: Polity Press, 1989), 34–46. On some postrevolutionary southern communities, see also Allan Kulikoff, *Tobacco and Slaves: The Development of Southern Cultures in the Chesapeake, 1680–1800* (Chapel Hill: University of North Carolina Press, 1986), 421–35.

husband's attempts to return stolen slaves to their Whig owners during the British occupation of the South Carolina low country (Doc. 7). Eliza Clitherall informed the assembly that, following his banishment in 1782, her husband James went to British East Florida, where he worked tirelessly to retrieve the slave property of his erstwhile countrymen in South Carolina (Doc. 13).

Although the conduct of such men fell far short of the republican ideal of selfless patriotism, the wives of those who adhered to the Crown to protect their families, their communities, or their race could ascribe to them qualities, such as courage, prudence, and benevolence, which boded well for their possible reintegration into political society. Perhaps that is one reason why the legislatures granted the overwhelming majority of such petitions. The petitions of other wives, who attributed their husbands' political errors to moral, intellectual, or physical weakness, were more problematic. Women who described their spouses as weak, irrational, or readily corrupted disclaimed their ability to act in a politically responsible fashion. In so doing, they rhetorically emasculated their spouses, endowing them with pejorative qualities that eighteenth-century Americans ordinarily associated with women and others they deemed unfit for republican citizenship.[18]

Some women who depicted their spouses as weak and ineffectual nonetheless won them reprieves from the penal laws. Petitioning the legislature in 1783 and again in 1785, Elizabeth Atkins of Charleston stressed her husband's physical debility, claiming that his "Indispositions, Pains and Infirmities," which allegedly prevented his leaving the city after 1780, led him to seek a change of climate when the British forces withdrew from it two years later (Doc. 4). North Carolinian Elizabeth Torrence maintained that her husband's Toryism was the product of his susceptibility to "the persuasion and instigation of the enemies of his country." Eleanor Mackey, the wife of a Charleston cooper, also characterized her husband as lacking independence and resolve, informing the assembly that he was "made a miserable Dupe to the Suggestions & persuasions of more artfull designing and malignant Men," who cajoled him into supporting the British. Another Charleston woman described her husband as "an absolute Madman" whose insanity led him to accept the

---

18. Gundersen, "Independence, Citizenship, and the American Revolution," 59–67; Kerber, *Women of the Republic,* chap. 1.

reinstatement of British rule.[19] Although such portraits encouraged little hope for the rehabilitation of their subjects, some of these men eventually were repatriated. Perhaps the legislators concluded that men so debilitated posed no danger to staunch patriots who had waged war for American independence and republican political values.

Unlike the wives of Tory exiles who were obliged to justify or to explain their husbands' political errors in hopes of reversing their banishment, the widows and children of deceased loyalists, who could neither seek repatriation nor pose a political threat, simply could seek relief from the penal statutes without attempting to defend the actions of their disgraced relatives. Because Tory families, even more than most of their Whig counterparts, suffered financially as a result of the war, the widows of loyalists often described themselves as distressed and destitute, suggesting that they and their children already suffered sufficiently under the penal laws to merit the mercy of the state government.

Widows of loyalists sometimes described themselves and their children as apolitical dependents who were not accountable for the political offenses of their husbands and fathers. The state of South Carolina conceded this point, according to petitioner Margaret Orde, when it respected dower rights and "never Confiscated the Property of Women" (Doc. 17), while another South Carolina woman averred that "it never was the Intention of the Legislature, to reduce to abject Poverty, a Wife, or a Child, for the Conduct of a Husband, or a Father." Eighteen year-old Elizabeth Trezevant, heir to the estate of a Charleston loyalist, thought it unjust that the penal statutes did not explicitly protect "the Interest of Infants and Minors," who were blameless and "utterly disqualified for taking care of or guarding their property themselves" (Doc. 21). Ann Field, wife of a banished North Carolina man, observed that her distressed offspring "might be useful members of Society, had they only the advantages of Learning, which they are . . . deprived of, by the want of the head of the family to provide necessaries for them" (Doc. 18). Similarly, when the children of Andrew Williamson, a backcountry Tory, petitioned for relief from the 12 percent amercement exacted from his estate, they asserted their own innocence and reminded the legislators

---

19. Petition of Elizabeth Torrence, 24 Oct. 1783, GASR, Apr.–June 1784, Nc-Ar; Petition of Eleanor Mackey, 5 Feb. 1784, LP, Sc-Ar; Petition of Elizabeth Mitchell, 10 Feb. 1783, ibid.

that "Justice . . . delight[s] not in visiting the Errors of the father on his Posterity."[20]

The wives and children of Tories, unlike the relatives of Whigs, could not invoke the patriotism of their kin to gain the respect and sympathy of those who weighed the validity of their grievances. In other respects, however, Tory and Whig supplicants and the petitions they presented were decidedly similar. Women who petitioned for relief from the anti-Tory laws, like women petitioners in general, were usually women alone—widows or wives of exiles. Most were at least able to sign their names, and they were slightly more likely than their Whig counterparts to have themselves penned the petitions they submitted. Women who petitioned on behalf of loyalists and their families occasionally referred to themselves and others as "Subjects" of the state (Doc. 9), thus signaling their innocence of a revolutionary political culture that transformed dependent subjects into volitional citizens who no longer were subservient to their government.[21] In most other respects, however, the language these women employed resembled that of other petitioners, mingling conventional expressions of deference with varying levels of informed argumentation.

The petitions of many women who sought relief from the penal laws show familiarity with and understanding of the statutory and administrative apparatus that pertained to loyalist claims. Knowing that South Carolina's Confiscation Act protected property conveyed to women in marriage portions, Ann McGillvray petitioned to recover property on those grounds in 1783 (Doc. 3). Mary Wells, wife of Charleston's loyalist printer, deferentially appealed to the "known humanity & bounty of the Legislature" to help her "distressed Family," but she tersely reminded the assembly that "the tenth clause of the Confiscation Act . . . holds out a final Provision for the families of those whose estates were sold by virtue thereof" (Doc. 22). After petitioning unsuccessfully to recover her husband's entire estate, Catherine Carne decided to settle instead for a portion of his property, declaring that she was "by Law entitled" to her dower

---

20. Petition of Elizabeth Atkins, 1 Mar. 1785, LP, Sc-Ar; Petition of Andrew Williamson et al., 24 Jan. 1789, ibid.

21. James H. Kettner, *The Development of American Citizenship, 1608–1870* (Chapel Hill: University of North Carolina Press, 1978), chaps. 1, 7. See also Petition of Martha Clifford, 17 Feb. 1783, LP, Sc-Ar.

rights, which the assembly duly granted (Doc. 23). Some petitioners knew that they held property in their own names, which should have been exempt from the penal laws (Docs. 8, 15). Others sought to recover inheritances they believed were immune from the anti-Tory statutes (Docs. 6, 16) or to correct disputed land titles that led to unwarranted confiscations (Doc. 20).[22]

In most cases, women who petitioned for relief from the penal statutes enjoyed certain advantages over the patriot women who sought payment of soldiers' wages, pensions, or other public debts. For one thing, the provisions of the laws pertaining to loyalism were well-known to those they affected. During the Revolution, each state enacted its own legislation to punish Tory dissidents within its jurisdiction. Because Congress left this issue in the hands of the respective states, federalism never complicated the settlement of loyalist claims as it did the recovery of most war-related debts. As a result, loyalists and their kin knew that the state legislature was the only forum in which they might seek relief from the anti-Tory laws. By knowing where to present their cases, they avoided many of the administrative obstacles that frustrated so many of their Whig contemporaries.

In addition, in presenting their cases, women who petitioned for relief from the penal statutes had a simpler task than those whose grievances pertained to soldiers' arrears, government pensions, or other public debts. The latter, as we have seen, were obliged to produce documents or sworn testimony to prove the validity of their claims against the government. Women who requested relief from the Tory laws, by contrast, could not be expected to prove that their husbands did not at some time support the Crown, a point they never disputed. The legislature decided these cases on more subjective grounds.[23] Did the individual in question actively support the Revolution before the British occupation?

---

22. Colonial southerners sometimes created separate estates for wives to protect property from creditors or shield women from insolvent spouses. This practice would become more widespread among southern planters in the economically unstable antebellum era. See Salmon, *Women and the Law of Property,* 81–97; and Suzanne Lebsock, *The Free Women of Petersburg: Status and Culture in a Southern Town, 1784–1860* (New York: W. W. Norton, 1984), 54–58, 60, 66.

23. Conversely, Tories seeking compensation from British authorities for American property lost as a result of their loyalty faced evidentiary problems similar to those encountered by patriot claimants. See Norton, *British-Americans,* chap. 7.

Did the service he rendered his neighbors offset the grave political error he committed? Did other circumstances satisfactorily mitigate or explain his wartime conduct? Had his wife and children suffered unfairly? Were they deserving recipients of the assembly's compassion and benevolence? Individual judgments, far more than objective evidence, determined the petitioner's answers to these questions and, more important, the assembly's assessment of the information the petitioner furnished.

Equally significant were bonds of kinship and friendship among loyalist petitioners, who presumably exchanged advice and information with one another and thereby demystified the rules and rituals of the petitioning process. Petitioners Sarah Jones and Sarah Glen, mother and daughter, submitted their separate petitions together, as did the sisters-in-law Judith and Ellinor Gaillard. Petitioners Mary Rowand and Mary Wells, wives of Charleston loyalists, were also sisters-in-law. Mary Deas Inglis and Mary Deas Brown were first cousins who petitioned to secure their spouses' repatriation in 1783. The wife of Robert Cunningham and the widow of Andrew Cunningham, both members of a prominent Tory backcountry family, petitioned for relief from the confiscation statutes in 1784 and 1785, respectively.[24]

In addition, many wives and widows of Tories could enlist the sympathies of powerful men who, for both personal and political reasons, supported a policy of leniency toward all but the most notorious loyalists in the immediate postwar era. In the Carolina low country as well as in coastal Georgia, the Revolution severely weakened the old colonial elite, of whom many took protection from the British during the occupation. When the war was over, those elites who remained active in the revolutionary movement and who, in many cases, held political office used their influence to help their loyalist friends and relatives recoup their wartime losses. Some prominent patriots opposed what they believed to be the excessively harsh penal statutes in their respective states. Others worked to keep their friends off the confiscation lists or, failing that, advised exiles on how to pursue their cases for repatriation. These same men often sup-

24. Petition of Mrs. [Ellinor Cordes] Gaillard, 20 Feb. 1783, LP, Sc-Ar; Petition of Margaret Cunningham, 14 Feb. 1784, ibid.; Petition of Margaret Cunningham, 7 Feb. 1785, ibid. On the Cunningham family, see Lambert, *S.C. Loyalists*, 44–45, 152–53, 207–9, 301–2. The other petitions mentioned in this paragraph are reproduced in this chapter or elsewhere in the present study.

ported the wives of exiles in their attempts to win clemency for their spouses. Motivated in part by ties of kinship and friendship, the loyalists' Whig benefactors were also political conservatives who feared and distrusted democracy and looked to the reconstitution of the old elite to stem the rising tide of popular government.[25]

Of course, not all petitioners enjoyed the benefit of such powerful patrons or even the camaraderie of others who shared their predicament. A well-connected widow like Mary Peronneau, who successfully petitioned on behalf of one brother-in-law in 1783, could depend on the "advice of her Friends" in her later effort to recover the property of another (Doc. 19). By contrast, widow Sarah Beaucham planned to leave North Carolina in 1782 because she had "no friends in this State" after the departure and subsequent death of her Tory husband (Doc. 1). More difficult still was the situation of the children of Richard Edwards, an obscure backcountry loyalist, who died in the war's final months. The bulk of his property confiscated and the remainder allegedly embezzled by state officials or their agents, Edwards left behind five motherless children under the age of thirteen, who lived with a neighboring family but had no legal guardian.[26]

The Edwards children were innocent bystanders in a war that robbed them of their parent, home, and patrimony. Although their case was perhaps extreme, women and children ranging from the politically committed to the apathetic or ignorant also suffered under laws enacted primarily to punish men who either actively or passively opposed the Revolution. In the postrevolutionary era, circumstances forced the female kin of Tories, like their Whig counterparts, into the public sphere to interact with their governors. In keeping with both the dynamics of the petitioning ritual and the era's prevailing gender stereotypes, most portrayed themselves as dependent and apolitical. Some, however, used the occasion to declare their personal independence by asserting a separate political allegiance and a distinct public identity.

---

25. Demond, *Loyalists in N.C.*, 163–66, 174–78; Nadelhaft, *Disorders of War*, 79–84; Lambert, *S.C. Loyalists*, 288–89, 294–95; Rogers, *Evolution of a Federalist*, 104–6; George R. Lamplugh, *Politics on the Periphery: Factions and Parties in Georgia, 1783–1806* (Newark: University of Delaware Press, 1986), 43–45.

26. Petition of John Campbell and Mary Campbell on behalf of the orphan children of Richard Edwards, 7 May 1782, GASR, Apr.–May 1782, Nc-Ar.

DOCUMENT 1

Sarah Beaucham

Like most natives of Pennsylvania who migrated to North Caro-
lina, this petitioner probably resided in the state's western section.
Sarah Beaucham, the mother of four young children, petitioned the
assembly on 25 April 1782, asking to leave the state with her chil-
dren, slaves, and livestock. A legislative committee admitted that
she "deserve[d] to have her petition granted" but nonetheless re-
jected it because the law allowed the wives and widows of Tories to
retain only a dower interest in their husbands' estates. Regardless of
the assembly's decision, Beacham probably left North Carolina. She
appears in neither the state census of 1784–87 nor in the federal
census of 1790.[1]

Humbly Sheweth—
Whereas Your Petition[er]s Husband was one of those Unhappy Men
that went to The English & is Now Dead & Your Petitioner being in Great
Distress with a family of helpless Children Humbly Requests You Grant
her Liberty to Remove to Pensylvania the Place from Where She Came
Having no friends In this State to Asist her in Any Wise Towards Raising
her Small Children. And further Your Petitioner begs That You Will Suffer her to take What Little Effects[2] She hath with her For the Support of
herself & Children. And She As in Duty bound will Pray.

(ADS, Nc-Ar)

DOCUMENT 2

Ann Legge

On 22 January 1783, Ann Legge (d. 1828) petitioned on behalf of
her husband, Edward, who in 1780 signed the congratulatory ad-

---

1. Committee report on the petition of Sarah Beaucham, 9 May 1782, GASR,
Apr.–May 1782, Nc-Ar.
2. Three slaves, six head of cattle, and two horses, besides her personal effects
(ibid.).

dress to Sir Henry Clinton and consequently later was banished
by the victorious Whigs. The legislature granted her petition, and
Edward returned to Charleston and recovered his estate, subject to
an annual 12 percent amercement. Edward and Ann had four sur-
viving children when he died in 1804. Ann never remarried, though
she survived her husband by twenty-four years.[3]

The Petition of Anne Legge in behalf of herself and her Husband Edward Legge Junr. Late of Charles Town Merchant Humbly Sheweth

That your Petitioners Husband is banished from this State and his Estate confiscated by an act of the last General Assembly commonly called the confiscation act. That your Petitioner is left with three inocent and helpless children, destitute of Support, as on their unfortunate father rested their whole Dependance, for Subsistence by his industry and attention to Mercantile affairs, being deprived of which they must necessarily in a Short time be reduced to a Situation Truly distressing to humanity. More especially if that act is permitted to have it's full operation, as Your Petitioner and her poor infants will thereby be divested of the *small remains* of property which they now have, and which *only* affords them a partial subsistence. That your Petitioner begs leave to annex hereto a petition from her unfortunate Husband.[4] She sincerely hopes upon a review of his conduct, it will be found that it has been inoffensive, and That your Honorable House will Extend your Mercy & forgiveness, which your petitioner Joins with her Husband Most humbly to Implore.

Your petitioner Respectfully Intreats your Honourable House to take the Premises into consideration, That you will please to Restore her to contentment by permitting her to possess the company of her unhappy consort, by releasing him from his banishment, but should policy dictate a refusal to this part of her prayer, She further Most Humbly Intreats

3. Sabine, *Loyalists of the Amer. Rev.*, 2:543; *S.C. House Journals, 1783–1784,* 552; Will of Edward Legge, 27 Mar. 1804, Charleston County Will Book, 1800–1807, typescript, 29:612–13, Sc-Ar; Will of Ann Legge, 11 Apr. 1828, Charleston County Will Book, 1826–34, typescript, 38:422–23, Sc-Ar.

4. Accompanying petition of Edward Legge Jr. is dated 10 December 1782. Legge claimed that, when the British captured Charleston, he believed himself "released from allegiance" to South Carolina but admitted that "his Mercantile concerns were a primary inducement" for seeking protection from British authorities (LP, Sc-Ar).

Your Honourable House to prevent her & her three poor inocent children from experiencing those calamities which a total Loss of her *little* remaining property must eventually produce, by vesting that Property in her or her children as to your Honorable House in your wisdom & goodness shall seem meet.

And your petitioner as in Gratitude Bound will Ever pray.

(DS, Sc-Ar)

DOCUMENT 3

Ann McGillvray

The petitioner was the widow of William McGillvray, who served briefly in the Tory militia but died before the war was over. On 25 January 1783, Ann McGillvray petitioned to recover William's property as well as her own marriage portion, which the state mistakenly confiscated. The assembly returned the property and relieved it from the customary amercement.[5]

Setting forth

That She is the Widow of John McGilvray[6] whose Estate is Confiscated by the Laws of this State, that she is left with two small Children, And if the laws should take the Estate, she must be reduced to the Necessity of Soliciting the Bounty of her friends or the Officers of the Parish, for the Support of herself and Children, That the greatest part was given her in Marriage by her Father And prays that the Said Estate may have relief from the pains and penalties of an Act entitled an Act for disposing of Certain Estates, &c.

(Petition quoted in South Carolina Senate Journals, 28 January 1783, Sc-Ar)

---

5. Clark, *Loyalists,* 1:174; *S.C. House Journals, 1783–1784,* 551–52.

6. Error in original. Legislative records identify her husband as William Henry McGillvray (*S.C. House Journals, 1783–1784,* 53).

DOCUMENT 4

Elizabeth Atkins

*The South Carolina assembly rejected this petition of 1 Febru-
ary 1783, in which Elizabeth Atkins sought clemency for her Tory
husband. Charles Atkins had fled the state in 1782 and never returned, settling eventually in London. In 1785, Elizabeth recovered
the proceeds from the sale of a portion of his property. She and her
children may have remained in South Carolina at least as late as
1790, when the first federal census listed an Elizabeth Atkins as the
head of a York County household composed of two white females in
addition to herself.[7]*

The Petition of Elizabeth Atkins, Wife of Charles Atkins late of
Charlestown, in the State aforesaid, Merchant, for herself and for and in
behalf of her two Children.

Sheweth That your said Petitioner with the deepest concern, beholds
her said Husband's Estate confiscated and himself banished from the
State aforesaid, in and by an Act of Assembly passed the twenty sixth Day
of February in the Year of our Lord, One Thousand seven Hundred and
eighty two.

That your said Petitioners said Husband for several Years before his
last Departure from the State aforesaid, having laboured under many and
severe Indispositions, Pains and Infirmities of Body, was advised by his
Physicians to change the climate, that being the dernier resort they could
have recourse to, to prolong his Life for the support and maintenance of
himself and Family.

That he in conformity to and in compliance with said Advice, did, on
or about the twenty fourth Day of Jany. in the Year of our Lord aforesaid,
depart from and leave the said State, but with full Intent, Purpose and
Resolution of returning thereto, whenever it should please God to restore

---

7. Petition of Elizabeth Atkins, 28 Feb. 1785, LP, Sc-Ar; Lambert, *S.C. Loyalists*,
188, 280; Sabine, *Loyalists of the Amer. Rev.*, 1:192; *Heads of Families . . . in the Year
1790: S.C.*, 28.

him to his former Health and not with Intention to withdraw himself entirely therefrom.

That should the said Act be strictly and liberally carried into Execution against the Person, Estate and Property of her said Husband, your said Petitioner with two helpless Children would be utterly and totally ruined and undone, and consequently become the Objects of Pity and Compassion and thereby obliged to become a Burthen and Expence upon and to the Parish, to prevent which, Y[ou]r Petitioner most humbly prays the Honourable House of Representatives to take into their tender Consideration the helpless and distressed Case and Condition of herself and Family and grant to her such relief in the Premises as to them in their great Wisdom shall seem meet, necessary fit and convenient.

And your said Petitioner as in duty bound will ever.

(ADS, Sc-Ar)

DOCUMENT 5
Elizabeth Leger and Elizabeth Leger Jr.

The petitioners, the widow and daughter of Charleston merchant Peter Leger, spent years trying to resolve financial problems arising from his partnership with Tory William Greenwood. Leger and Greenwood traded in furs and slaves in the early 1770s. Leger, who supported the Revolution, died in 1777; Greenwood remained in Charleston during the British occupation and later lost his estate and went to England as an exile. This petition, presented on 3 February 1783, was the first of three unsuccessful attempts on the part the Leger women to expedite the settlement of the firm's accounts.[8]

The Memorial and Petition of Elizabeth Leger, widow, and Elizabeth Leger, daughter, Legatees of the late Peter Leger, deceased.

Sheweth That the late Peter Leger, deceased, in his lifetime was largely concerned in Trade, as a Merchant, with Mr. William Greenwood, in a Co-partnership, under the Firm of Leger & Greenwood.

---

8. *Biog. Dict. of S.C. House, 1775–1790*, 429–30; Petition of Elizabeth Leger, 9 Feb. 1784, LP, Sc-Ar; Petition of Elizabeth Leger and Elizabeth Leger Hutchinson, 11 Jan. 1791, ibid.

That by an Act of the General Assembly, passed the 26th of February last, the estate of the said William Greenwood is confiscated, and his Person for ever banished, in consequence thereof, he was obliged, contrary to his inclination, to leave this State, and has carried with him the Books, Bonds, Notes &c, of the said Co-partnership.

That the Concerns of the said Co-partnership are yet unsettled.

That the said Co-partnership owes Debts to a very Large Amount.

That although debts to a very considerable amount are due to the said Co-partnership, yet there is great reason to suppose, from the Ravages of war, and the Ruin consequent thereupon, to many of their Creditors, and also the Losses sustained by the depreciation of Currency, that the debts, should any be received by the said Co-partnership, will fall short of paying the debts against it.

That the Concerns of the said Co-partnership have been so very extensive, and are so intricate and perplexed, that no person whomsoever, but the said William Greenwood, has such knowledge of them as to settle them without great Loss to the Co-partnership, and consequently to your Memorialists, Legatees, of the said Peter Leger, deceased, a Person who interested himself early & strenuously in the Cause of his Country.[9]

That the Commissioners of Confiscated Estates, nor any other persons for them, cannot possibly be supposed to be adequate to the settlement of those Concerns, more especially the Books of the said Co-partnership being carried away.

That your Memorialists have great reason to believe, that (without the greatest care and attention to the Concerns of the Co-partnership) when the debts of the said Co-partnership and the private debts of the said William Greenwood are all paid, he will have no property left, consequently the State will receive no benefits from the Confiscation of his Estate.

That no person can be supposed to pay so much care and attention to the Concerns of the said William Greenwood, or be so qualified for it, as the said William Greenwood, and any deficiencies or losses in the Co-partnership for want of such Care and attention, will ultimately fall on your Petitioners.

---

9. Leger, a conservative Whig, was an officer in the Charleston militia who represented the parish of St. Phillip and St. Michael in the Second Provincial Congress and in the first two state assemblies (*Biog. Dict. of S.C. House, 1775–1790*, 430).

That it is well known to your Memorialists that the said William Greenwood, during his connections with the British, never advised nor entered into violent measures. That the Commissions he took both in the Militia and the Civil Departments were imposed upon him. The Congratulatory Addresses he signed were on purpose to recover a large property in Indigo and other produce, the property of Leger & Greenwood captured by the British army.[10]

That his connections with the British since the surrender of Charles Town enabled him to put in execution his natural inclination to serve his American Friends and Acquaintances; and that he never pressed for Money, nor entered vexatious Lawsuits against any of the numerous Creditors of Leger & Greenwood, but, on the contrary, lent money to some, and furnished supplies of Necessaries to others of his distressed acquaintances, out of the Garrison.

That as the State in all probability will obtain no benefit from the Confiscation of the Estate of the said William Greenwood, & as it is certain the Estate of your Memorialists will be ruined for want of his Assistance to settle the Concerns of the said Co-partnership, Your Memorialists pray that your Honourable Senate will be pleased to take the Premises into consideration and prevent the operation of the Act of Confiscation and banishment against the Estate and Person of the said William Greenwood.[11]

And your Memorialists will pray &c.

(ADS [written by Elizabeth Leger and signed by her and by Elizabeth Leger Jr.], Sc-Ar)

---

10. In 1780, Greenwood signed both the address to Sir Henry Clinton, which accepted an offer of clemency in exchange for allegiance, and the address to Cornwallis, by which he took up a commission in the royal militia in exchange for the protection of British authorities. For the texts and signatories of these addresses, see David Ramsay, *The History of the Revolution in South-Carolina,* 2 vols. (Trenton, N.J.: Isaac Collins, 1785), 2:443–45, 466–68.

11. Between 1783 and 1791, Greenwood himself petitioned five times for readmission to South Carolina. The assembly granted none of his petitions, but by the early 1790s he had nonetheless returned to Charleston (Petitions of William Greenwood, 3 Feb. 1783, 12 Feb. 1785, 17 Feb. 1786, 14 Feb. 1789, 11 Jan. 1791, LP, Sc-Ar; Lambert, *S.C. Loyalists,* 295).

DOCUMENT 6

Anne Walker

The petitioner was the niece of Hopkin Price, a Welshman who settled in Charleston in the 1740s. Having no children of his own, Price encouraged his niece Anne to come to South Carolina. Perhaps expecting a large inheritance, she complied with his request, but when Price died, in 1781, he left her only £100 out of an estate worth £4,300. Posthumous confiscation of Price's estate prevented Anne from collecting even this sum, and on 4 February 1783 she petitioned to retrieve it. The assembly, however, did not act on her petition.[12]

The humble Petition of Anne Walker, late Anne David William Watkins, Neice of Hopkin Price late of Charlestown in the said State dec[ease]d.

Sheweth That the said Hopkin Price had wrote to his Family in Britain for some one or more of them to come out to him in South Carolina aforesaid.

That Colo. Probart Howarth[13] whilst visiting his Friends in the County of Caermarthen confirmed the said Hopkin Price's desire of seeing & invitation to some one or more of his Family to come out to him as aforesaid, and advised your Petitioner so to do, & assisted her to undertake the Voyage.

That some short time after her Arrival her Uncle departed this Life, & in his Will left her only One hundred pounds Sterl[in]g which she has not received nor any part thereof.

---

12. *Biog. Directory of S.C. House, 1719–1774*, 540–41; Will of Hopkin Prise, 13 Dec. 1780, Charleston County Will Book, 1780–83, typescript, 19:281–83, Sc-Ar.

13. Col. Probart Howarth was the commander of Charleston's Fort Johnson and a former officer in the British army. In 1777, he refused to take the Whig oath and became one of the first Tories to leave South Carolina (Robert W. Barnwell Jr., "The Migration of Loyalists from South Carolina," *Proceedings of the South Carolina Historical Association: 1937* [Columbia: South Carolina Historical Association, 1937], 34).

That by an Act of the Legislature the Estate of the said Hopkin Price decd. is confiscated as your Petitioner is informed but notwithstanding hopes that this Honourable House will be pleased to permit her to enjoy the same as a fit object of pity & compassion; and from her being in a strange Country & far removed from all her Relations Friends and Connections (in which Country she is very desirous of continuing) to grant her besides a small annual Sum or living out of her said Uncle's Estate.

Your Petitioner therefore humbly prays that this Hon[ora]ble House will take her Case & application into their humane Consideration & grant her the enjoyment of the said One hundred pounds Sterlg. Legacy and small annual Sum or Living besides out of her said Uncle's Estate.

As in duty bound will ever pray &c.

(DS, Sc-Ar)

DOCUMENT 7

Mary Inglis

Mary Deas, the daughter of a Scottish merchant, married Alexander Inglis in 1773. Inglis signed the addresses to the British commanders in 1780, and he and his family remained in Charleston during the British occupation. When the British departed in 1782, Alexander Inglis fled to East Florida, leaving his wife behind to seek clemency from South Carolina's state government. Mary Inglis successfully petitioned the assembly on 12 February 1783. Alexander returned to South Carolina and recovered his estate, subject to a 12 percent amercement. He died, insolvent, from wounds sustained in a duel in 1791.[14]

The Petition of Mary Inglis in behalf of her Husband Alexander Inglis—Humbly sheweth

That Your Petitioner out of the sincere Regard and Duty she owes to a kind and Affectionate Husband whose Estate is confiscated and his Per-

---

14. Rogers, *Evolution of a Federalist*, 102–3; Sabine, *Loyalists of the Amer. Rev.*, 2:535; *S.C. House Journals, 1783–1784*, 552; Lambert, *S.C. Loyalists*, 290, 295; Petition of Mary Inglis Junior et al., 8 Dec. 1791, LP, Sc-Ar.

son banished by a late Act of the Legislature at Jacksonborough, thinks it incumbent on her to state his Case to your Honourable House.

That her said Husband has resided in this State and in Georgia Twenty odd Years, during which Time, she flatters herself, he has ever supported the Character of a Man of Integrity.

That altho' he may have heretofore Unfortunately differed in some of his Political opinions from the rest of his Fellow Citizens, yet your Petitioner is certain that he never shew'd the most distant disposition to distress or offend Individuals, but on the contrary, avail'd himself of every oportunity that offer'd, so far as was in his power, to assist those that were under any Degree of Persecution from the British—having in several Instances rescued his Fellow Citizens out of the Provôt and Prison-Ships [15] and got them sent back to their own Homes, and at one time recover'd all the Negroes belonging to Mr. Jonah Collins of Santee, from some Plunderers that had brought them to Town, advancing out of his own Pocket One Hundred Guineas as a Compromise to get them restored, and also another Parcel of Mrs. Cattell's (the Widow of Colo. Wm. Cattell) [16] that were in the same predicament and were in like manner rescued by Mr. Inglis's Interposition—as your Petitioner can prove by the Testimony of the parties concerned.

That Mr. Inglis never took any Oath of Allegiance to the British Government since the unfortunate Fall of Charles Town, and waved accepting of any Office of Emolument, particularly a Seat at the Board of Police, refusing the Benefits of such an Appointment rather than hurt his own feelings by giving Offence to his Fellow Citizens.

That Your Petitioner is convinced her said Husband is most sincerely sorry that any part of his Conduct should have subjected him to the Resentment of the Country for which he has ever had the greatest Affection and Partiality, and she is certain that if he is permitted to return he will

---

15. After the fall of Charleston, some twenty-five hundred American prisoners were confined to British ships, where nearly one-third died of disease or starvation before the war was over. Prisoners on parole were confined to the city and prohibited from practicing their trades or professions. Those who broke the terms of their parole were arrested and interred in the Provost, a damp cellar under the Exchange (McCrady, *S.C. in the Revolution*, 2:349–59, 368–69).

16. Collins and Cattell were both Whigs. Jonah Collins served in the Charleson Battalion of Artillery after 1780, while Col. William Cattell was taken prisoner at the fall of Charleston (Moss, *S.C. Patriots*, 159, 188).

chearfully dedicate the remainder of his Life in rendering it every Service in his power—being well persuaded that few Men have a more grateful Temper than Mr. Inglis.

That her said Husband has under his Care several Minors and Orphan Children, particularly the Children of his Uncle Mr. George Inglis and those of his late worthy Partner Mr. Thomas Loughton Smith,[17] all of whom will suffer more or less in their affairs if he is not permitted to return.

That Your Petitioner has four small Children whose Maintenance and Support thro' Life will in a great measure depend on the Industry and Care of her said Husband, on whose account, she flatters herself Your Honourable House will think, with her, that the Punishment allotted her said Husband is more than adequate to the Faults that have been alledged against him. And therefore your Petitioner humbly prays your Honourable House to take his Case into your Consideration and that you will be pleased to restore him to his disconsolate Family and Friends and to the Enjoyment of his Possessions in this Country.

And Your Petitioner as in Duty bound will ever pray &c.

(ADS, Sc-Ar)

DOCUMENT 8

Ann Williams

Robert Williams was head of the currency commission under South Carolina's restored royal government. In January 1782, he conveyed part of his property to his wife to shield it from imminent confiscation. The penal laws subsequently invalidated all sales and conveyances made "with a view of eluding forfeiture," but on 12 February 1783 Ann Roper Williams nonetheless petitioned to recover the property in question. The assembly rejected her petition,

17. Thomas Loughton Smith, who died in 1773, had married Elizabeth Inglis, George's daughter and Alexander's first cousin. The Smiths had at least six children who survived to adulthood (Rogers, *Evolution of a Federalist*, 25; *Biog. Directory of S.C. House, 1719–1774*, 644–45).

*the Williamses moved to England, and neither Ann nor Robert
again attempted to reclaim their property in South Carolina.*[18]

The Petition of Ann Williams, of Charlestown.

Sheweth That as the character of your Petitioners Husband has undergone the several strictures, originating in private prejudice and resentment, your Petitioner, although fully sensible of their weakness and inefficacy upon liberal minds, cannot however refrain from lamenting, that through the assiduous exertions of those who promoted them, and a want of information in others who gave them credit, they have, in some instances, operated considerably to the disadvantage of said Husband.

That your Petitioner, uninfluenced by motives of resentment, but merely with a view to the suppression of falsehood and discovery of facts (in support of which, if required, she can produce undeniable proofs) is hopeful this Honourable House will excuse her premising a subject entirely unconnected with the substance of her Petition, to which she now solicits your Honours attention.

That the Persons deputed by the Commissioners of Confiscation waited on your Petitioner a few days ago, and in pursuance of their duty, took the dimensions of the House wherein she lives, together with an Inventory of the furniture, &ca, for the purpose, as she apprehends, of exposing the same to public Sale, agreeable to the Act of Confiscation.

That your Petitioner, with the charge of a numerous and helpless Family, and desirous of averting the ruin and distress they must infallibly be involved in, by the final operation of the said Act, conceives herself indispensably bound, in point of duty and affection, to lay before your Honours a just representation of the circumstances of her Case.

That your Petitioner's Husband, in pursuance of a certain Contract, with her Father the late William Roper Esquire,[19] in writing, bearing the date the sixth day of February, in the year of our Lord 1771, did, by deed duly executed, bearing date the nineteenth day of January 1782, and par-

18. Barnwell, "Migration of Loyalists," 34; Lambert, *S.C. Loyalists*, 187–88, 280–81; Sabine, *Loyalists of the Amer. Rev.*, 2:436; *S.C. Statutes*, 4:520.

19. Roper, who died in 1772, was a Charleston merchant and officeholder and a frequent member of South Carolina's colonial assembly. He owned a plantation as well as three town houses, one of which he apparently earmarked for Ann's marriage settlement (*Biog. Directory of S.C. House, 1719–1774*, 566–67).

ticularly reciting the aforesaid Contract, convey unto certain Trustees therein mentioned, to and for the separate use and behoof of your Petitioner, the Tenement and Messuage where she now resides, together with sundry Negro Slaves therein ascertained: But as your Petitioner is informed, the above deed of Settlement is counteracted and made void by a late Act of the General Assembly of this State,[20] She humbly submits to the generosity of this Honourable House to determine, whether, on consideration of the said Settlement's being made in consequence of a prior engagement subsisting previous to the commencement of the War, and before her Husband had incurred any legal disability, the said deed may not be permitted to operate, so as to entitle her to the benefit thereof, having been originally founded on the strictest principle of Justice and Equity. And your Petitioner further declares, without deviating from the truth or candor, that should the said Act of Confiscation be enforced in this instance, and the said property devested from her, which is all she depends on for support, herself and numerous family, consisting of eight helpless Children must inevitably be reduced to experience calamities, the relation of which would excite the tenderest feelings of humanity.

Your Petitioner therefore, in her own and their behalf, earnestly solicits the Interposition of this Honourable House in confirming the above settlement, or otherwise preventing the ruin which must ensue from the further process of Confiscation.

And your Petitioner, in gratitude, will ever pray, &ca.

(DS, Sc-Ar)

DOCUMENT 9

Mary Rowand

On 14 February 1783, Mary Elliott Rowand (1735–1802) petitioned for the repatriation of her husband, Robert. Although the as-

---

20. Section 12 of "An Act for disposing of certain Estates, and banishing certain persons therein named," enacted in February 1782, stipulated that all property held by Tories between the declaration of American independence and the fall of Charleston would be subject to confiscation "unless the same was really and bona fide sold and conveyed, for valuable consideration of money paid, or secured to be paid, and actual possession given to the purchasers, . . . without any secret trust or condition, and not with a view of eluding forfeiture" (*S.C. Statutes*, 4:520).

sembly rejected her petition and neither she nor Robert filed an-
other on his behalf, by 1790 he had returned to Charleston, where
he resided in a household with two white females, one "other free
person," and eighteen slaves.[21]

The Humble Petition of Mary Rowand Sheweth

That your Petitioner is descended from Ancestors who came into this Country at the first Settlement thereof, and whose industry, diligence, Valour & Perseverance, greatly contributed to the advancement and prosperity to which it is arrived.[22] That your Petitioner upwards of Seventeen Years ago intermarried with Robert Rowand then of this Town Merchant, by whom She had two Children, now alive. That in the disputes between this country and Great Britain Her Said Husband unfortunatly adhering to the attachment & preposession in favor of Great Britain, which he had imbibed from his birth and Strengthned by his Education,[23] declined taking the Oaths requird by the Laws of this State to Qualify him to be a citizen thereof, by which means he was obligd to withdraw from hence and return to Britain. That notwithstanding this his Conduct in Conformity to his Sentiments, yet he preservd Such a Grateful Sence of regard towards this Country & its Inhabitants, as never in the most distant degree to take any part in the Measures pursued to the disadvantage of America but contented himself with remaining in a quiet unoffensive & retired Situation. That after the conquest of this Town by the British Forces he returned to this Country to Visit his Family still persisting in his First resolution not to act or do any thing to the prejudice of this Country, and accordingly avoided accepting any public office what-

---

21. Mabel L. Webber, ed. "Records from the Elliott-Rowand Bible, Accompanied by an Account of the First Thomas Elliott and of Some of His Descendants," *South Carolina Historical and Genealogical Magazine* 11 (1910): 67–70; *Heads of Families . . . in the Year 1790: S.C.*, 42.

22. Thomas Elliott, a Quaker, arrived in South Carolina by 1696, when he received a land grant from the colonial government. The petitioner was his granddaughter and a member of the second generation of Elliotts born in South Carolina (Webber, "Records from the Elliott-Rowand Bible," 57–60).

23. Rowand, a native of Scotland, married Mary Elliott Mackewn on 12 September 1765. They had two children, a son and a daughter, who lived to maturity, and another daughter who died young. In addition, Mary had borne seven children during her first marriage, of whom only one adult daughter survived by 1783 (ibid., 67–70; Barnwell, "Migration of Loyalists," 36).

ever, or carrying Arms, or Signing any of the papers or addresses indicating any resentment against a people whom he lov'd & respected, living a domestic retird life, doing every Service in his power to every inhabitant in distress who Solicited his assistance. That on the evacuation of Charlestown by the British Troops her Said husband was Compell'd in obedience to the laws of this State again to remove himself tho' with Great reluctance and regret leaving behind him a disconsolate Wife and Child. That your Petitioner's husband the Said Robert Rowand is very desirous of becoming a determined & Zealous Subject of this State & dedicating the remainder of his days to Service, and has possess'd these Sentiments from a considerable time past looking on himself as totally absolved from his former Conexion and dependence on Great Britain.

Your Petitioner humbly prays this Honorable House will take her said husbands case into their merciful consideration, that he may be pardond the Banishment inflicted on him, and restord to the favor of this Country. And have the Comfort of living with his Family in a State to whose Interest and welfare he will be ever truly devoted. And your Petitioner as in duty and Gratitude Bound will ever pray &c.

(DS, Sc-Ar)

DOCUMENT 10

Mary Brown

Mary Deas, the daughter of a Charleston merchant, married Archibald Brown in August 1780. Both her father and her husband had taken British protection the preceding May, and in 1782 the state banished both men and confiscated their property. On 15 February 1783, Mary Deas Brown presented this petition on her husband's behalf. Some men from the Goose Creek neighborhood submitted a supporting petition five days later. Before the assembly ruled on these petitions, Archibald Brown himself petitioned for clemency, and in 1784 the state restored his citizenship and his estate.[24]

---

24. Moss, *S.C. Patriots,* 105; *Biog. Dict. of S.C. House, 1775–1790,* 178–79; Petition of the inhabitants of Goose Creek, 20 Feb. 1783, LP, Sc-Ar; Petition of Archibald Brown, 10 Feb. 1784, ibid.; *S.C. House Journals, 1783–1784,* 552.

The Petition of Mary Brown in behalf of her husband Archibald Brown. Humbly Sheweth

That your Petitioner out of the Duty and Regard she owes to a tender and Affectionate Husband whose Estate is confiscated and his Person banished by a late Act of the Legislature at Jacksonborough thinks it incumbent on her to State his Case to your Honourable House.

That the said Archibald Brown was born and bred up in this State and from the earliest dawn of these unhappy Disputes proved himself a zealous and active Friend in the Cause of his Country.

That at the time of every Invasion he was amongst the foremost at the Post of Danger.

That after the unfortunate Fall of Charles Town, when it was generally believed that the Country was irrecoverably lost, he amongst a Multitude of other Inhabitants became a British Subject.

That he accepted the Command of the Goose-Creek Company of Militia, from its appearing to him to be both the Wish of the Parish in general, and of the Privates in that Company in particular, but chiefly to prevent its being given to one Blackman a Cattle-driver in W[assemean?],[25] an obscure Man and of very illiberal Principles, who was absolutely named as one fit to take the command of that Company; That during his holding that Commission he received Instructions, similar to those sent to the other Captains of the Militia, ordering him to send down to the Sea Islands, as Prisoners of War, all the former Members of Assembly, all Commissioned Officers, Magistrates, and active Persons in the said District (which he had put in force would have nearly included every Gentleman in the Parish) but your Petitioner appeals to those Gentlemen, whether he did or did not send down any, in fact he sent none, but threw up his Commission rather than hurt his own feelings or those of his Fellow Parishioners.

That the taking the Command of one of the Militia-Companies in Charles Town he considered as his Duty, to keep the Peace of the Town as he had formerly done under the American Government.

That as to the Address to Sir Henry Clinton which he unfortunately signed and which has given so much Offense, Your Petitioner can only urge in excuse for her Husband, on that occasion, that he was led away by that kind of Contagion which spreads on such occasions, from the force of Examples set before him, by Men further advanced in Life, and of

---

25. Probably Wassamassaw in Berkeley County.

more knowledge of the World; and from its being held out to him as the only Terms on which he could expect to remain in this his Native Country, where it is well known he has many near Connexions who have much dependance on him, and whom he could not think of leaving in the unsettled State of Affairs at that time.

Your Petitioner, tho' loath to bear testimony of her Husband's Services to this State, yet humbly hopes that regard will be had to his former conduct as an Officer in the Militia, and as one of the State Agents sent to France, as also his firm and intrepid Behaviour in the Field, at Port-Royal and Savannah, and the Blood he there spilt in the Cause of his Country,[26] which he never would have deserted, had he not considered the State as conquered, and therefore your Petitioner humbly hopes that her Husband will be judged by his Country, on the general Line of his Conduct since the first beginning of these Troubles, and not by selecting particular Periods, when the general Distress rendered it difficult for Men of more Experience and of riper judgment to conduct themselves with propriety.

Your Petitioner, having with the outmost Horror heard that it was alledged before the late Honourable House of Representatives that her Husband was present at the burning of the Houses at Winyaw, begs leave to assure your Honourable House that said Report is not true, which she can prove by the Testimony of several of the Goose-Creek Company who were with him in George-Town, at the time those Houses were burnt by Major Wemyss at Black-Mingo or that Neighbourhood.[27]

---

26. Brown was among the defenders of Charleston in 1776, and the state later sent him to France to purchase clothing and other supplies. In February 1779, he was wounded at the Battle of Beaufort. He fought for the Whigs in Savannah, became a prisoner at the fall of Charleston in 1780, and thereupon accepted the restored royal government (Moss, *S.C. Patriots*, 105).

27. In August 1780, Maj. James Wemyss, with a force of some three hundred men, burned approximately fifty houses in the area surrounding Black Mingo, in Williamsburg County, about ten miles northwest of Georgetown (McCrady, *S.C. in the Revolution*, 2:746–47; Lambert, *S.C. Loyalists*, 115; Robert M. Weir, "'The Violent Spirit,' the Reestablishment of Order, and the Continuity of Leadership in Post-Revolutionary South Carolina," in Hoffman et al., eds., *Uncivil War*, 74; William Moultrie, *Memoirs of the American Revolution*, 2 vols. [New York: David Longworth, 1902], 2:248–49).

The supposed allegations against Brown do not appear in the legislative record. See A. S. Salley, ed., *Journal of the House of Representatives of South Carolina, January 8, 1782—February 26, 1782* (Columbia: State Company, 1916).

Your Petitioner further begs leave to assure your Honourable House, that if her Husband is restored to his Country and Friends, she knows his grateful Temper so well that she is confident that he will be happy in rendering his best Services in future, And has only further to offer that he has several worthy Connexions, besides your Petitioner and an innocent Babe, depending on him, to whom his return will be of the outmost consequence.

May it therefore please your Honourable House to take this Candid State of Facts into your consideration, and to restore your Petitioner's said Husband to his disconsolate Family and Friends, and your Petitioner as in Duty bound will ever pray.

(ADS, Sc-Ar)

DOCUMENT 11

Sarah Capers

When the petitioner married the wealthy widower Gabriel Capers in 1777, he was a supporter of the Revolution, a member of the first and second provincial congresses, and Whig assemblyman for Christ Church Parish. In 1780, however, Capers took protection from the British and became a major in the royal militia. As a result, in 1782, the state banished him and confiscated his property. On 21 February 1783, Sarah Lloyd Capers (d. 1808) petitioned on behalf of her exiled husband, whom the assembly permitted to return to South Carolina and recover his estate.[28]

The humble Petition of Sarah Capers, in Behalf of her husband Gabl. Capers now in East Florida, Sheweth

That your Petitioner is the Wife of Gabl. Capers who is Banished from this Country, and his Estate Confiscated, That She has four Small Children, and being deprived of her Husbands Estate, She had Nothing to Maintain them with, But she trusts the Generosity and Clemency of the Legislature, will Interpose, and not subject her and her helpless Innocent Family, to Misery, and Want, which thay Must Shortly Suffer;

28. *Biog. Dict. of S.C. House, 1775–1790*, 127–28; Sabine, *Loyalists of the Amer. Rev.*, 1:294; Clark, *Loyalists*, 1:183–84; *S.C. House Journals, 1783–1784*, 552.

Mr Capers's conduct has never been Oppressive to his fellow Citizens, nor she hopes Unpardonable with Respect to his Country, Many of his Fellow Parishioners are ready to attest, that he was ever inclined to render them every possible Service, to promote their Happiness, and welfare to the Utmost of his Power;[29] She therefore Prays your Honorable House will commisserate his Unfortunate Situation, and that of his innocent Family, and be pleased to Restore him to his Country, his Friends, and his Property, and as in Duty bound, your Petitioner will ever pray.

(ADS, Sc-Ar)

DOCUMENT 12

Judith Gaillard

Judith Peyre Gaillard (d. 1789) spent the early war years in exile with her husband, John, in Bristol, England, where she gave birth to the youngest of their thirteen children. The Gaillards returned to Charleston during the British occupation, but John fled to England in 1782, when the British evacuated the city. Judith remained behind, and on 22 February 1783, she successfully petitioned the assembly for relief from the anti-Tory statutes. John Gaillard owned two plantations and 115 slaves in 1790.[30]

The Petition of Judith Gaillard Humbly Sheweth

That your Petitioner with the deepest concern and unaffected grief sees her Husband John Gaillard in the list of those whose persons were banished, and there property confiscated. He falling under so heavy a censure of his Country, must ever give real cause of Anguish to his Bosom. But she still hopes that when his Country Men are informed, that his motives for accepting the Commission, which made him an object of

---

29. That same day sundry inhabitants of the parishes of Christ Church, St. Thomas, St. James, and St. Stephen presented another petition on Capers's behalf (LP, Sc-Ar).

30. Dorothy Kelly McDowell, comp., *Gaillard Genealogy: Descendants of Joachim Gaillard and Esther Paparel* (Columbia, S.C.: R. L. Bryan Company, 1974), 2, 6–7; *Biog. Directory of S.C. House, 1719–1774*, 264–65; *S.C. House Journals, 1783–1784*, 552.

the Law was to please his Parishioners, and protect a numerous and helpless Family from the insults of a conquering Enemy; and the many distresses he foresaw must attend the unhappy State this Country was
reduced to; she cannot but flatter herself that the lenity of this Honorable
House will pity the Man, whose tenderness and affection for his Family
brought him into this unfortunate situation. She therefore humbly hopes,
that, Your Honorable House will Commiserate the distresses of a Wife
and eight Children, an innocent offspring, and permit his returning to his
native Country by repealing that part of the Law that banishes his person
and Confiscates his property, and as in duty bound she will ever pray.

(DS, Sc-Ar)

DOCUMENT 13

Eliza Clitherall

*The petitioner was the wife of James Clitherall, an Edinburgh-
educated physician who in 1780 took up a commission as surgeon to
the South Carolina Royalists, a regiment of Tory militia. In 1782, he
fled to East Florida. On 16 February 1784, Eliza Clitherall invoked
the names of several prominent South Carolina Whigs when she
successfully sought permission for James to return and reclaim
his confiscated estate. James Clitherall was back in Charleston by
1 March 1785, when he sought compensation for land and slaves
that the state had sold in 1782. Unable to attain satisfaction, he renewed his petition the following year and again in 1791.*[31]

The Memorial of Eliza Clitherall in Behalf of her Husband Dr. Jas.
Clitherall now in Exile—Humbly Sheweth,

That Your Memorialists Husband, after the Surrender of Charleston to the British, was induced to accept a Commission in the Militia
of Berkly County where he resided, from a Wish that it might enable
him to grant Indulgences to his Neighbours, but finding soon after, that

---

31. Siebert, *Loyalists in East Florida*, 2:351; Joseph Ioor Waring, *A History of
Medicine in South Carolina*, 2 vols. (Columbia: South Carolina Medical Association,
1964), 1:200, 337; Petitions of James Clitherall, 1 Mar. 1785, 15 Feb. 1786, 20 Jan.
1791, LP, Sc-Ar.

more was expected of them than he could reconcile to his Feelings, he immediately resigned the Commission *without having done any duty whatever*—

That Afterwards merely for the Support of a large Family he was induced to accept the Office of Commissioner of Claims, and whilst he held it acquitted himself with great Justice & Integrity, & was very forward in promoting the Restitution of the Property of many now here—For the Truth of this an appeal may be made to Alexr. Fraser, Rawlins Lowndes, Roger Parker Saunders Esqrs. and many others who were benefited by his Care & Vigilance— [32]

His Humanity in his Attention to the American Hospital [33] was so conspicuous, that he was very severely censured for the Preference he gave to it; and his friendly Care of many Americans who stood in need of his Assistance is well known to many in this place particularly Maurice Simmonds Esq. [34]—he acted however from a benevolent Motive. Prisoners sick & in Distress had Superior Claims upon his Generosity & Compassion, to those who had their friends & Relations about them—

The active part he took in retaining the publick Records here at the Evacuation is well known to Many—

Since his Unfortunate Exile his anxious Wishes & Most earnest Endeavors have been invariably used to render every service in his power to the Citizens of this State be effecting the Restitution of their Negroes in East Florida; hitherto his Efforts by means of Govr. Tonyn have, in a great measure been rendered abortive, [35] but the unwearied pains & la-

---

32. All three men had impeccable Whig credentials. Fraser lent the state £92,225, furnished supplies to state militia units, and served in the assembly during the Revolution. Lowndes was president of South Carolina in 1778–79 and later served in the state assembly. Saunders was a captain in the state militia and, between 1776 and 1790, sat in all but one of the state assemblies (*Biog. Directory of S.C. House, 1719–1774*, 254–55; *DAB*, 6:472–73; *Biog. Dict. of S.C. House, 1775–1790*, 634).

33. During the occupation of Charleston, the British kept sick and wounded prisoners in the American Hospital. American officers often complained of the poor treatment soldiers received there and of British attempts to recruit troops from among the hospital's patients (Moultrie, *Memoirs*, 2:143–45, 151, 155–60).

34. Maurice Simons was a successful merchant and frequent member of the state assembly, though he took British protection after the fall of Charleston (*Biog. Dict. of S.C. House, 1775–1790*, 652–54).

35. Beginning in May 1783, Clitherall tried to recover slaves belonging to Whigs in South Carolina and Georgia. Patrick Tonyn, the royal governor of British East

bor he bestowed & the many hazards he has run, by his Zeal & Forwardness in this Business are well known to His Excellency Govr. Guerard, Genl. Barnwell, Thos. Savage & Benn. Garden Esqrs. & Mr. William Livingston Commissioners from this State to East Florida[36]—to all of whom and many others he makes a ready & Cheerful Appeal—So sensible is Govr. Guerard of the Doctors Services & good Wishes to the People of this Country that could he, consistent with his public Character have interceded in his Behalf, he would have cheerfully done it—

Your Memorialist therefore humbly hopes that upon a Consideration of the foregoing Facts Your Hon[ora]ble House will permit the Return of her Husband to the Country and a numerous Family.

(ADS, Sc-Ar)

DOCUMENT 14

Mary Cape

In 1783, Mary Cape and her husband, Brian, filed separate petitions for relief from the anti-Tory laws. The legislature rejected both petitions. On 18 February 1784, Mary petitioned again on her husband's behalf with satisfactory results. Brian Cape recovered both his citizenship and his estate, subject to a 12 percent amercement.[37]

The Petition of Mary Cape on the part and behalf of Brian Cape her Husband late Charleston Merchant—Humbly sheweth—

That by an Act of the Legislature of this State passed the 26h day of February 1782 the Estate and property of the said Brian Cape is confiscated and his person banished from this State.

Florida, frustrated Clitherall's efforts, refusing to surrender the slaves until the states repealed the laws authorizing the confiscation of loyalist estates (Siebert, *Loyalists in East Florida,* 1:123, 2:351).

36. In 1783, Governor Benjamin Guerard appointed commissioners to recover slaves who went to East Florida when the British evacuated South Carolina.

37. Petition of Brian Cape, 23 Jan. 1783, LP, Sc-Ar; Petition of Mary Cape, 22 Feb. 1783, ibid.; *S.C. House Journals, 1783–1784,* 552.

That the said Brian Cape in humble obedience and submission to the said Law retired from this State and has since resided without its Jurisdiction.

That when an impartial Enquiry and Investigation is made into the real case & situation of the said Brian Cape, it is hoped the same will be proved to have been greatly aggravated through misinformation.

That the attachment of the said Brian Cape to the Cause Interest and Welfare of this Country was not less notorious than sincere and not in the least degree even suspected until after the mortifying surrender of this Capital.

That previous to that Event the said Brian Cape discharged his Duty in your Service as a good Citizen with chearfulness and fidelity and upon all Occasions was ready to assist in the time of alarm.

That on the first intimation of General Provosts approach to storm the lines[38] he appeared a Volunteer in your Service—

That at the time this city was besieged by Sir Henry Clinton he had the strongest inclination and exerted every Effort to contribute his assistance but was rendered incapable and disqualified from performing that Duty by a fall from his Horse.

That immediately after his Recovery he returned to his Duty and joined his Company at Scotts Ferry with whom he continued until he unfortunately became the captive of Coll. Tarleton.[39]

That the said Brian Cape considered his situation as a prisoner very unfortunate having suffered great losses found himself embarrassed in many difficulties, the British having destroyed considerable part of his Property—

---

38. In May 1779, Maj. Gen. Augustine Prevost marched an army of some twenty-five hundred men within a few miles of the South Carolina capital but withdrew on learning that Gen. Benjamin Lincoln's troops were on their way to Charleston from Augusta (Christopher Ward, *War of the Revolution,* 2 vols. [New York: Macmillan, 1952], 2:683–87).

39. Clinton's six-week siege of Charleston began on 1 April 1780. Cape apparently recovered from his fall by 6 May, when Lt. Col. Banastre Tarleton surprised and defeated an American force at Lenud's Ferry on the Santee River. The British killed eleven, wounded thirty, and captured sixty-seven Americans, of whom Brian Cape appears to have been one (Howard H. Peckham, *The Toll of Independence: Engagements and Battle Casualties of the American Revolution* [Chicago: University of Chicago Press, 1974], 70).

That the said Brian Capes large Family were in want and greatly distressed and which forced him to seek relief by taking British Protection.

That the said Brian Cape to avoid all intercourse or connection with the British solicited for leave to retire to his plantation [40] which he was permitted for some time to do.

That the said Brian Cape daily heard and on some Occasions was a Witness of the ill Treatment the Friends to America received from the British with the greatest pain, displeasure and regret, he heard of and saw the cruelties and persecutions that were inflicted on their persons, the Distresses and wants of their Families and the waste destruction and Havock of their Estates and Property.

That the said Brian Cape in consideration thereof was induced to accept of a Deputation from Mr. Cruden who was sole Commissioner over Estates sequestered by British Authority [41] and his sole motive view and design was to prevent cruelties from being inflicted on his Frinds, to prevent as much as was in his power their persons from being persecuted, to assist and relieve their Families from their Distresses and to save and preserve their Estates and Property from that total Devastation which seemed to threaten.

That it was with such intention he accepted of that ingracious and disagreeable Deputation is evinced by his great Compassion for the sufferer, of the distressed, his exertions to relieve such from all persecutions, his tenderness and care over their Families, and the concern he took in preserving their property to the utmost of his power.

That the said Brian Cape did not stipulate for or receive any Emoluments profit or advantage on account of the said office from the s[ai]d Mr. Cruden or any other person whatsoever.

That he never held any other Commission under the British but that of a Magistrate and which he exercised for the good and relief of the oppressed—

That he truly and sincerely laments he ever took British Protection, but he had no other Alternative.

---

40. In St. Thomas Parish, Charleston District (*Heads of Families . . . in the Year 1790: S.C.,* 45).

41. John Cruden, a North Carolina merchant, was a committed Tory who, as the Charleston-based commissioner of sequestered estates, supervised the redistribution of land and slaves the British confiscated from Whigs in the Carolinas (Troxler, *Loyalist Experience in North Carolina,* 42).

That he heartily regrets and feels with the greatest concern he shou'd have incurred the resentment of his countrymen by a mistaken tho' well intended conduct, and assures this Honourable House that he considers himself truly unfortunate to be in exile from this State which deprives him of the society of his most regarded Frinds and all intercourse with his dearest Connections.

That your petitioner has a Family of five small children all under the age of twelve years totally unprovided for—

Your Petitioner relying on the wisdom Justice & Humanity of this Honble House humbly prays that you will take into consideration the helpless and distressed situation of her and her five small children, The upright and unoffending deportment of your petitioners Husband during a long residence in this State—And that he may be permitted to return and have his property restored to him—

And your Petitioner as in Duty will ever pray &c.

(DS, Sc-Ar)

DOCUMENT 15

Elizabeth Oats

Edward Oats died in 1781, but the state of South Carolina confiscated his estate posthumously the following year. In 1784, his widow, Elizabeth, asked that Edward's estate be returned to his heirs, but the assembly rejected her petition. On 19 February 1785, Elizabeth Oats petitioned to recover only two town lots and several slaves that Edward had set aside in trust for his wife and children. The assembly granted this more modest request.[42]

The Petition of Elizabeth Oats Widow of Edward Oats late of Charleston Merchant—Humbly Sheweth

That the Said Edward Oats intending to quit the State in Pursuance of an Act of Assembly passed the twenty Eight of March, seventeen hun-

---

42. *S.C. House Journals, 1783–1784*, 392; *S.C. House Journals, 1785–1786*, 188, 191; "An Act to afford a maintenance to the persons therein mentioned," 1785, *S.C. Statutes*, 4:666–67.

dred and seventy eight,[43] by Deeds of Lease an Release bearing Date respectively the twenty sixth and twenty seventh of June in said Year, did Convey and Assign all his Real and Personal Property (Consisting of Tracts of Land Lotts of Ground in Charleston, Household Furniture and Negroes,) to the Persons therein Nam'd in Trust for Your Petitioner and Children and in the Month of July following went to the West Indies—

That in the Year seventeen hundred and eighty he return'd to this State and continued in Business until his Death which happend in April, seventeen hundred and eighty one leaveing Four Children of Tender Years—

That from the time of his return to this State until his Death he Contracted several Debts to a greater Amount than the Value of his Real and Personal Property, which are yet unpaid, and no fund whatever left out of which they can be Discharg'd, save the Property Convey'd and Assigned as Aforesaid—

That your Petitioner's said Husband did not in any Instance, Act, Aid, or Assist the Enemies of this or any other of the United States from the Commencement of the War, nor did he in any Manner Interfere in the Prosecution thereof notwithstanding which his Name hath been Inserted in the Act of Confiscation, and part of his Real Estate sold by the Commissioners—

That Your Petitioner relying on the Rectitude and Clemency of this Honourable House, was Induce'd to become the Purchaser of such parts of said Estate, as were Sold, she being advis'd that on the Circumstance of her Case being humbly represented to Your Honour's, such sales would be set aside, and Your Petitioner be permitted to Remain in the quiet Possession of said Estate so convey'd for the Support of herself and large Family—

That Your Petitioner and her Children have not any Property whatever, save such as they Claim in Virtue of Said Deed of Release, and will be greatly distress'd if Your Petitioner shall be oblig'd to Comply with the Terms of said Sales, she having bid for the Lands so Sold, much more than their Value—

---

43. An act to enforce an "Assurance of Allegiance and Fidelity," which required all free males over sixteen years of age to swear allegiance to the state and promise to defend it against George III and other enemies (Lambert, *S.C. Loyalists*, 62; McCrady, *S.C. in the Revolution*, 1:266–67).

May it therefore please Your Honours to take the Circumstances of Your Petitioner's Case into Consideration and set aside the Sales so Made to Your Petitioner and make such further Relief as to Your Honor's Justice and Wisdom shall seem proper—And they will Ever Pray.

(DS, Sc-Ar)

DOCUMENT 16
Jane Villepontoux

South Carolina's anti-Tory laws doubly penalized Jane Dupont Villepontoux and her family. The state amerced the estate of her husband, Benjamin, a Whig who eventually took British protection so he could resume his business in Charleston. In addition, the Whig regime confiscated Jane's own inheritance because it was held in trust for her by her brother, a loyalist exile. She successfully petitioned to recover her property on 18 February 1786.[44]

The Humble Petition of Jane Villepontoux Sheweth—
    That your Petitioner had a Legacy of Two Hundred and Fifty pounds Sterling bequeathed her by an Uncle who died in England in the Year 1781—that Gideon Dupont Junr. Your Petitioners brother, made application for her bill in favour of John Nutt Merchant in London, to whom he stood Indebted, which she acquiesced in as her said brother was lawful Guardian of her Estate,[45] he having previous to this bill, a sum of

44. William Randolph Bauer, *The Sineath Family and Affiliated Family Lineages* (Columbia, S.C.: R. L. Bryan Company, 1970), 321; *S.C. House Journals, 1783–1784*, 86; Petition of Benjamin Villepontoux, 24 Feb. 1785, LP, Sc-Ar.

45. Gideon Dupont Jr., who died in 1785, initially supported the American cause but professed allegiance to the Crown after the fall of Charleston and held civil commissions in the restored royal government. Dupont went to England when the British evacuated the city in 1782. He was a business associate of John Nutt of London. Jonas Dupré, brother of the petitioner's mother, Jane Dupré Dupont, was the uncle who left her the legacy in question (*Biog. Directory of S.C. House, 1719–1774*, 211–12; Gideon Dupont Jr. to Jane Dupont Villepontoux, 13 June 1781, on verso of Petition of Jane Villepontoux, 18 Feb. 1786, LP, Sc-Ar).

money of hers in trust, as will more fully appear by his account Currant dated 1 July 1781—that on the Evacuation of Charleston her said brother (unfortunately for her) being an adherent of the british went off with them—and has since died Insolvent, his principle Creditors being in England, that Your Petitioner has been deprived of her immediate remedy on his Estate by the confiscation act passed in the Year 1782, Your Petitioner therefore begs leave to Subjoin the Copy of his Letter and account Currant[46] which refers to the above and Humbly Submits her particular Case to the Justice of Your Hon[orab]le House hopeing for such relief as in Your Wisdom shall see fit, and Your Petitioner as in duty bound will ever Pray*

*Your Petitioner further begs leave to mention for Information that her Brothers Property sold by the Commissioners amounted to upwards of £10,000 St[erlin]g, of which £4000 Sterling is to be paid in Specie.[47]

(DS, Sc-Ar)

DOCUMENT 17

Margaret Orde

The petitioner spent most of the war years in England with her Tory relatives. On returning to South Carolina, she married Capt. James Orde, a British naval officer. Orde lost his estate, including his wife's marriage portion, under the confiscation statutes. He fled South Carolina and assumed the governorship of the British colony of Dominica some time before 9 February 1787, when Margaret Stevens Orde asked the assembly to restore her marriage portion to her. The assembly granted Orde's request, and she may have left the

---

46. Two accounts accompanied the letter (cited in n. 45). One shows that as of 1 July 1781 Dupont owed his sister £349.13.8, which included her inheritance from their uncle. Another recorded £113.3.11 1/4 in interest accumulated from that date, making the grand total due her £462.17.7 1/4.

47. Text following the asterisk appeared vertically in the petition's right margin. Dupont estimated the value of his estate at £59,158 sterling when he submitted his claim to the British government (*Biog. Directory of S.C. House, 1719–1774*, 212).

state shortly thereafter. Margaret Stevens Orde does not appear in the 1790 census.[48]

The Humble Petition of Margaret Orde late Margaret Stevens—
Sheweth

That your Petitioner is a native of this State, and was carried to Europe by her friends antecedent to the Commencement of the late War, where she remained till the Year one thousand seven hundred and Eighty one—That after she quitted Europe and while she was yet a Minor, she intermarried with Captain John Orde. That by such Intermarriage and a Settlement made in Consequence thereof, Captn Orde became entitled to a life Estate in her Lands in this Country, which life Estate has been Confiscated by the Assembly held at Jacksonborough—That such Confiscation has tended greatly to the Distress and Injury of your Petitioner, as she has been thereby prevented from improving, or selling her Estate as no person will purchase it while so incumberd. That your Petitioner is informed this State has never Confiscated the Property of Women, and she trusts a Deviation from this Rule will not be made to her prejudice.

Your Petitioner therefore hopes your honourable House will Consider her Situation, and grant her such Relief as will be consistent with their Goodness and Humanity—

And as in Duty bound She will ever pray.

(ADS, Sc-Ar)

DOCUMENT 18

Ann Field

The erstwhile Regulator Robert Field was one of four brothers whom the victorious Whigs captured at Moore's Creek Bridge and

---

48. *S.C. House Journals, 1787–1788,* 292; "An Act for restoring unto Mrs. Margaret Orde such part of her Estate as has been confiscated . . . ," 1787, *S.C. Statutes,* 5:19–20.

later banished for Toryism. Robert fled to England, where in 1782
former governor Josiah Martin recommended him and his brother
William as North Carolinians having "real and great claims to the
notice of the [British] Government." Meanwhile, Ann Field re-
mained in Guilford County seeking the repatriation of her banished
husband. In 1785, the assembly rejected her first petition on his be-
half. On 22 November 1787, however, Field resubmitted her re-
quest, which the assembly granted.[49]

————————

The Petition of your petitioner Wife of Robert Field most Humbly Sheweth, that her Unfortunate Husband has been Exiled from her this Several years on Account of Some Misdemeanor done by him at the time of the Late troubles, to the Great loss of his unhappy wife and small family who Suffers Grievously, and Labours under Innumerable Difficulties by the Loss of him; which has almost deprived them of the necessaries of Life; These are therefore Honoured Gentlemen, Petitioning Begging and, Praying, that your Honours would be pleas'd to Grant her Petition and Restore her Banish'd Husband to his much-Distressed Family; a Family that by divine Assistance might be useful members of Society, had they only the advantages of Learning, which they are unhappily, entirely deprived of, by the want of the head of the family to provide necessaries for them; and Honoured Gentlemen if his crime was great, his Punnishment has been very great, as also the whole of his disconsolate family. I pray that your Honours through your Generosity will Seriously Look into my much Distress'd Situation And Grant me relief; and by your Honours Condescending to this my weak Petition you will Gain an Eternal Blessing, and the prayers of a much Distressed family Shall Continually be offered for your Honrs. (Tis God Like to forgive;) and by your Honours Giving way to the Tears Prayers and Petition of a Disconsolate woman you will be the Means of Preserving her Distressd family, and She as in Duty Bound Shall Ever Pray. I am Gentlemen with Due Respect yours Honours Most Obedient And Disconsolate Petitioner.

(ADS, Nc-Ar)

————————

49. *N.C. Recs.*, 10:599, 841; 20:10, 13, 14, 17, 18, 318, 440; 22:618; DeMond, *Loyalists in N.C.*, 48.

DOCUMENT 19

Mary Peronneau

Widowed by 1774, Mary Hutson Peronneau spent the war years in South Carolina, and she assiduously attempted to recover the property of her Tory in-laws once the war was over. In 1783, she petitioned successfully for the restoration of the estate of her brother-in-law Robert Peronneau. Then, on 7 February 1788, she asked the assembly to remove the amercement from the estate of another brother-in-law, Henry Peronneau, a Tory who died in London in 1786. A legislative committee recommended granting this petition, but the house never acted on the committee's recommendation.[50]

The Petition of Mary Peronneau Widow Sheweth,

That her deceased Husband Arthur Peronneau by a long course of painful industry, and close application to mercantile business in this City had so far improved his patrimony, as to be enabled to leave her and a family of five Small children at the time of his Death in 1774 in easy and affluent circumstances. That the Estate consisted of a Lot and Buildings in Broad-Street, and a considerable amount in good and well Secured Bonds. That almost the whole of the Bonds have in the course of the late contest been paid off in the Paper Currency in a State of great depreciation, and the Buildings on the lot in Broad-Street were first burned down in the Fire of 1778[51] and having been rebuilt were again reduced to Ashes in 1786. Your Petitioner farther Sheweth, that Mr. Henry Peronneau, the Brother of her deceased Husband has, by his Will bearing date the 29th July 1786 after directing payment of several considerable Legacies, devised the Residue of his Estate, at the death of his Widow Ann Peronneau

---

50. John W. Moore, *Some Family Lines of James Peronneau DeSaussure and His Wife Annie Isabella Laurens* (Washington: n.p., 1958), 7–8; *Biog. Directory of S.C. House, 1719–1774*, 517–18; Petition of Mary Peronneau, 23 Feb. 1783, LP, Sc-Ar; *S.C. House Journal, 1783–1784*, 164, 552; *S.C. House Journal, 1787–1788*, 424–25.

51. In January 1778, a fire in Charleston destroyed some 250 houses (Nadelhaft, *Disorders of War*, 64).

now living, to William Peronneau one of her Sons.[52] That the said Estate is at present by Law subject to the payment of an amercement. That your Petitioner, with a large Family having been, from the combined effect of the two Calamities afore-mentioned, much reduced in her circumstances is induced by the advice of her Friends to prefer this her Petition to have the Said amercement taken off from this Estate, which relying upon the filial affection of her Son she is led to consider as the chief object of her hope for the future support of herself and family, and your Petitioner as in duty bound Shall ever pray.

(DS, Sc-Ar)

DOCUMENT 20

Judith Dowd

The loyalism of Connor Dowd resulted in years of litigation for his wife and family. After the war, Connor returned only occasionally to North Carolina, but his wife, Mary, recovered his estate and began to sell property to pay his outstanding debts. Mary's sister-in-law, Judith Dowd, claimed a portion of that property for herself and her six children. On 1 December 1789, Judith asked the legislature to verify her title to a tract of land her late husband, Owen Dowd, had purchased from his brother Connor. The assembly granted her petition. Judith Dowd owned four hundred acres, including this land, when she died in 1803.[53]

52. Henry Peronneau was the treasurer of the colony of South Carolina. He was banished in 1777 for his refusal to swear allegiance to the new state government. Peronneau returned to Charleston briefly during the British occupation. He and his wife, Ann Motte Peronneau, had no children. Arthur and Mary Hutson Peronneau had five, of whom William and three daughters survived to adulthood (Moore, *Some Family Lines,* 6–7; Biog. Directory of S.C. House, 1719–1774, 517–18).

53. Troxler, *Loyalist Experience in North Carolina,* 32–35; Will of Judith Dowd, 3 Nov. 1802, Chatham County Will Book A, pt. 2, 88–89, Nc-Ar.

The Petition of Judith Dowd Humbly sheweth—

That your Petitioner and her Husband in his life time, hath been possessed for twenty four years past of a certain tract of Land in Chatham County lying in the fork of Smiths Creek and Deep-River, Containing one hundred Acres. In Virtue of a Deed or Article, a true coppy whereof is hereunto Anexed, Signed by Connor Dowd, as Will appear by reference thereto.[54]

Your Petitioner further humbly represents that as the said Connor Dowd at the time of executing the Referred to Article with his Brother Owen Dowd, had it not in his power to obtain a Grant for said land, The Earl of Granville's Office then been shut up; But afterwards, when the land office of this State was opened the said Connor Dowd did obtain a Grant for the same.[55] But unfortunately for your petitioner and a large family of Children the said Connor Dowd did Attach himself to the Brittish Army, and left this country before he had convenient opportunity of Conveying to his Brother Owen Dowd his Heirs &c the said tract of land, Agreeable to his Article and many repeated promises to that effect well known to many.

Wherefore your petitioner conceives herself not to have as Legal a Title to her said land as she in equity and right ought to have.

Therefore your petitioner further prays that the Honourable General Assembly will take her case into consideration and pass an Act to secure to her the said Judith Dowd Her Heirs and Assigns forever, the said Tract or parcel of Land containing one hundred Acres, in Fee Simple.

And your Petitioner as in duty bound shall ever pray.

(ADS, Nc-Ar)

---

54. A copy of the articles of agreement between the two brothers, dated 10 January 1765, accompanied the petition. The tract in question was located in present-day Lee County, immediately south of the boundary between southern Chatham County and the northwest corner of Lee.

55. John Carteret, later earl of Granville, was the only Carolina proprietor who did not sell his share of colonial land to the Crown in 1729. His holdings, known as the Granville District, contained more than 26,000 square miles, which he sold and rented to tenant farmers. When Granville died in 1763, his North Carolina land office closed, leaving many settlers unable to register and secure their titles. The new state land office opened in 1783 but closed the following year due to excessive speculation (A. Roger Ekirch, *"Poor Carolina": Politics and Society in Colonial North Carolina,*

DOCUMENT 21
Peter Trezevant and Elizabeth Willoughby Farquhar Trezevant

On 19 January 1791, this daughter of a Tory merchant and her husband, the son of a prominent Whig, petitioned jointly to settle a debt incurred by her late father. The legislature rejected their petition, recommending that they "should apply to the Courts of Judicature for relief as it it not in the power of the Legislature to grant it." [56]

The humble Petition of Peter Trezevant of the City of Charleston in the State aforesaid & Elizabeth Willoughby his Wife, late Elizabeth Willoughby Farquhar, only Child of Robert Farquhar, late of Charleston aforesaid Merchant deceased, & now an Infant of the Age of Eighteen Years.

Sheweth That William Russell, late of Charleston aforesaid Vendue Master, but now resident in the Island of Dominica & in very indigent circumstances,[57] was indebted to the Father of your Petitioner, Elizabeth, in the sum of Two Thousands & twenty Eight Pounds Eighteen Shillings & tenpence half penny Sterling, exclusive of Interest. That the Property of the said Russell, was confiscated & sold by the Commissioners appointed for that purpose, & at the sale thereof your said Petitioners Father purchased in a small House & Lot of Land, in Stolts Alley in Charleston, on or about the 17th June 1783, for the sum of Seven hundred & ten Pounds, with an idea of discounting the amount of the Purchase money, out of the debt due to him, by the said Russell. That, your Fathers Petitioner gave his bond for the Purchase, when Titles were made to him, but before he could take it up by the discount, against the

---

1729–1776 [Chapel Hill: University of North Carolina Press, 1981], 127–43, 177–78; Morrill, *Fiat Finance,* 37–39).

56. *Biog. Directory of S.C. House, 1775–1790,* 722–23; *S.C. House Journals, 1783–1784,* 55, 209; *S.C. House Journals, 1791,* 133.

57. Russell, a Tory who fled to East Florida in 1782, unsuccessfully petitioned for relief from the penal statutes the following year. He did not renew his attempt to regain his property in South Carolina (*S.C. House Journals, 1783–1784,* 46, 618 n).

said Russell's Estate, as above mentioned, he was lost at Sea, going from Charleston to Savannah in January 1784. That your said Petitioners Father left a Will duly executed, wherein your Petitioner Elizabeth, is made the sole Devisee & principal Legatee. That her Fathers Executor, positively and solemnly avers, that he always thought, that your Petitioners Father, had discounted the Amount of the purchase money of the said House & Lot, out of his Claim against said Russell, nor did he ever know a Syllable, of their being a bond against his Testators Estate in the Public Treasury, till an Action was commenced by the Attorney General to recover it, & thinking that the State had no Claim against his Testators Estate, & that the said Russell, had little or no property besides the House & Lot aforesaid, was the reason, why he did not render a State of his Testators Claim against said Russell. That the Action commenced on the said bond, against your Petitioners Fathers Estate, was instituted about or soon after the intermarriage of your Petitioners, that the Attorney General is now carrying on the Proceedings & Execution must shortly issue thereon, unless your Petitioners shall be relieved by your Honorable House. Your Petitioners lament that there is not in the confiscation Laws (as there generally is in all Laws of that nature) some Clause or Proviso, to protect the Interest of Infants & Minors, who are utterly disqualified for taking care of or guarding their property themselves, & who thro' an accident similar to the one they now labour under might be materially hurt or perhaps entirely ruined. And for as much as your Petitioners can seek relief, in this distressing situation from no other Power, than your honorable House, who they trust will ever prove themselves the Lovers of Equity, Supporters of Justice & Protectors of the property of Orphan Infants, who by reason of their tender Age, & incapacity to guard their own Interest are ever liable to innumerable Losses & disadvantages. Your Petitioners must humbly beseech your Honorable House to take their very uncommon case into consideration, that you will consider that they will not be allowed at this late Period to give in their Claim against said Russell, which far exceeds the amount of the Purchase of the said House & Lot, altho' they understand that no Person has had audited or ever preferred any Claims against the said Russell, & that if they should not be relieved & Execution should issue against the Estate, owing to the present & depreciated Value of property & appreciated Value of Indents, not only the House & Lot aforesaid, but in all probability the greater part of their Fathers Estate must be given away at a Sheriffs sale, in order to pay the Amount of that purchase. And, that your Honorable House will also consider, that this misfortune is not brought on by any imprudence or neglect in themselves, but on the contrary it has happened thro' an Accident, by which, an Orphan Infant now only Eighteen Years old is now on the point of losing her Property, & has taken this very first Opportunity of applying in Conjunction with her Husband to the only Power that can do her Justice & riscue her from the impending Loss. And Your Petitioners, do lastly Humbly Pray that your Honorable House, will direct the Commissioners of the Treasury, to deliver up the bond of the said Robert Farquhar to your Petitioner, or that your Petitioners may be permitted to have their account audited, & discounted from the Debt due by the said Russell to the said Robert Farquhars Estate, & they will chearfully discharge such costs & Charges, as may have accrued on the suit, brought on the same bond, if this House shall think fit to order them to do so. And your Petitioners as in duty bound will ever Pray.

(ADS [written by Peter Trezevant and signed by him and "Elizabeth Willoughby Trezevant"], Sc-Ar)

DOCUMENT 22

Mary Wells

Mary Rowand and Robert Wells married in Scotland in 1750 and three years later emigrated to South Carolina. Robert prospered in Charleston as a printer, bookseller, and newspaper publisher, but he and Mary left for England at the onset of the Revolution. Despite his success as a London merchant, Wells was bankrupt by 1785, as a result of his inability to collect his American debts. On 1 February 1791, Mary Rowand Wells (1728–1805) unsuccessfully petitioned to recover a portion of his confiscated estate. Her brother, Robert Rowand of Charleston, later renewed this request on her behalf, but the assembly also rejected his petition.[58]

The Petition of Mary Wells, Wife of Robert Wells, formerly of Charleston, but now of London, humbly sheweth—

---

58. Louisa Susannah Wells, *The Journal of a Voyage from Charlestown to London* (New York: New York Times and Arno Press, 1968), 77, 79–81, 84; Sabine, *Loyalists of the Amer. Rev.*, 2:406–7; Petition of Robert Rowand, 29 Nov. 1792, LP, Sc-Ar.

That your Petitioner's Husband, Robert Wells, resided in Charleston for many Years previous to the American Revolution, during which time he always demeaned himself as a good Member of Society, & endeavoured to promote the progress of useful knowledge in this state by the establishment of a Press, and the importation and sale of the largest collection of valuable books that had ever appeared in America: striving by his Industry to maintain & educate a large family of Children all born in this Country.[59]

That at the Commencement of the Troubles in America & upwards of fifteen months before the declaration of Independence, your Petitioner's Husband went to Great Britain, leaving behind him his family & all his Property, & hoping and intending to return in a short time; but the difficulties and distresses that follow'd induced him to remain in London, where he has continued ever since.

That after his departure his Attornies purchased for him a House & Lot in King Street, which, together with two others on the Bay of Charleston, constituted the whole of his real Estate: his personal property being chiefly in Books, Types, Printing Presses, & other Articles in the way of his Business.

That by the Fire in Charleston in 1778 his Houses on the Bay with part of the Property therein, were entirely consumed, & this added to the former Losses, reduced his family to a scanty subsistence.

That by the Act of Confiscation, passed at Jacksonborough, in the Year 1782, all the Estate of the said Robert Wells was confiscated, and has been sold, on the public account, as appears by the Books of the Commissioners to the amount of £13,646 : 1 : 8 in Specie and Indents.

That your Petitioner's Husband having applied in England for a compensation of his Losses, out of the Fund allowed for that purpose, received only £1400 St[erlin]g for all his Losses, and for the two Lots on the Bay.[60] The House and Lot in King Street having been purchased after the

---

59. Mary and Robert Wells had five children who survived infancy, of whom four appear to have spent the war years with their parents in London. The fifth, John Wells, took over his father's Charleston print shop and was an active Tory who later resettled in the Bahamas (Wells, *Journal of a Voyage*, 97; Kathryn Roe Coker, "The Artisan Loyalists of Charleston, South Carolina," in Calhoon et al., eds., *Loyalists and Community in North America*, 99–100; Sabine, *Loyalists of the Amer. Rev.*, 2:407).

60. According to his daughter Louisa, Wells obtained only £1,200 in compensation from the British government. From 1775 through 1779, however, the family

declaration of Independence no compensation cou'd be obtained for any part thereof.

That your Petitioner's Husband having thus lost his whole Estate in this Country, either by the Fire in the Year 1778, or by the subsequent sale for public use, & having also met with considerable losses in America since the peace by bad debts; Your Petitioner is reduced to the urgent necessity of applying to the known humanity & bounty of the Legislature of South Carolina hopeful that, as they have restored the Property of many who were objects of resentment in this Time of War and Confusion, she and her distressed Family may partake of their Liberality.

She is the more emboldened in this hope, as the tenth clause of the Confiscation Act abovementioned, holds out a final Provision for the families of those whose Estates were sold by virtue thereof.[61]

Your Petitioner, therefore, humbly requests that, in consideration of her situation & that of her Children, such reasonable allowance may be made her, as the Legislature, in their wisdom & Humanity, may think her entitled to, upon a review of the Circumstances she has above represented.

And Your Petitioner, as in duty bound, will ever Pray &c.

(DS, Sc-Ar)

DOCUMENT 23

Catherine Carne

Physician Samuel Carne arrived in South Carolina in 1740. In 1759, he married Catherine Bond, the daughter of a prosperous planter. Five years later, the couple moved to London, where Samuel started a lucrative career in the Carolina trade. The Carnes returned to South Carolina in 1774 but left again in 1777, when

---

also received an annual pension that ranged from £60 to £150 (Wells, *Journal of a Voyage,* 80).

61. That clause empowered the commissioners of confiscated estates to "make such provision for the temporary support of such families of [the dispossessed], as shall appear to the said commissioners, or a majority of them, necessary, until the said commissioners shall render a full account of the sales hereby directed to be made" (*S.C. Statutes,* 4:520).

Samuel refused to swear allegiance to the Whig regime. He died in London in 1786, and in 1787 Catherine tried in vain to recover his estate in South Carolina. On 1 February 1791, when she petitioned to retrieve only her dower rights, the assembly granted her indents to satisfy her claim.[62]

The Humble Petition of Catherine Carne, widow and relict of Samuel Carne late of South Carolina Doctor of Physick Sheweth

That your Petitioner on her Intermarriage and at the death of her Father the late Jacob Bond of Christ Church Parish Esqr. deceased Carried to her said Husband a fortune of full three thousand pounds sterling in Money and Negroes.

That the Estate of the said Samuel Carne was confiscated & sold under the act passed at Jacksonborough on 26th Feby 1782 and a Lott & House in Orange Street & a Vacant Lot So. End King Street were sold together for £2615, Sterling in Indents.

That the said Samuel Carne in Consequence of his losses in this Country became Bankrupt & has left your Petitioner without any provision whatever from his Estate—

That your Petitioner is by Law entitled to dower in the said Lands but is prevented from applying at Law without first Coming for Redress from the Legislature.[63]

She therefore Humbly prays your Honors to Consider her hard Case and to grant such Redress as to your Justice may seem meet.

(DS, Sc-Ar)

DOCUMENT 24

Paulina Telfair

The petitioner, who was a native North Carolinian, married Alexander Telfair, a Scottish merchant residing in Halifax County.

---

62. *Biog. Directory of S.C. House, 1719–1774,* 85, 141–42; Petition of Catherine Carne, 1 Mar. 1787, LP, Sc-Ar; *S.C. House Journals, 1791,* 287.

63. Wives or widows could claim dower portions of confiscated estates only with the express approval of the legislature. For the process of claiming dower rights in the courts, see "An Act for the more easy and expeditious obtaining the admeasurements of Dower to Widows . . . ," 1786, *S.C. Statutes,* 4:742–43.

In 1777, the Tory Telfair fled to England with his family. Although he later claimed £3,578 in losses as a result of his loyalty to the Crown, the British government approved only about one-seventh of his claim. Depressed and deeply indebted, Telfair committed suicide, and his family returned to America soon thereafter. On 4 December 1792, Paulina Telfair petitioned for permission to recover Alexander's North Carolina debts, a request the assembly granted.[64]

The Petition of Paulina Telfair

Humbly Sheweth That your Petitioners late husband Alexander Telfair left this State with his family, under the Expulsion law in the year 1777 and resided in Great Britain until the time of his tragical death, leaving your Petitioner in great distress with five children in a land of strangers. That it has been with the greatest difficulty she has been able to struggle through life until October 1791 when she returned with all her children to her native Country with an intention of spending the remainder of her days in it hoping to procure those blessings of life which have been denied to her elsewhere. to effect so desireable an end your said Petitioner humbly applies to this Honorable Assembly Praying leave for permission to collect the debts due to her said late husband Alexander Telfair—at least such a part thereof as have not been yet collected under the law for confiscating debts in this State[65] and as most of those debts lay in the County of Halifax where your Petitioner has been informed Commissioners have been appointed, and collections made, the balance must be comparatively small,—but as small as the sum may be and of little consequence to the public, Yet to your Petitioner it may be very considerable, indeed it is all her future prospects in life, it would serve to afford a decent support to her children and enable her to educate them in such a manner as to qualify them in future to become useful members of the community—Those debts have been contracted under the different Firms of Alexander Telfair Alexander Telfair & Co. Alexander & Hugh

---

64. Ekirch, *"Poor Carolina,"* 35; Troxler, *Loyalist Experience in North Carolina,* 40.

65. "An Act to Carry into Effect . . . An Act for Confiscating the Property of all such Persons as are inimical to the United States . . . ," 1778, gave the commissioners of confiscated property the authority "to Demand, make Distress for and receive all sums of Money due and owing" confiscated estates and declared such debts "forfeited to the State" (*N.C. Recs.,* 24:212).

Telfair, Hugh Telfair and David Telfair & Co. at their stores at Halifax, Enfield and at Tarborough. Hugh Telfair and David Telfair both died without issue.[66]

(ADS, Nc-Ar)

DOCUMENT 25

Margaret Williams

Margaret Campbell was about thirteen years old when her great-grandmother filed this petition on her behalf. Margaret was the orphan daughter of Capt. Archibald Campbell, a British army officer, and Margaret Philp, the daughter of a Charleston Tory, both of whom died in 1782. Thereafter, she resided with her maternal grandmother, Mary Philp, who three times petitioned to regain a parcel of confiscated property and, having done so, to free it from amercement, before she, too, died in 1785. Philp bequeathed the amerced property to her young granddaughter. As Margaret Campbell's new guardian, Margaret Williams continued to seek relief from the punitive tax without success, filing this petition on 12 December 1793.[67]

The Petition of Margaret Williams of Stono parish Widow in behalf of her Infant great grand Daughter Margaret Campbell—Sheweth—

That on the Marriage of Mrs. Mary Philp now deceased the grand Mother of Miss Campbell with Robert Philp now also deceased, she the said Mary Philp was possessed under the Gift of her Father[68] of a certain House and Lot of Land in Queen Street in Charleston.

That on the Confiscation of the Estate of the said Robert Philp by the Legislature of this State the House & Lot of Land in Queen Street afore-

---

66. Both Alexander Telfair and Hugh Telfair were listed by name in the North Carolina confiscation statutes (ibid., 24:263, 424).

67. Will of Robert Philp, 25 Sept. 1781, Charleston County Will Book, 1783–86, typescript, 21:420–23, Sc-Ar; Will of Mary Philp, 26 February 1785, ibid., 21:672–74; Petitions of Mary Philp, 22 Jan. 1783, 11 Feb. 1784, LP, Sc-Ar; *S.C. House Journals, 1785–1786,* 206; McCrady, *S.C. in the Revolution,* 2:592 n.

68. James Harvey, the petitioner's first husband.

said was seized & sold as his property altho the said Robert Philp had been dead several months previous to the surrender of Charleston.

That the said Mary Philp relying on the Justice & Humanity of her Country presented her humble Petition to the Legislature praying that as the object of their Resentment no longer existed they would be pleased to take her Case into their Consideration and restore to an aged infirm & distressed widow the Property which She inherited from the Bounty of her Father & which from the early & particular attachment as the Family Residence she had been induced to purchase at the Sale of Confiscated Property for a Considerable Sum. That the said Legislature in their bounty was pleased to restore the said Property to the said Mary Philp subject nevertheless to a heavy amercement.[69] That shortly afterwards the said Mary Philp departed this Life leaving Miss Campbell her Grand Child & Heiress an infant of very tender Years. That the Bond of the said Mary Philp still remains in the public Treasury unsatisfied. Your petitioner therefore humbly prays in behalf of her infant relation to take her peculiar Case into Consideration and to order the said Bond to be delivered cancelled and further should your Honorable House deem it meet—To Relieve the said Lot of Land from the Amercement for which it is liable she will pray.

(ADS, Sc-Ar)

---

69. See *S.C. House Journals, 1783–1784,* 553.

Chapter 4

WOMEN, ALLEGIANCE, AND CITIZENSHIP

Mary Willing Byrd portrayed herself as both a patriot and a citizen when she solicited the support and sympathy of Virginia's revolutionary governors. Requesting a pass across enemy lines to recover property seized by British troops in 1781, she declared her allegiance to the United States and to Virginia, asserting that "no action of my life has been inconsistent with the character of a virtuous American." [1] As a property holder, taxpayer, and stepmother of a Continental soldier "who lost his life in the Service of [his] Country," however, the widow Byrd also claimed republican citizenship, which gender barred her from attaining in its fullest form. Alluding to the prerevolutionary debate over the nature of representation and the colonists' refusal to pay taxes to which they did not consent, Byrd protested, "I have paid my taxes, and have not been Personally or Virtually represented." Lacking the right to vote or other means by which to influence government policies, she observed, "my property is taken from me and I have no redress," save petitioning her governors. [2]

Gender conditioned Byrd's definition of political allegiance and her society's construction of citizenship. Although Virginia law explicitly recognized women as citizens of the state, law and custom prevented them

1. Mary Willing Byrd to Thomas Jefferson, 23 Feb. 1781, in Julian P. Boyd et al., eds., *The Papers of Thomas Jefferson* (Princeton: Princeton University Press, 1950–), 5:691.
2. Mary Willing Byrd to [Thomas Nelson], 10 Aug. 1781, in ibid., 703–4. For the distinction between "virtual" and "actual" representation, which the colonists invoked initially in 1765, see Edmund S. Morgan and Helen M. Morgan, *The Stamp Act Crisis: Prologue to Revolution* (Chapel Hill: University of North Carolina Press, 1953), 105–19.

from exercising most of the rights and obligations that contemporaries increasingly regarded as hallmarks of republican citizenship.[3] The issue of women's political allegiance was equally ambiguous. Statutes that monitored men's political allegiance usually assumed either that women were apolitical or that their allegiance automatically followed that of their male relatives. Even women who claimed separate political identities articulated a gendered understanding of allegiance. While men could point to arms bearing, voting, officeholding, and other specific activities as proof of their allegiance, women commonly stressed their quiet acquiescence to the revolutionary regime and basked in the reflected glory of their heroic sons and husbands. Accordingly, Mary Byrd portrayed her own patriotism as passive and vicarious, rather than active and autonomous, citing her lawful conduct and her stepson's military service as evidence of her allegiance to Virginia's revolutionary government.

Reflecting their ambiguous political status, most women petitioners, like Byrd, portrayed themselves as marginal members of a political community who, while lacking full legal and political identities, nonetheless merited equitable treatment from their governors. When she described herself as a "citizen" and a "virtuous American," Byrd simultaneously assumed the role of a "defenceless Woman, who could not injure her Country" but who could "as a female, [and] as the parent of eight children" supply patriotic sons to fight its battles.[4] For her and for many of her contemporaries, such modest pronouncements belied the reality of their participation in the Revolution and the resulting enhancement of their political consciousness.[5]

---

3. William Waller Hening, ed., *The Statutes at Large: Being a Collection of All the Laws of Virginia from the First Session of the Legislature in the Year 1619* (Philadelphia: William Waller Hening, 1819–23), 11:129–30. On defining rights and obligations of republican citizenship, see Linda K. Kerber, "A Constitutional Right to Be Treated Like American Ladies: Women and the Obligations of Citizenship," in *U.S. History as Women's History: New Feminist Essays,* ed.Linda K. Kerber, Alice Kessler-Harris, and Kathryn Kish Sklar (Chapel Hill: University of North Carolina Press, 1995), 23, 27–35.

4. Mary Willing Byrd to Thomas Jefferson, 23 Feb. 1781, in Boyd et al., *Papers of Thomas Jefferson,* 5:691; Mary Willing Byrd to [Thomas Nelson], 10 Aug. 1781, in ibid., 703–4.

5. On the politicization of women during this period, see Linda K. Kerber, *Women of the Republic: Ideology and Intellect in Revolutionary America* (Chapel Hill: University of North Carolina Press, 1980), esp. chap. 3; Mary Beth Norton, *Liberty's*

Although neither statutes nor conventional wisdom conceded women's capacity for patriotism or political allegiance, during and after the Revolution they repeatedly demonstrated those qualities both publicly and in private. Women's letters revealed a new awareness of political issues as well as strong allegiances during the war and in subsequent partisan controversies. Politicized women tacitly or explicitly challenged the conventions that previously constrained their discussion of political matters, and a few even questioned their formal exclusion from public life. Although men excluded women from the Independence Day parades and dinners that became the republic's dominant civic rituals, some found other ways to assert their patriotism in public.[6]

Beginning with the Stamp Act crisis of 1765, southern women showed a growing awareness of and interest in political issues, which increasingly affected their family's welfare and their daily lives. Whig and Tory women alike reported political news and expressed strong opinions in their letters, though many initially felt obliged to justify their discussion of matters that most traditionally regarded as unsuitable for their sex.[7] As the imperial crisis deepened, however, Whig women became publicly active in the colonial boycotts of British goods, appearing clad in homespun at balls and church services in the late 1760s.[8]

A few years later, the tea boycott politicized others who, by proscribing the consumption of tea in their homes and urging others to do likewise, showed their allegiance to the cause of American liberty. The tea boycott inspired some women to declare their allegiance publicly by writing essays under feminine pseudonyms and forming the first organizations devoted to women's political activism. Some female essayists pointedly appealed to their "sisters" to abjure the dutied British tea. Others reported the activities of patriotic women in the southern colonies

---

Daughters: The Revolutionary Experience of American Women, 1750–1800 (Boston: Little, Brown, 1980), chaps. 6–9.

6. On the evolution of civic rituals during and after the Revolution, see Cynthia A. Kierner, "Genteel Balls and Republican Parades: Gender and Early Southern Civic Rituals, 1677–1826," VMHB 104 (1996): 185–210.

7. Kerber, Women of the Republic, 73–80; Norton, Liberty's Daughters, 170–71.

8. Charles Woodmason, The Carolina Backcountry on the Eve of the Revolution, 1763–1789, ed. Richard J. Hooker (Chapel Hill: University of North Carolina Press, 1953), 20–21; Virginia Gazette (Purdie and Dixon), 14 Dec. 1769; Virginia Gazette (Rind), 14 Dec. 1769.

and elsewhere to provide models of feminine public spirit that their readers could emulate. In August 1774, some "Respectable Ladies" in Charleston organized a "Meeting of that amiable Part of our Species . . . to converse and agree upon some general Plan of Conduct with Respect to the Article of TEA." Two weeks later, writing under the pseudonym "Andromache," a Charleston woman reported that she and her associates had "engaged in a Promise . . . to reject, and totally renounce the baneful herb" and devised a plan to promote the boycott among their towns-women.[9] North Carolina women also organized publicly to show their support for the tea boycott and for the more general nonimportation agreement that the First Continental Congress adopted in October 1774. Fifty-one women from the coastal town of Edenton signed a petition endorsing the nonimportation resolutions to safeguard "the peace and happiness of our country," while the women of Wilmington "burnt their tea in a solemn procession" through the streets of their community.[10]

Participation in the imperial crisis and in the war that followed encouraged many women to discuss politics and inspired some to question explicitly the conventional assumption that their sex lacked political consciousness. Young Nelly Blair, who learned about politics and war firsthand by fleeing the invading British forces, later complained of men who "treat women as Ideiots" instead of recognizing them as "reasonable beings" who could comprehend serious issues and topics. Although Eliza Wilkinson claimed that she did "not love to meddle in political matters," her difficult wartime experiences led her to criticize "the men who say [women] have no business with them. I won't have it thought," Wilkinson declared, "that because we are the weaker sex as to *bodily* strength . . . we are capable of nothing more than minding the dairy, visiting the poultry-house, and all such domestic concerns." A few brave women even challenged the laws and customs that prevented their formal participation in public life. Like Mary Willing Byrd, Hannah Lee Corbin invoked the revolutionary dictum "no taxation without representation" to protest the

---

9. *South Carolina Gazette and Country Journal,* 2 Aug. 1774, 16 Aug. 1774. See also Clementina Rind's *Virginia Gazette,* 15 Sept. 1774, which featured on its front page two long political essays written by and for women.

10. Inez Parker Cumming, "The Edenton Ladies' Tea-Party," *Georgia Review* 8 (1954): 289–91; Samuel Ashe, *History of North Carolina,* 2 vols. (Greensboro, N.C.: C. L. Van Noppen, 1908–25), 2:427–29; *South Carolina Gazette,* 3 Apr. 1775.

status of widows and other propertied women, who paid taxes but yet remained disenfranchised and thus politically marginal.[11]

In the postrevolutionary era, rising literacy rates and the increasing availability of magazines and newspapers also promoted women's political awareness, while the acrimonious partisan debates of the postwar decades stimulated the interest of many in public life. In the 1790s, as Americans divided into Federalists and Republicans, some women eagerly sought political news and declared their allegiance to one of the contending parties. The sisters Judith Randolph and Ann Cary Randolph used the title *Citizen* to address their correspondents, thus showing their support for the French Revolution and the emerging Republican Party. At the other end of the political spectrum, Eleanor Parke Custis condemned "those barbarous *democratic murderers*" in France and "those poor misguided multitudes" who supported them in America. "I am becoming an outrageous politician, perfectly *federal*[ist]," observed this granddaughter of Martha Washington who, along with her friends, wore special insignias and cockades that denoted her support for the Federalist Party. In the years before the War of 1812, Republican women invoked the sartorial traditions of their revolutionary foremothers, showing their support for the embargo against European imports by appearing dressed in homespun gowns at Independence Day celebrations.[12]

Most women probably shared the political allegiances of their male relatives, but some pointedly questioned men's political opinions, at least

---

11. Nelly Blair to William Blair, 20 Aug. 1784, quoted in Mary Beth Norton, "'What an Alarming Crisis Is This': Southern Women and the American Revolution," in *The Southern Experience in the American Revolution,* ed. Jeffrey J. Crow and Larry E. Tise (Chapel Hill: University of North Carolina Press, 1978), 220; Caroline Gilman, ed., *Letters of Eliza Wilkinson, during the Invasion and Possession of Charleston, SC, by the British in the Revolutionary War* (1839; reprint, New York: Arno Press, 1969), 60–61; Richard Henry Lee to Hannah Lee Corbin, 17 Mar. 1778, in *The Letters of Richard Henry Lee,* 2 vols., ed. James Curtis Ballagh (New York: Macmillan, 1911–14), 1:392–93; Louise Belote Dawe and Sandra Gioia Treadway, "Hannah Lee Corbin: The Forgotten Lee," *Virginia Cavalcade* 29 (1979): 70–77.

12. Ann Cary Randolph to St. George Tucker, 29 Oct. 1797, Tucker-Coleman Papers, Vi-W; Judith Randolph to St. George Tucker, 5 Nov. 1797, ibid.; Ann Frances Bland Tucker Coalter to John Randolph, 30 Dec. 1798, Grinnan Family Papers, Vi-Hi; Eleanor Parke Custis to Elizabeth Bordley, 23 Nov. [1797], 14 May 1798, in *George Washington's Beautiful Nelly: The Letters of Eleanor Parke Custis Lewis to Elizabeth Bordley Gibson, 1794–1851,* ed. Patricia Brady (Columbia: University of

in private. John Chesnut, a South Carolina Federalist, complained that his sister-in-law was "so much of a Democrat," but the two engaged in a good-natured debate over the virtues of their respective parties. Elizabeth Gamble, a much more belligerent Federalist, mocked the politics of a Republican suitor, informing him that she and her Federalist friends ignored the festivities that marked Jefferson's inauguration in 1801, preferring instead an elegant ball commemorating Washington's birthday "at which . . . not more than two or three Democrats attended." Catherine Read of Charleston asserted that she did not "always think it necessary to think as my Husband does," and she criticized him and other southern men for their foolish willingness to involve the United States in European wars.[13]

During the Revolution, when the stakes were much higher, some women also disagreed politically with their husbands. Not surprisingly, the wives of Tories were far more likely than the wives of Whigs to disavow publicly the political views of their spouses. Because the laws required men, not women, to take oaths of allegiance, differences between Whig husbands and Tory wives remained private in most cases, unless the wife attempted to aid the British or otherwise drew public attention to her political sentiments.[14] Conversely, when wives and other female kin of loyalist men professed their own support for the Revolution—for either ideological or pragmatic reasons—their disagreement often became public, as women emphasized their distinct political allegiance to protect themselves and their families from the wrath of their neighbors and from the economic penalties imposed on their now discredited Tory relatives.

South Carolina Press, 1991), 41, 52. On women's patriotic and partisan dress, see Kierner, "Genteel Balls and Republican Parades," 206.

13. John Chesnut to Mary Cox Chesnut, 24 Feb. 1799, 21 May 1799, Cox-Chesnut Papers, Sc-U; Elizabeth Washington Gamble to Thomas Bayly, 11–12 Mar. 1801, Elizabeth Washington Gamble Wirt Letter, Vi-Hi; Catherine Read to Eizabeth Read Ludlow [1798], Read Family Papers, Sc-U. Though cataloged under 1798, the undated Read letter probably dates to circa 1806, as its text indicates that Read opposed an expected war with Britain, not France. In 1798, the United States fought an undeclared naval war with France; Britain was America's chief foe after 1800.

14. For instance, see Elaine Forman Crane, "Religion and Rebellion: Women of Faith and the American War for Independence," in *Religion in a Revolutionary Age,* ed. Ronald Hoffman and Peter J. Albert (Charlottesville: University Press of Virginia, 1993), 75–79; Joan R. Gundersen, "Independence, Citizenship, and the American Revolution," *Signs* 13 (1987): 68.

In keeping with contemporary gender ideals, most women who professed a separate political allegiance described themselves as passive supporters of the Revolution and provided mainly negative evidence of their allegiance to the new state governments. Such women did not attempt to prove that they had purposefully contributed to the revolutionary effort but, rather, that they had done nothing either to hinder it or to undermine the authority of the Whig regime. Accordingly, the wife of one backcountry Tory requested relief from the confiscation statutes on the grounds that, "although her husband imprudently took part with the enemies of America, yet she and her children have been hitherto conformable" to the laws of the state (Doc. 1). A Georgia woman likewise cited her own "inoffensive conduct" as reason to restore the confiscated property of her recently deceased husband.[15] After admitting her husband's political errors and begging pardon on his behalf, South Carolinian Eleanor Mackey informed the legislators that she was "deserving of your Compassion" because "her own conduct has been irreproachable" (Doc. 6). Ann Elizabeth Saylor complained that the amercement imposed on her husband's estate unfairly penalized herself and her three children "to whom no crime can be alleged" (Doc. 12).

Only a few petitioners, by contrast, described themselves as active supporters of the Revolution, and fewer still offered positive evidence of their activities on behalf of the patriot cause. Of those who did so, Florence Cooke, wife of a Charleston carpenter, most tenaciously asserted her separate allegiance, forcefully distinguishing her own conduct and opinions from those of her banished husband. Petitioning the legislature in 1783, Cooke declared that she was "inocent of any crime" against the state, and she professed "a Sincere affection for the independence and freedom of her Country." In addition, she maintained that the confiscation of her husband's estate was unfair to her and her daughter not merely because they depended on his property for their subsistence but because that property "has been caused, not more by the hand of industry of her husband, than by her own Domestic toil, frugality and attention." Cooke also offered the assembly positive evidence of her active allegiance to the revolutionary cause. Along with her petition she

---

15. Petition of Mary Beattie, 17 Jan. 1785, in "Journal of the House of Assembly of Georgia, Session Jan. 21, 1784 to Aug. 15, 1786," Works Progress Administration typescript, 1938, 163.

presented an affidavit, signed by eight Charleston men who swore that she "entertained a Zealous & Affectionate Attachment to the Cause of America, and . . . has been remarkable for her humane attention and Generosity in relieving the distresses of those who were Prisoners of War in Cha[rle]s Town, helping them with a liberality that must have been inconvenient to her" (Doc. 3).

Like some other women who sought to convince Whig legislators of their patriotism, Cooke also argued that the way in which she discharged her maternal duties demonstrated her allegiance to the American cause. Cooke emphasized her efforts to instill in her only daughter a "real attachment to the liberty of her Native Country," adding that, "if providence had blessed her with a Number of Sons," she would have used "all the influence & Care of a Mother, to render them fit for the defense and Support of their Country." A somewhat less assertive Elizabeth Mitchell, who characterized her husband as "a man of very distracted Mind," also implied that she, not her spouse, had molded her children's political sentiments. Mitchell informed the assembly that, despite her husband's Toryism, she and her children were "well affected" to the Revolution and that one of her sons became a soldier to support the American cause (Doc. 4).

When they portrayed motherhood as an expression of patriotic allegiance, Florence Cooke and Elizabeth Mitchell alluded to the nascent ideal of republican womanhood, which would become the most widely accepted representation of female patriotism in postrevolutionary America. Articulated both privately and publicly by women and by sympathetic men in the decades following the Treaty of Paris, this new feminine ideal proscribed women's formal participation in public life while investing their traditional domestic responsibilities with new public significance. Proponents of republican womanhood believed that patriotic wives could inspire their husbands to civic virtue and, more important still, that conscientious mothers could instill in their children values essential to good citizenship.[16] Presented in 1783, the petitions of Cooke and Mitchell were early attempts of women to formulate and to assert publicly this peculiarly feminine construction of patriotism.

---

16. Kerber, *Women of the Republic,* chap. 15; Jan Lewis, "The Republican Wife: Virtue and Seduction in the Early Republic," *WMQ,* 3d ser., 44 (1987): 689–91, 698–703.

Unlike Cooke and Mitchell, petitioners who came from Whig families were unlikely to claim a separate political identity or allegiance, for they had no practical incentive to do so. North Carolinian Mary Moore was unusual in distinguishing her own wartime "Services" from those of her spouse when she submitted two separate petitions to the state legislature in 1786. The first she filed as the widow of a revolutionary soldier seeking back pay due her husband's estate, but in the second she asked compensation for the "many signal Services" she had performed in wartime, including "Saving many Hundred thousand pounds" currency from the British army (Doc. 10). Ann Timothy, South Carolina's state printer, who succeeded her deceased husband in that office, also declared her own allegiance to the state when she averred that "her patriotism would induce her to serve the public for no other reward than the satisfaction she would enjoy in the reflection of having served her country" (Doc. 11).

For most Whig women who, unlike Timothy and Moore, did not serve their states directly, the issues of feminine identities and allegiances were more abstract and ambiguous. The conventional image of woman as weak and apolitical retained a powerful influence on the rhetoric—and perhaps the minds—of many petitioners, some of whom simultaneously avowed and denied their politicization and its significance. When twenty-one coastal North Carolina women, themselves professing "steady adherence to the Whig principles of America," asked that the wives and children of Wilmington's Tories be allowed to remain in the town after the British evacuation, they declared it "beneath the character of the independent State of North Carolina to war with women and children," who presumably were politically apathetic or ineffectual (Doc. 2). Even more equivocal was the petition of Margarett Brisbane of Charleston, the wife of a banished loyalist, who described the condition of women as "weak and Defenceless" but then asserted that her own "Sentiments *with regard to the present Contest* . . . were always contrary to her Husbands" (Doc. 5).

By their words and by their actions, some women thus claimed political allegiance, though they rarely described themselves as citizens of the polities they inhabited. While political allegiance presupposed opinions and sentiments that many could entertain and even express, citizenship entailed reciprocal rights and obligations that women did not possess. The Revolution did not inspire a repudiation of the English common-law tradition with its extreme gender bias. Coverture endowed women with obligations to their husbands that superseded most civic obligations and most civil rights. As a legal construct, coverture applied to wives only, but the gender conventions that justified coverture by describing women as irrational and dependent pertained to the entire female sex. For all women, coverture and the assumptions from which it derived therefore had important political implications.[17]

At a time when revolutionary political culture increasingly construed citizenship as volitional, culture and law alike envisioned women as passive dependents. In theory at least, republicanism transformed dependent subjects of the Crown of Great Britain into independent citizens, free to choose or reject their governors. In keeping with classical republican theory, Americans made personal independence the chief criterion for citizenship, thus defining it in a way that potentially excluded not only wives, whom coverture rendered legally dependent, but all women whose presumed de facto dependence on men barred them from the formal activities—voting, officeholding, jury and militia service—which constituted the rights and obligations of republican citizenship. Consequently, with rare exceptions even widows and single women who met the property qualifications for voting were turned away from the polls, usually on the pretext that they, as women, lacked the independence, knowledge, and experience necessary to participate in political life.[18]

Rituals and rhetoric alike reflected women's exclusion from full citizenship. In the postrevolutionary decades, southern communities celebrated American independence and nationhood every Fourth of July, staging militia parades, artillery drills, and patriotic orations. Military exercises, which potentially included all white adult propertied men, dramatized the masculine ideal of republican vigilance and the rough equality of the participants by virtue of their shared citizenship. Similarly, Fourth of July orations downplayed class distinctions to celebrate the patriotism of male citizens past and present. By contrast, speakers rarely ac-

---

17. Kerber, "A Constitutional Right to Be Treated Like American Ladies," 27; Norma Basch, "Equity vs. Equality: Emerging Concepts of Women's Political Status in the Age of Jackson," *JER* 3 (1983): 305–6.

18. James H. Kettner, *The Development of American Citizenship, 1608–1870* (Chapel Hill: University of North Carolina Press, 1978), chaps. 1, 7; Gundersen, "Independence, Citizenship, and the American Revolution," esp. 60–68. The most significant exceptions occurred in New Jersey, where widows and single women, like all other "free inhabitants" of the state, were enfranchised between 1776 and 1807.

knowledged women's capacity for patriotism, and those who mentioned the "ladies" at all usually portrayed them as victims of war and politics, rather than active participants. In the deeply gendered political language of the times, orators and other male observers also characteristically distinguished "ladies" from "citizens" when they described the audiences that attended such civic functions.[19]

Some women clearly internalized this gendered construction of citizenship. Few described themselves as citizens, though they often employed that term to refer to their husbands and other men when they petitioned their state assemblies. In 1796, for instance, two daughters of a South Carolina Tory sought to regain his property—and their inheritance—by invoking the citizenship of their late husbands. When they petitioned the South Carolina assembly, they described themselves as "Widows . . . of American Citizens." Claiming citizenship for their husbands only, the petitioners thus implied that even dead men enjoyed a status and consideration that women could not (Doc. 13).

Women's exclusion from the republic's chief political rights, responsibilities, rituals, and institutions also inhibited development of the group consciousness that citizenship appears to have presupposed. During and after the Revolution, men petitioning in groups often prefaced their memorials with observations about their rights as citizens and the contractual origins of civil government. Seeking to adapt the petitioning ritual to their increasingly egalitarian political values, male petitioners also gradually replaced their habitual deference to a supposedly beneficent ruling class with ideals that endowed all white men with equal political and economic rights.[20] In 1781, for example, male petitioners from the Salisbury District of North Carolina alerted the assembly to the many problems that plagued their community, declaring, "It is at all times the Priviledge of free Men in Republican Governments to address their Rulers, and

---

19. Kierner, "Genteel Balls and Republican Parades," 196–205. For the rhetorical distinction between *ladies* and *citizens*, see, for instance, *Raleigh Register,* 4 Aug. 1801; *Richmond Enquirer,* 9 July 1811, 11 Jan. 1814, 11 July 1817.

20. Jay Fliegelman, *Prodigals and Pilgrims: The American Revolution against Patriarchal Authority* (Cambridge: Cambridge University Press, 1982), chap. 4; Ruth Bogin, "Petitioning and the Moral Economy of Post-Revolutionary America," *WMQ,* 3d ser., 45 (1988): 391–45. As Bogin shows, the North Carolina Regulators used this tactic in their prerevolutionary petitions, but the use of declaratory preambles later became much more widespread.

have Reason to expect their Grievances and Distresses will have such Degree of Attention paid to them, as Circumstances will admit." Six years later, a group of men from North Carolina's western counties, in a similar vein, announced their desire to form a separate state, claiming the "undeniable right" to "Enjoy the essential Benefits of Civil Society under a form of Government which our Selves alone can only Calculate for such a purpose."[21]

Individual petitioners of either sex rarely made such ringing declarations. The fact that only group petitioners aggressively claimed the prerogatives of citizens suggests that southerners saw citizenship as communal, in keeping with the ideals of classical republicanism, despite the growing acceptance of liberal individualism among some postrevolutionary Americans.[22] If a collective consciousness born of shared civic or occupational activities and interests were prerequisites for claiming citizenship, it is significant that southern women were signatories to only eighteen group petitions between 1776 and 1800 and that none of these included general political statements or appeals to libertarian ideologies. At a time when men increasingly used group petitions, legislative instructions, and other techniques to state their collective interests and to influence public policy, women's political consciousness was more private than public, more individual than collective.[23]

Of the eighteen group petitions women filed on their own or with men in the four southern states before 1800, at least seven dealt with family or domestic issues reflecting conventional notions of woman's place and status. In 1780, fifty-one South Carolina women—"deserted by their

---

21. Petition of inhabitants of the District of Salisbury, Dec. 1781, GASR, Apr.–May 1782, Nc-Ar; Petition of inhabitants of the western country, 1787, GASR, Nov.–Dec. 1787, Nc-Ar.

22. For an insightful analysis of the coexistence of these traditions, see James T. Kloppenberg, "The Virtues of Liberalism: Christianity, Republicanism, and Ethics in Early American Political Discourse," *JAH* 74 (1987): 9–33.

23. I have defined a group petition as one filed by two or more signatories not related by blood or marriage. On legislative instructions, see Gordon S. Wood, *The Creation of the American Republic, 1776–1787* (Chapel Hill: University of North Carolina Press, 1969), 189–91, 370–72; Edmund S. Morgan, *Inventing the People: The Rise of Popular Sovereignty in England and America* (New York: W. W. Norton, 1988), 213. North Carolina's state constitution expressly encouraged citizens to instruct their representatives.

husbands gone over to the Enemy"—requested relief from the punitive taxes imposed on Tories, noting that a total of 203 children depended on them for shelter and sustenance. In 1782, twenty-one Whig women from North Carolina's Cape Fear region petitioned to prevent the expulsion of the "helpless and innocent" wives and children of Wilmington's Tories (Doc. 2). In 1796, 191 women cosigned Mary Fraser's petition for the repatriation of her banished husband, and three women joined with their male neighbors in defense of a Randolph County, North Carolina, man who pulled down a house where women "were Very Loose with their Virtue & their tongues Such as Making mischief between men and their Wives." On three other occasions, widows petitioned in pairs to collect government pensions or recover wartime losses.[24] In all of these cases, the petitioners asked the state government to step in to help or protect suffering families. Such requests represented the expansion into the public sphere of values and activities that contemporaries readily identified with virtuous women.

Only rarely did women act collectively to pursue objectives that were less readily compatible with their conventional domestic roles. As we have seen, in 1783 a group of Charleston widows petitioned to protest new market regulations that undermined their economic interests and in 1789 sixty-seven seamstresses unsuccessfully sought the imposition of duties on imported clothing to shield their trade from foreign competitors. These petitions, like that of North Carolina's Moravian "single women," who requested and received a tax exemption for their school at

---

24. Petition of 51 women and 301 children, 4 Feb. 1780, in *S.C. House Journals, 1776–1780*, 274–75; Petition of Mary Fraser et al., 11 Nov. 1796, LP, Sc-Ar; Petition of Elizabeth Richards et al., 13 Dec. 1796, GASR, Nov.–Dec. 1796, Nc-Ar; Petition of Jane Dixon and Sarah Millyard, 1776, LP, Norfolk City, Vi-Ar; Petition of Mary Figg and Jane Buck, 1777, LP, Misc., Vi-Ar; Petition of Delia Barnes and Mary Tripp, 8 June 1784, LP, Princess Anne County, Vi-Ar. An eighth petition, submitted by the "Ladies of Augusta" to the Georgia legislature in 1783, appears to have solicited the return of a banished man to his family. This document has not survived, but it is mentioned in *Rev. Recs. of Ga.*, 367.

South Carolina and Virginia women also joined with men in signing religious petitions, which, though they pertained to extradomestic matters, exploited contemporary assumptions about women's superior piety. See Petition of the Presbyterian Congregation of Edisto Island, 31 Jan. 1784, LP, Sc-Ar; and Raymond C. Bailey, *Popular Influence upon Public Policy: Petitioning in Eighteenth-Century Virginia* (Westport, Conn.: Greenwood Press, 1979), 44, 53.

Salem, were unusual in bringing together southern women with common occupational interests to lobby their state government.[25]

On other occasions, widows and single women joined with men of their class to express publicly their common grievances. In 1784, Mary Simpson, a Charleston baker, along with fourteen male members of her profession, petitioned to raise the price of bread. In 1790, forty-nine Virginia tenant farmers who leased land from the College of William and Mary asked their state assembly to abolish the college, which they believed offered unfair leases and, as a royally chartered institution, was an incongruous legacy of the imperial past in postrevolutionary America. Even more boldly, free black women and men joined together to seek the repeal of South Carolina's discriminatory poll tax in 1794.[26]

These few exceptional group petitions were significant as early instances of women's collective public activism, but they did not represent an articulation of women's citizenship. Indeed, women petitioning in groups were even less likely than those petitioning alone to describe themselves as citizens—a significant inversion of the pattern among men who, as we have seen, most aggressively invoked their status as citizens when they petitioned together. Perhaps the implicit radicalism of collective activism made women who petitioned in groups more circumspect. At any rate, between 1776 and 1800, only five southern women petitioners described themselves as citizens when they petitioned their state assemblies.

Those five either claimed citizenship implicitly and indirectly or, like Mary Willing Byrd, articulated a version of citizenship that was decidedly gendered and limited. Both Florence Cooke and Elizabeth Beard implied that they themselves were citizens when they appealed to their "fellow citizens," whom the assembly represented, to allay their families' hardships (Docs. 3, 14). In 1783, Elizabeth Ronaldson, wife of a Georgia Tory, petitioned to be "Admitted to the Priviledges of a Citizen," but the fact that the legislators seriously considered her request suggests that

---

25. Petition of the Single Women at Salem in Stokes County, [Dec. 1797], GASR, Nov–Dec. 1797, Nc-Ar. For the widows' and seamstresses' petitions, see chap. 2, above.

26. Petition of the bakers of Charleston, 19 Feb. 1784, LP, Sc-Ar; Petition of the Tenants of the lands [belonging] to the College of Wm. & Mary . . . , 5 Nov. 1790, LP, Williamsburg City, Vi-Ar; Petition of the people of Colour of South Carolina, 1794, LP, 1794, Sc-Ar.

both she and they regarded the privileges of female citizens as inferior and gender specific.[27]

Even Jane Spurgin, by far the most outspoken petitioner to approach a southern legislature during this period, used the language of citizenship selectively and reluctantly. Her frequent and frustrating interactions with the North Carolina assembly show how, while the Revolution and its consequent dislocations brought women into the public sphere and enhanced their political consciousness, they nevertheless remained on the fringes of public life. Spurgin was the wife of a slaveholding Tory from Rowan County in western North Carolina. When the state government banished William Spurgin and confiscated his estate, Jane remained in Rowan County with their large family, and she attempted to preserve her dower portion of William's twenty-one hundred acres, slaves, livestock, and other property. During the war, she was "almost Continually harrassed from the Military who took from her grain, meat, and many other Articles without the least recompense."[28] After the war, she petitioned both to recover her dower and to obtain compensation for produce state troops had taken.

Between 1785 and 1792, Jane Spurgin sent the North Carolina assembly three petitions in which she articulated not only her grievances but also her understanding of women's political status in postrevolutionary America. The escalating assertiveness of Spurgin's three successive petitions suggests that each setback in her dealings with the government forced her to rethink the basis of her claims and, in so doing, enhanced her political consciousness. Throughout the process, Spurgin demonstrated a thorough knowledge of state laws pertaining to Tories and their families as well as an unusual willingness to chide the legislators for their insensitivity and injustice.

Spurgin's career as a petitioner began with a simple assertion of her dower rights and ended with a bold declaration political allegiance and citizenship. A 1784 North Carolina statute sought to "promote that equality of property which is of the spirit and principle of a genuine republic" by abolishing primogeniture and endowing all sons with equal shares of their fathers' estates. Although the new law did not explicitly invalidate the dower rights of widows, it undermined the economic rights and interests of many by stipulating that, when a man left more than two chil-

---

27. *Rev. Recs. of Ga.*, 216, 465.
28. Petition of Jane Spurgin, 11 Nov. 1788, GASR, Nov.–Dec. 1788, Nc-Ar.

dren as his heirs, his widow was to "share equally with all the children, she being entitled to a child's part" of his estate.[29] As a mother of eight, Spurgin could expect to be penalized heavily if her husband's estate were divided according to the terms of this new legislation. Instead of her customary "widow's third," she would receive only one-ninth of the property that had belonged to her banished husband. In 1785, she therefore approached the assembly as a woman whose husband was "politically dead" and thus possessed of an "indefeasible right" to her dower portion under the penal statutes, which antedated the new inheritance law (Doc. 7).

Although the assembly rejected her initial petition, Spurgin tried again three years later, this time attempting to distance herself from her Tory husband. Decrying William's political errors, Jane implicitly claimed a separate allegiance when she recounted the wartime suffering of herself and her children and declared that the assembly could not "make the Wife and Small Children entirely miserable on account of the Husbands and fathers transgressions" (Doc. 8). The legislators, however, again refused to reinstate her dower rights.

Spurgin's final petition, presented in December 1791, may be the most forceful piece of political writing produced by a southern woman in the postrevolutionary decades. First, she called this document a "memorial," not a petition, adopting the less deferential terminology that was used increasingly after the Revolution, especially by male petitioners. Second, though her husband was still living, Spurgin explicitly disavowed her marriage to the Tory William as "an evil that was not in her power to remidy" once the Revolution commenced. Third, she claimed a political allegiance distinct from William's, asserting that she actively supported the Revolution by selling provisions to its armies and that she now petitioned to recover the state's resulting debt. Finally, and most important, Spurgin described herself as a "good Citizen" who was loyal, long-suffering, and wrongly "deprived of the Common rights of other Citizens" (Doc. 9).

Like many other postwar petitioners, Spurgin believed that her personal and economic hardships entitled her to equitable treatment at the hands of her government, but she was unusual among women petitioners in calling herself a "Citizen" and in claiming a citizen's "Common rights."

---

29. *N.C. Recs.*, 24:575. See also Marylynn Salmon, *Women and the Law of Property in Early America* (Chapel Hill: University of North Carolina Press, 1986), 168–72; Kerber, *Women of the Republic*, 146–47.

Spurgin's frequent and assertive interaction with her government had no colonial precedent nor did her use of the rhetoric of rights and citizenship. Still, even she requested not the political and economic rights of white male citizens but, rather, only the rights of dower and debt recovery which the common law traditionally afforded. In all three instances, the legislators rejected her petitions.

The ambiguous rhetoric of even the most assertive women's petitions reflected the reality of their political exclusion and their own reluctance to claim the rights and obligations of citizenship. For Jane Spurgin, the "Common rights" of women citizens consisted chiefly of dower rights in widowhood and the ability to collect justly contracted debts. "Anne Matilda," a South Carolina essayist, and one of the few other southern women who described themselves as "citizens" possessing "rights" during this era, constructed women's citizenship in equally gendered terms.

In 1806, Anne Matilda penned an extraordinary newspaper essay attacking licentious men who seduced and corrupted virtuous women. Declaring herself to be a "citizen of the world, free and independent," Anne Matilda nevertheless went on to suggest that freedom from seduction was the loftiest prerogative of women citizens. She also described normative citizenship in conventionally masculine terms. "Tho' precluded by the laws of propriety from wielding a sword, or shooting a pistol in the field," she averred, "yet I shall maintain the post of a private citizen, and chastize the insolence that [dares] to riot upon the rights of my sex."[30]

Despite her familiarity with the rhetoric and ideals of republican political culture, Anne Matilda claimed for herself a lesser form of citizenship that was more "private" than public, more passive than participatory, more governed by her relationship to men than by her status in the polity. Like her, most southern women did not defy the conventions that barred them from wielding swords and pistols, though they too must have recognized that their exclusion from these and other activities effectively prevented them from being citizens in the fullest sense. Some, however, used their right to petition to enter the public sphere to seek emancipation from onerous customs and institutions that shaped their private lives.

---

30. *South Carolina Gazette* (Columbia), 5 July 1806. On seduction as a recurrent theme in postrevolutionary writing, see Lewis, "Republican Wife," 716–20; and Cathy N. Davidson, *Revolution and the Word: The Rise of the Novel in America* (New York: Oxford University Press, 1986), esp. 45–47, 101–12, 129–50.

DOCUMENT 1

Margret Cotton

The petitioner was the wife of James Cotton, a lieutenant colonel in the Tory militia, who was captured at Moore's Creek Bridge in 1776, fled to England the following year, and probably never returned to North Carolina. On 15 August 1778, Margret Cotton petitioned to retrieve her husband's property for herself and her children. When the assembly rejected her petition, she may have followed James to England. In 1783, however, their two sons, whom the legislature regarded as "good and faithful citizens," recovered for themselves and their sister the unsold portion of their father's estate.[1]

The humble petition of Margret Cotton of the County of Anson—Humbly sheweth—

That your petitioner is in a most distressed condition, that although the supreme power of this State were so humane as to make provision for petitioner and her family,[2] yet the persons whom they were pleased to appoint, did not execute their trust, that instead of contributing to the support of your petitioner and family, they in great measure converted what she doth acknowledge as your Bounty to their own private use and benefit, that many persons supposing her to be deprived of the benefit of the Law do take her property without makeing her that least recompence, that although her husband imprudently took part with the enemies of America, yet she and her children have been hitherto conformable, and are willing to bind themselves by every tye to any rule that

1. *N.C. Recs.*, 10:119, 125–29, 160–61, 201; 11:290, 768; 19:186, 191, 193, 312–13, 316, 321–22; "An act to vest the title of certain lands, and other property therein mentioned, in Thomas Cotton, James Cotton, and their sister," North Carolina sessions laws, microfiche, 1783, chap. 41.

2. North Carolina's 1777 anti-Tory statutes mandated that traitors and others who refused to take the oath of allegiance forfeit their property to the state but provided that the courts "shall and may order and appropriate so much of the Traitor's Estate, as . . . may appear sufficient, for the Support of his or her Family" (*N.C. Recs.*, 24:10–11, 123–24).

the Honorable the Legislature shall think proper to devise and require of them. Petitioner therefore humbly prays, that the property which was formerly her husbands may be vested in her and her children, to prevent a too frequent troubling of this Honourable House.

And your Petitioner as in duty bound Shall ever Pray.

(D, Nc-Ar)

DOCUMENT 2

Women of Wilmington

The British evacuation of the southern port towns compelled loyalists to choose between exile and prosecution and forced their families to choose between starting life over in an unfamiliar place and extended separation from their banished loved ones. These petitioners, who were obliged to flee Wilmington when the British occupied the town in February 1781, sought to spare their Tory counterparts a similar fate when they submitted this petition in 1782. Perhaps because they addressed their petition to the governor instead of the assembly, it was not acted on.[3]

To His Excellency Governor Martin[4] and the Members of the Honorable Council.

We, the subscribers, inhabitants of the town of Wilmington, warmly attached to the State of North Carolina and strenuously devoted to our best wishes and endeavours to the achievement of its independence, feeling for the honor of and desirous that our Enemies shoud not have

---

3. Andrew J. Howell, *The Book of Wilmington* (Wilmington, N.C.: Wilmington Printing Company, 1959), 68–72; DeMond, *Loyalists in N.C.*, 123.

4. Alexander Martin, president of the North Carolina senate, was acting governor for four months following the enemy's capture of Governor Thomas Burke in September 1782. By February 1782, when the women submitted their petition, Burke had escaped and resumed the governorship, and the text of the document was copied into his letterbook. The results of the next election, however, made Martin governor in his own right. He succeeded Burke in April 1782 (*Dict. of N.C. Biog.*, 4:223; Governors' Letter Books, 4:62–65, Nc-Ar).

the smallest pretext to brand them as cruel and precipitate, that the dignity of our public characters may not be degraded to the imitation of examples of inhumanity exhibited by our Enemies.

Humbly shew to His Excellency the Governor and the Honorable the Council that we have been informed that orders have issued from your honorable board that the wives and children of Absentees should depart the State with a small part of their property in forty eight hours after notice given them.

It is not the province of our sex to reason deeply upon the policy of the order, but as it must affect the helpless and innocent it wounds us with the most sincere distress and prompts our earnest supplication that the order may be arrested and the officers forbid to carry it into execution.

If it is intended as retaliation for the expulsion of some of us, the subscribers, by the British from the town of Wilmington, and to gratify a resentment which such inhumanity to us may be supposed to have excited, its object is greatly mistaken.

Those whom your proclamation holds forth as marks of public vengeance neither prompted the British order nor aided the execution of it. On the contrary they expressed the greatest indignation at it and with all their power strove to mitigate our sufferings. Still some instances attended which made the execution of it less distressing to us than yours must be to those upon whom it is intended to operate. We were ordered without the British Line and then our friends were ready to receive us. They received us with a cordial welcome and ministered to our wants with generosity and politeness. With pleasure we bear this public testimony. But our Town women now ordered out must be exposed to the extreme of human wretchedness.

Their friends are in Charlestown,[5] they have neither carriages or horses to remove them by land nor vessels to transport them by water and the small pittance allotted them of their property could they be procured would be scarce equal to the purchase of them. It is beneath the character of the independent State of North Carolina to war with women and children. The authors of our ill treatment are the proper subjects of our

---

5. Loyalists from the Carolinas and Georgia gathered in Charleston, from which they left the United States in the final months of 1782 (Lambert, *S.C. Loyalists,* 248–56).

own and the resentment of the public. Does their barbarity strike us with abhorrence? Let us blush to imitate it, not justify by [our] own practice what we so justly condemn in others. To Major Craig[6] and him alone is to be imputed the inhuman edicts, for even the British Soldiers were shocked at it.

If we may be allowed to claim any merit with the public for our steady adherence to the Whig principles of America, if our sufferings induced by that attachment have given us favor and esteem with your honorable body, we beg leave to assure you that we shall hold it as a very signal mark of your respect for us if you will condescend to suffer to remain amongst us our old friends and acquaintances whose husbands though estranged from us in political opinions have left wives and children much endeared to us and who may live to be an honor to the State and to Society if permitted to continue here. The safety of this State, we trust in God, is now secured beyond the most powerful exertions of our Enemies, and it would be a symtem of abject weakness to fear the feeble efforts of women and children.

And as in Duty bound we shall ever pray.

Anne Hooper[7]
Mary Allen   Ann Towkes
Sarah Nash[8]   M. Hand
Mary Nash[9]   S. Wilkings

---

6. With a force of 400 to 450 men, Maj. James H. Craig captured Wilmington on 1 February 1781. He was the British commander there until the town was evacuated on 18 November (Boatner, *Ency. of Amer. Rev.*, 1211–12).

7. Anne Clark Hooper and her children were forced to flee Wilmington in 1781. British forces destroyed the Hooper home outside of Wilmington, and the family resettled in Hillsborough after the war was over. Anne's husband, William, was a prominent Whig and a signer of the Declaration of Independence (*Dict. of N.C. Biog.*, 3:200–201; Claghorn, *Women Patriots*, 105).

8. Sarah Moore Nash was the widow of Brig. Gen. Francis Nash, who died in 1777 as a result of wounds sustained at the Battle of Germantown. She supplied provisions for the North Carolina forces (Claghorn, *Women Patriots*, 399).

9. Mary Whiting Nash was the wife of North Carolina's governor when the British invaded the state in 1781. She and her children fled the approaching British forces under Maj. James Craig, who burned the Nashes' house in New Bern (*Dict. of N.C. Biog.*, 4:356–57).

Mary Moore[10]   M. Lord
E. Nash   Isabella Read
Sarah Moore   Sally Read
M. Loyd   Mary Grainger
Catharine Young   Jane Ward
J. M. Drayton   Hannah Ward
E. Wilkings   Kitty Ward

(DC, Governors' Letter Books, 4:62–65, Nc-Ar)

DOCUMENT 3

Florence Cooke

According to her neighbors, Florence Cooke "entertained a Zealous & Affectionate Attachment to the Cause of America, and . . . [was] remarkable for her humane attention and Generosity in relieving the distresses of . . . Prisoners of War" in occupied Charleston. Her husband, James, however, was a Tory who held minor official posts and persuaded the authorities to bar Whigs from doing business in the capital. On 23 January 1783, Florence petitioned on James's behalf, and the assembly rescinded his banishment only to reverse its decision under pressure from angry Whig artisans and mechanics. Florence Cooke may have remained in Charleston, but James never returned to South Carolina.[11]

The Petition of Florence Cooke Humbly Sheweth—

That your Petitioner is the Wife of James Cooke of this Town whose property hath been Confiscated and himself banished by a Law of this State. That She is informed that herself is deprived of her right of Dower,

---

10. Mary Moore, wife of Col. James Moore, furnished supplies to North Carolina troops, as did her copetitioners Sarah Moore, Mary Grainger, and Kitty Ward (Claghorn, *Women Patriots*, 392, 393, 381, 478).

11. Walsh, *Charleston's Sons of Liberty*, 92, 97–98, 118; Kathryn Roe Coker, "The Artisan Loyalists of Charleston, South Carolina," in *Loyalists and Community in North America*, ed. Robert M. Calhoon et al. (Westport, Conn.: Greenwood Press, 1994), 97–98; Affidavit of John Winn et al., 1 Feb. 1783, LP, Sc-Ar.

and her Child a Daughter of Twelve years of age, of all future claim on the inheritance of her father. This Law she humbly thinks the more severe as her Child received early & strong impressions of real attachment to the liberty of her Native Country; with a Confirmed aversion to our Enemies; principally inculcated by yr. Petit[ione]r who if providence had blessed her with a Number of Sons, would have thought herself happily engaged in employing all the influence & Care of a Mother, to render them fit for the defence and Support of their Country. Conscious of this, she the more regrets that herself and Child should be put out of the protection of the former Laws of this State, with respect to her own Dower, and her Daughters right of future Succession to her fathers inheritance: a property that has been caused, not more by the hand of industry of her husband, than by her own Domestic toil, frugality and attention.

Your Petitioner is not only inocent of any crime, but if a Sincere affection for the independence and freedom of her Country, avowed and testified in the worst of times, be any Merit, She flatters herself she has some to plead. With regard to her banished husband, She has but little to say. Being a laborious hardworkingman in a Mechanic employment, and not versed in the knowledge of publick troubles, it is not likely he could do any political good or harm. The change that happened in Charles Town was too powerful for his Situation and Circumstances to withstand; he might have said an Idle thing, but your petitioner believes he had neither inclination nor influence to execute any Mischievous one.

One House & Lott on the Bay & half of a House & Lott in St. Michaels alley in this Town, with three Negroes, was all that on his leaving his Country he could leave her. As She now lives on the rent of one alone, and has many debts to pay, his Child and a sickly old Lady, a relation & dependant, to support, she is already reduced to very great distress; and shou'd this little property be sold, she is utterly undone. She makes this application to the members of the legislature as her Country men & fellow Citizens, humbly entreating to allow her husband & the father of her Child to return and have a hearing, if he has commited any Crime. If he be acquited as She trusts he will, she Pledges herself that She will Exert all the ascendency of a wife & friend to make him a goodman and useful Citizen.

And lastly she humbly implores of this honorable house, that She may not be deprived of the only resource for herself and the maintenance & Education of her Daughter, who must otherwise be turned into the world, without friend or protector, exposed to that misfortune and affliction which seldom fail to pursue an unhappy female fallen from afluence to poverty.

And your Petitioner as in Duty bound will ever pray.

(DS, Sc-Ar)

DOCUMENT 4

Elizabeth Mitchell

On 10 February 1783, the widow of Charleston merchant John Mitchell petitioned the assembly to recover his confiscated estate, which included three plantations, slaves, livestock, and several lots in Charleston. The petitioner carefully distanced herself and her children from Mitchell's political errors, which she attributed to insanity, though he described himself as possessing "a sound and disposing Mind and . . . understanding" when he wrote his will in 1780. The assembly, however, concluded that John Mitchell "was generally thought to be a man not in his perfect senses" and granted his widow's petition.[12]

The petition of Elizabeth Mitchell, Widow of John Mitchell deceased, in behalf of herself and the heirs and devisees of John Mitchell Setting forth

That her husband has been dead almost two Years, and left his Estate real and personal to herself and children,[13] And with Concern observes the Said Estate is Confiscated by an Act of Assembly of this State. And begs leave to observe that for many Years preceeding his death he was a man of very distracted Mind and if he has been Guilty of any Acts to Occasion the displeasure of the Legislature, Such misconduct must have been the result of insanity only And that he was confined frequently as an

---

12. Will of John Mitchell, 28 Nov. 1780, Charleston County Will Book, 1780–83, typescript, 20:269–71, Sc-Ar; *S.C. House Journals, 1783–1784,* 210.

13. When the assembly heard Mitchell's petition, her husband had been dead for slightly more than one year, as his will was proved on 2 February 1781. The Mitchells had three children: Elizabeth Mitchell Campbell and two sons, John and William Nisbet, both under the age of twenty-one (Will of John Mitchell, 28 Nov. 1780, Charleston County Will Book, 1780–83, typescript, 20:269–71, Sc-Ar).

absolute Madman. That he never held a Commission under the British that herself and the heirs of the Said deceased are well affected to this State, And one of the heirs tho' a Youth of tender Years hath lately turned out a Volunteer in the States Service. And prays relief from an Act entitled an Act for disposing of Certain Estates &ca.

(Petition summarized in South Carolina Senate Journals, 15 February 1783, Sc-Ar)

DOCUMENT 5

Margarett Brisbane

James Brisbane was a Tory from the beginning of the Revolution. He went into exile in 1778, leaving behind the petitioner, who was his second wife, and children from two marriages. James returned to Charleston in 1780 and in 1783 sought permission to remain in South Carolina. Hoping to keep her family intact, Margarett seconded James's request on 22 February 1783, but the assembly rejected her petition. Neither she nor James renewed their petitions in subsequent legislative sessions, but in 1786 James's son William recovered his father's confiscated property for himself, his minor brothers, and half-brothers.[14]

The Petition of Margerett Brisbane Humbly Sheweth
That about the Year of our Lord 1762, she intermarried with Doctor George Frasier, then living in the State of Georgia, by whom, she had three Children. That her Husband dying, she, sometime afterwards, intermarried with Mr James Brisbane, formerly of this State; A Gentleman, whose political sentiments differed from those of his fellow Citizens, which, induced him to quit this Country, at a very early period, in this unhappy Contest. The part he has taken, has, unfortunately, drawn

14. Lambert, *S.C. Loyalists,* 60, 188; Petition of James Brisbane, 30 Jan. 1783, LP, Sc-Ar; Petition of William Brisbane, 15 Feb. 1786, ibid.; *S.C. House Journals, 1785–1786,* 486.

on him the heavy displeasure of the Legislature, at the last meeting.[15] And your Petitioner, apprehensive least this Hon[ora]ble House, under an Idea of Retaliation, or, from political Motives, may think proper, to send away from this Country, the Unfortunate & distressed Wives & Children of those persons who have become so obnoxious, has taken the Liberty of requesting that she may be considered, not only in the view of a wife, but that of a Mother—a Mother, who must be parted, (should such an Event take place) from her Children by her former Husband, Children, whose Interest lies in America, the place of their Nativity & Residence, and where your Petitioner wishes to reside with her Offspring.

And your Petitioner further sheweth unto this Hon[ora]ble House, That she has, by her Husband, the aforesaid Mr Brisbane, a Child about eighteen Months old, and is now pregnant with a second, both of which, with herself, must suffer, should not the Hon[ora]ble House appropriate for their Support and Maintenance, some portion of her Husband's late property. Call'd on, as she is, by Humanity towards her Offspring, she finds herself *impell'd* to make this Request, & flatters herself with Hopes, that when the House reflects on the weak and Defenceless Situation of woman & children, who are not the promoters of the War, nor, from their Sphere in Life, can possibly be disadvantageous to the Contest; and whose Opinions seldom avail, and do not frequently operate on the Judgment of Men; when they recollect this, and are informed that her Sentiments *with regard to the present Contest* never coincided with, but were always contrary to her Husbands.

That they will take into Consideration the facts above set forth, and extend its Benevolence towards her, by permitting her to remain in this Country; and towards her Children jointly with herself, by granting some part of that Property, which she *once* considered, as, in some degree, her own, and ultimately, as the Inheritance of her now destitute Children; and thereby enable them to go through Life, without the prospect of penury & want.

And your Petitioner as in duty Bound will ever Pray &c.

(ADS, Sc-Ar)

---

15. The petitioner is referring to her husband's inclusion in the banishment and confiscation statutes that the legislature enacted in its previous session.

DOCUMENT 6

Eleanor Mackey

In 1783, James Mackey, a Charleston cooper, petitioned for relief from the anti-Tory statutes. Mackey asserted that "persons whose prudence and Judgement he thought he might rely on" induced him to sign the congratulatory addresses to the British commanders— a claim his wife, Eleanor, echoed when she petitioned on his behalf on 5 February 1784. Although the assembly rejected James's petition, it granted Eleanor's, thereby enabling him to return to South Carolina and recover his estate, subject to the customary amercement of 12 percent.[16]

The humble Petition of Eleanor Mackey Sheweth

That her husband James Mackey Cooper is unhappily among the number of those Persons who are banished and whose Estates are confiscated.

That your Petitioner is advised by some who are well acquainted with the Character & Conduct of her husband and urged by her present Distress & pain to invoke again the Clemency & benignity of this honorable house, Praying a reconsideration of her case.

That she trusts she can make appear that her husband during a residence of eighteen years in Charleston deported himself as a quiet industrious inoffensive Man, and was never ambitious of attracting any other Notice or acquiring any higher Character than that of an honest industrious mechanic.

That during the domination of the British he was not remarkable for any activity or services injurious to the views & success of the United States.

That if he incautiously made himself in any degree conspicuous for an adherence and attachment to the British Government it was because his simplicity and timidity made him a miserable Dupe to the Suggestions & persuasions of more artfull designing and malignant Men.

---

16. Petition of James Mackey, 23 Jan. 1783, LP, Sc-Ar; *S.C. House Journals, 1783–1784,* 552.

That her husband since his Exile has been pursued by a series of unlucky Accidents and now sinking under the pressure of accumulated misfortunes can find no relief but from the humane & forgiving temper of this honorable house.

That the chief part of her husbands property earned by a long course of unremitted industry & frugality is the House No. 8 Bedons Alley, which being sold under the Confiscation, she was advised to purchase by some Gentlemen who knew and pitied her Situation, in hopes that the Legislature upon a further application might alleviate her distressfull condition.

That if she had not purchased it she would have been without a habitation or the means of procuring one, and if the terms of the Sale be exacted, she must be compleatly wretched & deplorable cast forlorn on the wide World, friendless & hopeless destitute of all resource & Subsistence with a mind preyed upon by Sorrow and a Body weaken'd by care and the approaches of Age.

That she is a native of this Country and presumes that her own conduct has been irreproachable and that she is deserving of your Compassion.

Your Petitioner therefore earnestly implores this honorable house to view with compassionate regard her calamitous condition and that it will be pleased to consider and mercifully decide upon the case of her unhappy husband to lessen his punishment and to grant him & her such other relief as may appear in this honorable house consistent with its Justice and Mercy and the Character of a brave and humane People.

(DS, Sc-Ar)

DOCUMENT 7

Jane Spurgin

The petitioner was the mother of eight children and the wife of William Spurgin, who settled in Rowan County, North Carolina, in the 1750s and was a justice of the peace there before the Revolution. A committed Tory, William served in the British forces, attaining the rank of major. When the state banished him and confiscated his property, he probably fled to England, leaving his wife, Jane, in North Carolina. On 3 December 1785, she submitted the first of three petitions in an attempt to recover at least a portion of her family's property. The assembly rejected her petition.[17]

The Petition of Jane Spurgin Humbly Sheweth that She being the Wife of William Spurgin a late unhappy Man, is entirely deprived of Any thing to Subsist upon, as follows there were Different Suits commenced against the estate of Said Spurgin by Way of Original Attachment, And Judgments Were Obtained for considerable Sums & executions issued & Were livied upon the Whole of the Property of the Said Spurgin & Sold, notwithstanding the commissioner of confiscated property had directed that her thirds[18] of the land Should not be Sold & Very Justly too, for Agreeable to the Act of Assembly, the legislature does not even When a Man's estate is confiscated require that the Whole Shall be Sold, but that the county court Shall Previous to any Sales Set apart so Much of the personal property as Will be Sufficient for the reasonable Support of the Wives, Widows & Children of any person Whose estate is, or may be confiscated & one third of the lands if Sufficient for their Support, but at their discretion to Assign the Whole of the land, therefore it cannot be expected that any Government Would place any individual or Set of individuals in a better Situation than the whole community. Nor Would they She hopes after Giving her a right to a Sufficiency clear from the Publick do it for the purpose of Satisfying Some individuals Who had a Claim against her husbands estate Generally, On Account of his Trespasses during the late Warr Which Occasioned the forfiture of his estate. Therefore She hopes that as her husband is politically dead, & has no expectation of his return to assist in the Maintainance of herself & eight Small children, the Assembly after due consideration of her circumstances, will restore & give to her an indefeasible right to Seven hundred & four acres of land her husbands that is to Say her thirds of the two tracts one tract containing three hundred & four acres & the Other four hundred. She hopes to get it out of both Tracts. All She requests of the personal property is a ne-

17. Sabine, *Loyalists of the Amer. Rev.*, 2:325; Carole Watterson Troxler, *The Loyalist Experience in North Carolina* (Raleigh: North Carolina Division of Archives and History, 1976), 55; *N.C. Recs.*, 22:618.

18. A dower portion, also known as a "widow's third."

gro fellow Named Simon, relying on the humane & upright disposition of the General Assembly Your Petitioner waits with Great expectation.

(D, Nc-Ar)

DOCUMENT 8

Jane Spurgin

> *On 11 November 1788, the exasperated Spurgin again attempted to regain her dower rights in William's estate. On consideration of her petition, a legislative committee recommended that "an Act be passed . . . Securing to the Said Jean [sic] and all others in Similar circumstances the Lands so assigned them" in the 1779 confiscation law. The assembly, however, rejected the committee's report without comment.*[19]

The Petition of Jean Spurgin of Rowan County humbly Sheweth

That where as her husband William Spurgin by mistake and bad Conduct did in the last war draw on him the resentment of the Law, in so much that his Estate real and personal was Seized for the State and made Sale off, and he banished and not permitted to live at home and assist her, Your Petitioner has Sufferd great Callamities and hardships; for during the late War She was almost Continually harrassed from the military who took from her grain, Meat, and many other Articles without the least recompense, that eaven for Several Years She and her family of Small Children enjoyed hardly any of the produce of her plantation; and Since the War, perticularly by this rigour and Severity that eaven that part of the plantation which was by Law allotted to her and had been laid off according to Law for the Subsistance of her and her Small Children, is now Seized and lays under ejectment, and She is now threatened every day to be turned out, She and her Children without Mercy. Other Women under the Same Circumstances are not treated in so hard a manner, nor can Your Petitioner believe it to be the meaning of the Law to punish without

---

19. Report on the petition of Jean Spurgin, 20 Nov. 1788, GASR, Nov.–Dec. 1788, Nc-Ar.

lenity, to give, only to be taken away again, and to make the Wife and Small Children entirely miserable on account of the Husbands and fathers transgressions. Your Petitioner and her Children are thus worse Situated than a Widow and Orphants, and cannot forbare herewith to look up to the Honorable the Representatives of the State for redress, imploring your Mercy and justice to look into the premises, to take your Petitioners and her Childrens Circumstances into Consideration, and to give her and her them Such releif as by Law originally intended. And your Petitioner as in Duty bound Shall ever pray &c.

(DS, Nc-Ar. Signed by "Jane Spurgin" and seventy-eight men who supported her petition)

DOCUMENT 9

Jane Spurgin

> On 28 November 1791, the assembly heard the last of Spurgin's three petitions, in which she most forcefully dissociated her actions and opinions from those of her Tory husband. This time Spurgin attempted to collect a debt she claimed the state owed her for supplies she had sold to its troops during the Revolution. The assembly rejected her petition, noting that she had already submitted her claims to the district commissioners, "who refused to grant them, owing in all probability to the want of proper Vouchers." By 1800, Spurgin and her children had left Rowan County, possibly joining William in Upper Canada, where he received a twelve hundred–acre land grant in recognition of his loyalty and military service.[20]

The memorial of Jennet Spurgen Humbly Sheweth
That during the late war She fur[ni]shed the regular Troops and Militia of this State with Provisions and Forriage some part of which, the officers that took it gave her certificates for. But the greater part that was taken from her She never got any vouchers for, owing to her husbands being disaffected to the government and owing to the same reason, the

---

20. Report on the petition of Janet Spurgin, 3 Jan. 1792, GASR, Dec. 1791–Jan. 1792, Nc-Ar; Troxler, *Loyalist Experience in North Carolina*, 55.

vouchers She did obtain would not be received and audited by the auditors of Salisbury District to whom they ware presented for that Purpose.[21] And tho it was your memorialists misfortune to be married to a man who was Enemical to the revolution it was an evil that was not in her power to remidy—and as She has always behaved herself as a good Citizen and well attached to the government She thinks it extreamly hard to be deprived of the Common rights of other Citizens. Your memorialist is advanced in life, and very much failed and had six Children to provide for,[22] and no one to assist or help her, and is also in very low Circumstances her husband not having lived with her Since the war. She has therefore Stated her account for Such articles As She obtained vouches for and humbly hopes your honorable body will grant her Such relief in the Premises as you in your great wisdom's may think her entitled to. And your Memorialist as in duty bound will ever pray &c.

(DS, Nc-Ar)

DOCUMENT 10

Mary Moore

The petitioner was the widow of Sergeant Stephen Moore of the North Carolina Continentals, and she herself appears to have traveled for a time with the American forces. Mary Moore, a resident of Fayetteville, claimed to have been present at Gen. Horatio Gates's defeat at Camden, where she prevented a cache of money from falling into enemy hands. On 29 December 1786, she petitioned for

---

21. A signed and sworn affidavit attesting to "her furnishing the troops with Provisions & forage and her having Presented the vouchers she received for the Same to the Auditors" accompanied this petition (Affidavit of "Janet Spurgin," 25 Nov. 1791, GASR, Dec. 1791–Jan. 1792, Nc-Ar).

22. The 1790 federal census lists Jean Spurgin as the head of a Rowan County household composed of herself, three white males, and two other white females. The William Spurgin who appears in the census as the head of a different Rowan County household was perhaps an adult son of Jane and William, as Jane claimed to be supporting only six of her eight children by 1791 (*Heads of Families . . . in the Year 1790: N.C.*, 174). The 1800 census lists no Spurgins in North Carolina, suggesting that the family left the state some time during the 1790s.

compensation for her services to the state, but the assembly rejected her petition.[23]

The Petition of Mary Moore Humbly Sheweth

That whereas your petitioner hath during the late War performed many signal Services well known to many of the members of this assembly to the Cause of the United States of America in Saving many Hundred thousand pounds at Gates's Def[ea]t hitherto has had no manner of Compensation for the Same.

Your petitioner most humbly requests that your honourable Body may be pleased to take her case into Consideration and order such Redress may be made to her Grievance as in your wisdom may be deemed adequate to her said Services and your Petitioner as in Duty bound will ever pray &c.

(DS, Nc-Ar)

DOCUMENT 11

Ann Timothy

The war years had been difficult for Peter and Ann Donovan Timothy (c.1727–92), both of whom were ardent Whigs. The British captured Peter in 1780 and forced his wife and children to flee Charleston. The family reunited in Philadelphia in 1781, but Peter and two daughters died at sea the following year. Ann Timothy returned to Charleston, where she resumed the family printing business and, beginning in 1785, served as state printer. As this petition of 16 January 1790 suggests, Timothy found it difficult to collect her public debts. The legislature did not act on this petition, though it satisfied her accounts partially in subsequent sessions.[24]

---

23. Petitions of Mary Moore [2], 29 Dec. 1786, GASR, Nov. 1786–Jan. 1787, Nc-Ar. On women who traveled with the Continental Army, most often as nurses, cooks, and laundresses, see Holly A. Mayer, *Belonging to the Army: Camp Followers and Community during the American Revolution* (Columbia: University of South Carolina Press, 1996), chap. 4; Kerber, *Women of the Republic,* 55–60.

24. *NAW,* 3:465; Hennig Cohen, *The South Carolina Gazette, 1732–1775* (Columbia: University of South Carolina Press, 1953), 244–47; Petitions of Ann Timothy,

The humble Petition of Ann Timothy, Printer to the State—Sheweth
That by a particular Resolve passed by both Branches of the Legislature at the last Session, Certificates were granted to your petitioner for the amount of the demand she had at that time against the State,[25] which were to have been received in payment of all duties & taxes after being countersigned by the Treasurers, that she applied to the Treasurers to countersign the said Certificates, but they refused to do so altho they were previously signed by the Honorable the President of the Senate & the Honorable the Speaker of the House of Representatives, that after such application she advertised the said Certificates for sale & disposed of some of them, but when they were tendered by the purchasers in payment of duties, the Treasurers absolutely and positively refused to receive them—that in consequence of this, application was made to his Excellency the Governor and Council, who were unanimously of the opinion, that the said Certificates ought to be received at the Treasury and passed a Resolve to that effect & when the same was sent to the Treasurers your petitioner was informed that they would then receive the said Certificates, upon which she endeavoured to dispose of the rest of them, but was not able to sell more than one half of the amount due her by the State, and Such as she did get rid of she was obliged to sell at a discount of twelve and one half per Cent. Your petitioner assures your Honorable House that the sum allowed for her services is very small in comparison to the work done annually for the Public & would not reimburse her for the expence she is at on account of the State, even if it were punctually paid to her—that she is only allowed the wages of one journeyman & her public Taxes, altho' she declares that one journeyman alone would not have been able to do all the work done for the Public this year—& thus has she received no compensation for her own services or the use of her press and tipes and she has frequently been obliged to displease her customers & leave out their advertisements for which she would have received cash, in order to make room for inserting the public business, and by reference to the State Gazette[26] sent to the Clerk of this Honorable

---

12 Feb. 1785, 21 Jan. 1788, 30 Oct. 1788, 21 Feb. 1789, 18 Jan. 1791, 3 Dec. 1791, LP, Sc-Ar; *S.C. House Journals, 1789–1790*, 372n; *S.C. House Journals, 1791*, 129, 402; *S.C. House Journals, 1792–1794*, 152.

25. On 7 March 1789, the legislature passed such a resolution in response to Timothy's petition (*House Journals, 1789–1790*, 175, 214–15, 237).

26. The *State Gazette of South Carolina* was the Charleston newspaper Timothy published.

House it will appear that generally a large proportion & sometimes one whole side of it has been taken up by publications for the State, besides which she has had to furnish the amount of 8 or 10,000 Blanks[27] for the different public Offices.

Your Petitioner begs leave to remind your Honourable House of a Resolution passed in March 1785 whereby she was appointed State printer in consequence of & as a reward for the services of her late Husband,[28] this she received with gratitude & assures your Honourable House that her patriotism would induce her to serve the public for no other reward than the satisfaction she would enjoy in the reflection of her having served her country (the only recompense her predecessor received) would it be in any degree consistent with her circumstances. She wishes for no compensation for the services of her Husband—she wishes to be rewarded merely for her own, at the same time leaving it to your Honorable House to determine whether your good intentions in granting her the State Office, have been answered, when she was called on in the years 1786, 1787 & 1788 to contend with men, who wished to deprive her of that Office; by which means she was reduced to the necessity either of working for a very trifling consideration, or of giving up the office of State Printer, which would have been still more mortifying, whereas she had conceived on her appointment that she was to hold that office during her life. As you petitioner still has an orphan family to provide for,[29] she humbly hopes that her situation will be taken into serious consideration & that some provision may be made in order to discharge the Debt due to her by the State. Your petitioner with deference conceives that the request she is now about to make, will appear no more than just and reasonable & doubts not but every member of your Honorable House possesses such sentiments of Justice, Equity & Humanity as will induce

---

27. Unused paper.

28. In response to Ann Timothy's petition of 9 February 1785, on 11 March the legislature adopted a joint resolution that named her state printer "in Consequence of the Services rendered to [the State] by her late Husband" (*S.C. House Journals, 1785–1786*, 81, 179, 202, 217).

29. The Timothys had at least seven children who survived infancy, of whom four were still living by 1790. Although they were grown, Timothy's offspring included an invalid son and an unmarried daughter, both of whom were her dependents (Will of Peter Timothy, 22 Apr. 1780, Charleston County Will Book, 1783–86, typescript, 20:95–96, Sc-Ar; Will of Ann Timothy, 5 May 1790, Charleston County Will Book, 1786–93, typescript, 24:1138–43, Sc-Ar; *NAW*, 3:465).

him to determine in his own mind that this request is so, which is, that she may be allowed Interest on her different accounts from the time they became due & may be reimbursed for the loss she has sustained by the sale of her Certificates, which she avers she disposed of to the best possible advantage.

Your petitioner informs your Honorable House that it will not be possible for her to remove to Columbia,[30] but at the same time assures you, that any service which is in her power to render the State, by Printing for the Public in Charleston, shall be most cheerfully done as far as can be accomplished by her exertions, and that she will at all times hold herself in readiness to execute your Command.

Your petitioner will ever pray.

(ADS, Sc-Ar)

DOCUMENT 12

Ann Elizabeth Saylor

> *David Saylor, a prosperous Charleston cooper, initially supported the Revolution but then changed sides in order to continue his business under the restored British government. In 1782, the state confiscated his property, but in 1783 he petitioned successfully to reclaim his estate subject to the standard amercement of 12 percent. David Saylor died a few years later. This petition, dated 13 December 1791, was the first of two unsuccessful attempts on the part of his widow, Ann Elizabeth Saylor, to exempt his estate from the punitive amercement.*[31]

The humble Petition of Ann Elizabeth Saylor Sheweth

That your Petitioner is the Widow of the late David Saylor of Charleston Cooper deceased whose Estate is under an Amercement of

---

30. South Carolina moved its capital to Columbia in 1790, though Timothy remained in Charleston and continued to serve as state printer until her death in 1792.

31. Walsh, *Charleston's Sons of Liberty*, 5, 24, 122n; Coker, "Artisan Loyalists of Charleston," 93; *S.C. House Journals, 1783–1784*, 26–27, 552; Petition of Ann Elizabeth Saylor, 3 Dec. 1792, LP, Sc-Ar; *S.C. House Journals, 1792–1794*, 87.

12 p[e]rc[en]t. which had your Petitioners Husband have lived He by his well known diligence and industry might have been able to have paid and still have procured a comfortable living for his family.

But in April 1791 Your Petitioners Husband after a very severe and expensive illness died and left her in a very infirm state of health with three small Children the youngest not seven weeks old at the time of its fathers decease, his property barely sufficient for their maintenance and education and that under the aforesaid amercement which if your Petitioner should be compelled to pay must involve herself and three Children (to whom no crime can be alleged) into very great difficulty and distress.

Your Petitioner therefore relying on the well known clemency of your honorable house humbly prays that her unfortunate situation may be taken into your serious consideration & that you will be pleased to grant her such relief as you in your wisdom may think proper—And in Duty bound your Petitioner will ever pray.

(DS, Sc-Ar)

DOCUMENT 13
Hannah Ash and Margaret Ash

This petition, submitted on 9 December 1796, was the second of four that Hannah Deveaux Ash (1761–1822) and Margaret Deveaux Ash presented to the assembly in an attempt to obtain compensation for the confiscated estate of their Tory father. Although the women emphasized their own political innocence and the patriotism of their husbands, the assembly did not act on their petition. The sisters persisted in petitioning, without success, as late as 1810.[32]

32. Petitions of Hannah Ash and Margaret Ash, 21 Nov. 1795, 9 Dec. 1796, 4 Dec. 1804, 30 Nov. 1810, LP, Sc-Ar. The 1795 petition is reproduced in chap. 2, above.

The Petition of Hannah Ash, Relict of Samuel Ash deceased, and Margaret Ash, Relict of the late John Ash junr. in behalf of themselves and Sisters—Respectfully Sheweth

That their Father's Estate, after having been Confiscated, was by an Act of the General Assembly, past in the year 1784, restored to him, subject to the payment of an amercement of 12 per Centum.[33] That the said Estate having been previously disposed of by the Commissioners of Confiscated Estates for Bonds payable in Specie, the purchasers were by a law past two years afterwards permitted to discharge the same in the Indents of this State,[34] which being greatly depreciated at that time, their Father was induced to let them remain in the Treasury of this State—and having acquired a legal and just right to them under a positive law of the state aforesaid, He then gave them to his four Daughters who are married to Citizens of this State,[35] as a portion, to be equally divided among them. That some time afterwards, as late as the year 1794 the Legislature past a Resolution that the Treasurers should only pay unto the Creditors of this State, one pound Specie for five pounds Indents[36]—having previously exonerated such purchasers of Confiscated property, as had not before that time settled for the same, from four fifths of their debts. But your Petitioners humbly conceive that altho' the Legislature had an undoubted right to compromise with their Debtors, as they thought fit, yet, with all due submission and difference for the laws of their Country, they are induced to believe that they could not be Constitutionally divested of their property, which they had a just and legal Title to, under the afore-

---

33. In February 1784, the assembly released the estate of Andrew Deveaux in response to the petition of his son John (*S.C. House Journals, 1783–1784*, 81, 438).

34. "An Act to amend the Confiscation Act," 1786, *S.C. Statutes*, 4:756–57.

35. Hannah Deveaux and Margaret Deveaux were the widows of Samuel Ash and John Ash, respectively, both of whom were Whigs. The first husband of Catherine Deveaux (1759–1829) was a Tory, Nicholas Lechmere, but he died in 1782, and Catherine married another John Ash in 1785. Mary Deveaux (d. 1845) married William Brisbane, who served in the American army. All four sisters lived in South Carolina (Stephen B. Barnwell, *The Story of an American Family* [Marquette: n.p., 1969], 54).

36. This May 1794 resolution was part of a general attempt to fund and retire the state debt (*S.C. House Journals, 1792–1794*, 554; "An Act to make such provision for the Debt of the State of South Carolina," 1794, *S.C. Statutes*, 5:239–40).

said Law now of force, by virtue to any subsequent Resolution to the Contrary.

Your Petitioners, however, with pleasure appeal to the justice of your Honorable House for redress, and flatter themselves that the same impartial justice will be extended to the Widows and Orphans of American Citizens as has already been done in the case of a young Gentleman whose wharf was appraised and paid for, agreeably to the decision of a former Legislature.

Your Petitioners beg leave farther to represent to your Hon[ora]ble House, that by a Resolution past by the Legislature at their last Session Commissioners were appointed by His Excellency the Governor,[37] for the purpose of appraising the property formerly their Father's, in order that the present Legislature might take the same into consideration, and devise some mode of doing justice to their claims—they therefore beg leave to mention, that they are willing to accept of, either the amount agreeably to the first sale in Specie, or the valuation of the Indents as afterwards commuted, or, agreeably to the valuation of the property by the Commissioners appointed by the Governor, and to be provided for either in the funds of this State, or in any other way which your Hon[ora]ble House shall think fit.

And they as in duty bound will ever pray &ca &ca.

(DS, Sc-Ar)

DOCUMENT 14

Elizabeth Beard

> *The petitioner was the widow of a Charleston tinsmith who initially supported the Revolution but who, in 1780, capitulated to the restored British government. Robert Beard described himself as a committed loyalist when he sought remuneration from British officials after the war, but he recovered his property in South Carolina by claiming that he switched sides only to avoid subjecting his family to severe economic hardship. Elizabeth Beard reiterated the*

---

37. There is no evidence that the assembly passed such a resolution nor that Governor Arnoldus Vander Horst appointed commissioners specifically to handle the De-

latter story on 16 November 1797, when she unsuccessfully sought relief from the amercement that she continued to pay as a result of Robert's opportunism.[38]

The Petition of Elizabeth Beard, Widow of Robert Beard, late of Charleston, deceased; Sheweth,

That when the British Army took possession of Charleston, her late husband was unfortunately situated; having then to provide for an aged Mother in Europe, as well as an infirm and helpless Mother in Law[39] and her Family, exclusive of his own Family. Under the pressure of these Circumstances, he was reduced to the Alternative, either of abandoning all these or of taking Protection under the British Government. The latter was to him the most eligible, as it enabled him to provide for their immediate Necessities. He therefore yeilded to the Claims of Consanguinity and of domestic Affection. But your Petitioner, while candidly confessing his political Errors, solemnly avers that he never directly or indirectly took the least active part under the british Administration; but always studied to be quiet, and peaceably pursued his own Business.

That the deceased was unfortunately included among the Enemies of his Country and his Estate was consequently confiscated; but on his return to this place the Legislature in their Clemency placed him on the Amercement List.[40] That there now appears due to the State, on

---

veaux estate. A resolution of 19 December 1795, however, charged the state commissioner of public accounts to account for all outstanding indents. William Brisbane, son-in-law of Andrew Deveaux, submitted the family's claim for some £3,400 principle plus roughly £2,900 in interest, but he received a certificate for only £852.1.9 plus interest on 8 September 1796 (Records of the General Assembly: Governor's Messages, microfilm, Sc-Ar).

38. Walsh, *Charleston's Sons of Liberty*, 94, 122n; Coker, "Artisan Loyalists of Charleston," 93–94; Petition of Robert Beard, 29 Jan. 1784, LP, Sc-Ar; *S.C. House Journals, 1783–1784*, 552.

39. Elizabeth Colles was the petitioner's mother and the mother-in-law of Robert Beard. Colles petitioned the assembly on Beard's behalf in 1783, seeking his repatriation and the return of his confiscated estate (Petition of Elizabeth Colles, 25 Jan. 1783, LP, Sc-Ar).

40. Robert Beard twice petitioned to have the punitive amercement removed from his estate (*S.C. House Journals, 1787–1788*, 352–53; *S.C. House Journals, 1791*, 136).

the Amercement, the following Sums, namely, Thirty One Pounds ten Shillings in Specie, Thirty one Pounds ten Shillings in Special Indents and Three hundred and Seventy Eight Pounds fourteen Shillings and four pence in Principal Indents, (with Interest) on which Judgement has been obtained and Execution issued.

Your Petitioner craves the Indulgence of your honorable House, while she represents, that the Estate of her late husband is very considerably involved in Debt; in so much so that she is apprehensive there will be but very little left to enable her to support herself and an helpless Sister; which Little is the only Source from whence she can hope for a Maintenance.

Impressed with the fullest Confidence in the Candor and Humanity of her fellow Citizens, who compose your honorable Body, she ventures to solicit an exemption from the remaining Penalties incurred by the Political Errors of her late Husband. The weight of which Penalty will now fall severely on her, in her present helpless situation. She therefore casts herself on the Mercy of the Legislature. Their Compassion and Clemency on this Occasion, will be ever gratefully acknowledged by their Petitioner.

(DS, Sc-Ar)

Chapter 5

THE LIMITS OF REVOLUTION

The American Revolution unleashed, in one historian's words, "a contagion of liberty" that inspired people to question and in some cases to remedy injustice. American revolutionaries in the southern states and elsewhere thus made voting and officeholding accessible to more white men, abolished the colonial religious establishments, and made taxation more progressive and legislative representation more equitable.[1] Some Americans, including a few southerners, questioned the propriety of slavery in a republic based on liberty. Others tentatively reconsidered the laws pertaining to marriage and property which victimized many women.[2]

---

1. The metaphor is from Bernard Bailyn, *The Ideological Origins of the American Revolution* (Cambridge, Mass.: Harvard University Press, 1967), 230–32. On political reform in the southern states during and after the Revolution, see John E. Selby, *The Revolution in Virginia, 1775–1783* (Williamsburg, Va.: Colonial Williamsburg, 1988), chaps. 3, 6, 12; Delbert Harold Gilpatrick, *Jeffersonian Democracy in North Carolina* (New York: Columbia University Press, 1931), 23–30; Nadelhaft, *Disorders of War,* chaps. 6–7; Rachel N. Klein, *Unification of a Slave State: The Rise of the Planter Class in the South Carolina Backcountry, 1760–1808* (Chapel Hill: University of North Carolina Press, 1990), 118–48, 257–66; George R. Lamplugh, *Politics on the Periphery: Factions and Parties in Georgia, 1783–1806* (Newark: University of Delaware Press, 1986), 18–23, 88–91.

2. David Brion Davis, *The Problem of Slavery in the Age of Revolution, 1770–1823* (Ithaca, N.Y.: Cornell University Press, 1975), 169–84, 196–212. The antislavery sentiment of revolutionary southerners should not be overstated. See Frederika Teute Schmidt and Barbara Ripel Wilhelm, "Early Proslavery Petitions in Virginia," *WMQ,* 3d ser., 30 (1973): 133–46.

Significant public criticisms of the laws of marriage and property as they pertained to women included "A Tract on the Unreasonableness of the Laws of England . . . ," *Columbian Magazine,* 2 (1788): 22–24, 189; "Woman's Hard Fate," *American Museum* 6 (1789): 417–18; "The Propriety of Meliorating the Condition of Women in

The revolutionary era saw modest changes in the laws and customs that governed slavery, divorce, and women's property rights, but this reformist impulse stopped far short of eradicating the inequalities of race and gender which undermined the autonomy of women and African Americans. Revolutionary ideology rejected patriarchy as the basis of political and social relations among white men who now, in theory at least, came together as cosigners of a "fraternal social contract" to establish political institutions and to select the men who ran them. Yet patriarchy, however discredited as a political ideal, continued to influence relations between husband and wife, father and children, and master and slave in postrevolutionary America. In the southern states especially, many of the same men who repudiated political patriarchy in the form of kingship still accepted it as an entirely appropriate model for governance within their households.[3]

The documents in this chapter include petitions from slaves and free blacks as well as from white women seeking divorces, separate estates, or other exemptions from laws and customs that often undermined their interests and complicated their lives. Most of these petitions express the concerns of members of previously quiescent social groups and have no colonial precedents. The sudden appearance of such petitioners suggests that the libertarian ideals of the Revolution inspired some politically marginal southerners to state their grievances publicly and to expect a fair hearing from their republican governors. The frequent failure of their petitions, however, reveals the limited impact of those ideals on the entrenched inequalities of race and gender in postrevolutionary America.

Civilized Societies, Considered," ibid. 9 (1791): 248–49; "A Hint," ibid. 7 (1790): 208; Charles Brockden Brown, *Alcuin; A Dialogue* (New York: T. and J. Swords, 1798).

3. Carole Pateman, "The Fraternal Social Contract," in Pateman, *The Disorder of Women* (London: Polity Press, 1989), 33–45. On the southern states, in which scholars characterize the dominance of white men as "patriarchal" or "paternalistic," see Victoria E. Bynum, *Unruly Women: The Politics of Social and Sexual Control in the Old South* (Chapel Hill: University of North Carolina Press, 1992), chaps. 3–4; Elizabeth Fox-Genovese, *Within the Plantation Household: Black and White Women of the Old South* (Chapel Hill: University of North Carolina Press, 1988), esp. 60–66; Bertram Wyatt-Brown, *Southern Honor: Ethics and Behavior in the Old South* (New York: Oxford University Press, 1982), esp. chaps. 10–11; Stephanie McCurry, "The Two Faces of Republicanism: Gender and Proslavery Politics in Antebellum South Carolina," *JAH* 78 (1992): 1245–64.

The Revolution brought limited changes in the laws of marriage, divorce, and property which circumscribed the rights and activities of most women in eighteenth-century America. Although coverture remained in force in every state, courts and legislatures were increasingly amenable to granting separate estates to individual petitioners. Most states made divorce available to their inhabitants for the first time, though in practice it remained difficult and costly to dissolve unhappy marriages.

The case of Sarah Coakley Hawley demonstrates how coverture, coupled with the absence of legal divorce, could jeopardize the welfare of women and their families in postrevolutionary America. In 1780, Sarah married Benjamin Coakley on the Caribbean island of St. Martin, where she resided with him for six years before they mutually agreed to terminate their marriage. With the advice of a lawyer, the couple concluded a formal separation agreement by which Benjamin gave Sarah his bond for five thousand pounds as a pledge of his "never thereafter intermeddling with or disturbing [Sarah] either on her person or her property." In effect, by agreeing to dissolve his union with Sarah, Benjamin also acknowledged that she was no longer subject to his coverture. Sarah used her new freedom to migrate to North Carolina, where she married William Hawley in 1788. The Hawleys had several children, and their marriage lasted until William died of yellow fever in 1799. Although he died intestate, Hawley left behind "considerable property both real and personal, the hard earnings of . . . William and of [Sarah]," which they believed "would have decently supported them in their decline of life" and provided for their children. As a wife, Sarah contributed the fruits of her labor to her husband's estate, expecting him to furnish her with a just maintenance if he predeceased her.[4]

William Hawley died intestate, and the ensuing controversy surrounding his estate and Sarah's legal status shows how the laws and customs governing marriage and property, despite their supposedly protective intent, could be disproportionately injurious to women and minors. When Sarah attempted to claim William's estate for herself and her children, she learned that North Carolina law did not recognize the dissolution of her first marriage, which, in turn, nullified her subsequent union with Hawley. Although neither Benjamin Coakley nor the de-

---

4. Petition of Sarah Coakley [Hawley], Nov. 1800, GASR, Nov.–Dec. 1800, Nc-Ar.

ceased William Hawley suffered as a result of the state's ruling, its consequences were disastrous for Sarah and her children. By insisting that
Sarah and Benjamin's marriage remained intact, the state of North Carolina invalidated his renunciation of any claims to property she later acquired, though coverture obviously prevented Sarah from taking any of
Benjamin's property while he lived and gave her only her dower rights
after his death. Even more important, Sarah lost her interest in Hawley's
estate—part of which she herself earned—and her children by him became bastards who had no legal right to inherit the property their parents
accumulated. If Benjamin Coakley had remarried, his second wife and
her children would have suffered a similar fate.

   Sarah Coakley Hawley tried to make the best of a horrid situation.
Having learned that North Carolina authorities would recognize neither
the validity of the "separation contract" between herself and Benjamin
Coakley nor of her subsequent marriage to William Hawley, Sarah resigned herself to the loss of the latter's estate. Looking to the future, she
attempted instead to shield herself and her children by Hawley from possible demands on the part of her first husband. Petitioning the legislature
for a separate estate in 1800, she described herself as "destitute and almost helpless, [having] no resource but her own industry and exertions"
by which to support her family. Her industry, however, was "damped by
the apprehension lest the little she may hereafter acquire be wrested
from her and from those for whom she toils by . . . Benjamin or by his
representatives." Conceding that the petitioner faced a "peculiar hard
situation," the legislature granted Sarah's petition. While she lost the economic fruits of a seemingly happy and prosperous eleven-year marriage,
as well as the prospect of remarrying while Benjamin lived, she at least
secured the right to acquire property and to use it as she saw fit.[5]

   Although North Carolina authorities did not regard Sarah's marriage
to Benjamin as dissolved by virtue of their separation agreement, Americans in that state and elsewhere increasingly sought and received legal
divorces in the postrevolutionary decades. As the case of Sarah Coakley
Hawley suggests, women were the chief beneficiaries of the liberalization
of divorce law in the postrevolutionary decades. If Sarah and Benjamin

   5. Ibid.; Committee report on the petition of Sarah Coakley [Hawley], 29 Nov.
1800, ibid.

had divorced, their separation would have been a matter of public record and therefore legally unassailable. In addition, bad marriages usually hurt wives more than husbands, as the latter were more likely to abandon or abuse their spouses or to commit adultery. In most states, women were more likely than men to seek civil divorces, and, though the states remained reluctant to compromise the authority of white men over their dependents, the existence of divorce as a legal option offered women at least the possibility of escape from severely abusive husbands.[6]

Divorce laws were most liberal in New England, where civil divorce had been available during the colonial period, and in Pennsylvania, where lawmakers included the liberty to dissolve an unsatisfactory marriage among the reforms of the revolutionary era. Elsewhere state legislatures or courts initially considered individual divorces on a case-by-case basis, though they gradually enacted general divorce statutes. By 1800, most northern states had such laws, and the southern states gradually followed suit in the ensuing decades. Tennessee passed the first southern divorce law in 1799, with Georgia following two years later. North Carolina enacted its first divorce legislation in 1814, and Virginia did so in 1827. Only South Carolina remained obdurate. With the exception of a brief period during Reconstruction, when a short-lived divorce law was in force, civil divorce was not available to South Carolinians until the twentieth century.[7]

Procedures for seeking divorces varied from state to state. In the nineteenth century, each state gradually transferred jurisdiction over divorce from the legislatures to the courts, though most state legislatures continued to pass private divorce bills even after the statutes allowed the courts to hear divorce cases and formally dissolve marriages. In North

---

6. Jane Turner Censer, "'Smiling through Her Tears': Ante-Bellum Southern Women and Divorce," *American Journal of Legal History* 25 (1981): 24–47; Bynum, *Unruly Women*, 72–77; Linda K. Kerber, *Women of the Republic: Intellect and Ideology in Revolutionary America* (Chapel Hill: University of North Carolina Press, 1980), 162–63, 179–84; Nancy F. Cott, "Divorce and the Changing Status of Women in Eighteenth-Century Massachusetts," *WMQ*, 3d ser., 33 (1976): 594–96, 605–6. See also Frank L. Dewey, "Thomas Jefferson's Notes on Divorce," ibid., 39 (1982): 219.

7. Kerber, *Women of the Republic*, 174–81; Cott, "Divorce and the Changing Status of Women," 586–92; Censer, "'Smiling through Her Tears,'" 24–26.

Carolina, for example, the legislature received and resolved all divorce petitions before 1814, when the superior courts were empowered to decide divorce cases subject to ratification by the state assembly. Many North Carolina petitioners continued to submit their cases to the legislature directly, however, until a new divorce law gave the judiciary sole jurisdiction in 1835. In Virginia, the state assembly received all divorce petitions and forwarded to the courts only those they deemed worthy of further consideration. If the court granted the divorce, the legislature then passed a bill to dissolve the marriage. Virginia's courts played an increasingly large role in adjudicating divorce cases, but legislative divorce nevertheless predominated in that state until constitutionally prohibited in 1850.[8]

The earliest attempts of southerners formally to escape unhappy marriages occurred in the eighteenth century's closing decades, when petitioners may have pursued divorce as a seemingly logical outgrowth of the Revolution's libertarian ideology. In 1779, Alexander Dickson of North Carolina became the first petitioner to seek a divorce from a southern state legislature. The fact that his petition failed did not deter four wives, four husbands, and six couples from filing similar petitions—all but one of which the North Carolina assembly rejected—between 1780 and 1800. Susannah Wersley filed Virginia's first divorce petition in 1786, and in the next fourteen years seven women besides her, along with twelve men and two couples, sought divorces in that state without success, as did two South Carolinians, who petitioned their legislature in 1788 and 1791, respectively.[9] Fragmentary evidence suggests that the inhabitants of Georgia, whose legislative records are not extant for most of

---

8. Guion Griffis Johnson, *Ante-Bellum North Carolina: A Social History* (Chapel Hill: University of North Carolina Press, 1937), 218–19; Glenda Riley, "Legislative Divorce in Virginia, 1803–1850," *JER* 11 (1991): 51–52; Censer, "'Smiling through Her Tears,'" 47.

9. Petition of Alexander Dickson, 22 Oct. 1779, *N.C. Recs.*, 13:292. In 1766, Solomon Ewell had submitted an unsuccessful petition for divorce to North Carolina's colonial legislature (ibid., 7:352). For other early attempts to obtain divorces, see Petition of Susannah Wersley, 20 Nov. 1786, LP, Hanover Co., Vi-Ar; Petition of Fielding Woodruff, 24 Jan. 1788, LP, Sc-Ar; Petition of John Christian Smith, 19 Jan. 1791, ibid. The Virginia legislature sent three of these twenty-two cases to the courts for further consideration, but apparently none of the petitioners won their cases, as the legislature did not enact the state's first "act of divorce" until 1803.

this period, also began to seek divorces during the postrevolutionary years. In January 1796, a legislative committee noted "the reluctance with which former legislatures have acted on this business," and from 1796 to 1800—years for which some records have survived—the Georgia assembly received at least eleven divorce petitions.[10]

In every state except South Carolina, the numbers of divorce petitions rose dramatically as the nineteenth century progressed, though authorities were more accommodating in some states than in others, and in every state personal connections or a changing political climate might determine the fate of one's request. Legislators in North Carolina, generally regarded as the most liberal of the seaboard southern states on the issue of divorce, brusquely asserted, in response to the 1792 petition of an abandoned wife, that, "should the Legislature enter into the business of granting divorces, it would be productive of many dangerous and evil consequences." Yet six years later, when Robin Braswell of Nash County petitioned to have his marriage dissolved apparently on the grounds of simple incompatibility, the legislators responded by passing a bill that granted the first civil divorce in North Carolina's history.[11] Georgia's legislature granted no divorces before 1796, but when a newly elected assembly convened in January of that year it granted all but one of seven divorce petitions submitted. The members of the legislative committee charged with considering divorce petitions boldly declared that because "it was never the intention of the great Creator that man and wife should

---

10. None of the Georgia petitions are extant, but the contents of some can be deduced from the legislative record and, when successful, from the resulting statutes. See Journals of the Georgia House of Representatives, Jan. 1796–Feb. 1797, microfilm, 102, 213, 267, 326, Ga-Ar; Horatio Marbury and William H. Crawford, comps., *Digest of the Laws of the State of Georgia, 1775–1800* (Savannah: Seymour, Woolhopter and Stebbins, 1802), 192–98.

11. Committee report on the petition of Teresa Butler, 29 Jan. 1791, GASR, Dec. 1791–Jan. 1792, Nc-Ar; "An Act to carry into effect the petition of Robin Braswell of Nash County, by granting him a divorce from his wife Calley," North Carolina sessions laws, microfiche, 1798, chap. 106. Braswell's petition is not extant. In 1798, a legislative committee also reported favorably on the divorce petition of Jane and Sydney Witherow, but the assembly did not act on this report (Committee report on the petition of Jane and Sydney Witherow, 1798, GASR, Nov.–Dec. 1798, Nc-Ar). On the relative liberality of North Carolina's antebellum divorce policies, see Bynum, *Unruly Women*, 63–64.

be bound together for the sole purpose of making each other miserable" worthy petitions "ought to be granted."[12]

Acceptable grounds for divorce were unclear before the enactment of general statutes. In the absence of explicitly defined legal grounds for divorce, men occasionally invoked the ideals of the Revolution when they sought to dissolve unhappy marriages. In the early 1770s, when lawyer Thomas Jefferson prepared to argue before the House of Burgesses in support of what would have been Virginia's first legislative divorce, he planned to base his client's claim to the "liberty of divorce" on a contractual theory that portrayed the origins of a marriage as analogous to those of civil government. In 1791, in language reminiscent of the Declaration of Independence, a South Carolina man employed this same analogy. "Since Marriage was instituted for the purpose of promoting the happiness of individuals and the good of society," declared John Christian Smith, "when it becomes impossible for [husband and wife] to remain longer united when mutual wretchedness must be the consequence of continuing their connection," that marriage "should be dissolved and . . . the parties should be left free to form such other domestic connections as may contribute to their felicity."[13]

Like all South Carolina divorce petitions before Reconstruction, Smith's failed, not the least because of the fatal flaw in his contractual analogy. American revolutionaries in South Carolina and elsewhere, indeed, rejected the metaphorical familial bonds that tied "daughter" America to a tyrannous "father" king and a corrupt "mother country," but severing the bonds between parents and children was not analogous to cutting those between marriage partners within a patriarchal family.[14] In revolutionary America, the liberalization of divorce laws proceeded more as a consequence of the sentimentalization of marriage and woman-

---

12. Committee report on the petition of Benjamin and Elizabeth Butler, 1796, in Journals of the Georgia House of Representatives, Jan. 1796–Feb. 1797, microfilm, 213. The upper house subsequently rejected three of seven divorce petitions the assembly granted during this session.

13. Petition of John Christian Smith, 19 Jan. 1791, LP, Sc-Ar; Dewey, "Jefferson's Notes on Divorce," 219. Because his client died, Jefferson never presented his case to the legislature.

14. Jay Fliegelman, Prodigals and Pilgrims: The American Revolution against Patriarchal Authority (Cambridge: Cambridge University Press, 1982), esp. chap. 4; Pateman, "Fraternal Social Contract."

hood than as an outgrowth of libertarian ideology. In the southern states, where patriarchal values remained strongest, governments were most reluctant to grant divorces. They appear to have done so most often, however, to defend men's honor or protect women's virtue rather than to provide petitioners with the liberty of pursuing their conjugal happiness.[15]

Petitioners sought divorces either to alleviate conjugal misery or to gain legal sanction for an existing separation. One North Carolina couple, who petitioned jointly in 1787, asserted that their parents forced them into a marriage that became "the Source of all their Miseries and Misfortunes." They separated after three years of living together in "mutual disgust and inveterate hatred" but waited an additional twelve years before seeking a divorce so that they might remarry and thus be spared the "Solitude and other inconveniences of a single Life" (Doc. 1). John and Elizabeth Kemp Nelson married in 1778 but found that "after many attempts and tryals . . . [they] lost all manner of Affection for each other." Concluding that "it is not possible they ever can live together as Man & Wife," they separated, discussed a division of their "little property," and "some time" later requested to "be divorced and seperated by Law."[16] James and Comfort Tomlinson also were already living apart when they petitioned for divorce in 1793. Married in 1785, the Tomlinsons lived together for two years, when James left his wife to "take up with a single woman." The two lived separately for six years before filing a joint petition requesting the dissolution of their ill-fated marriage (Doc. 8).

Wives and husbands who petitioned for divorce alone, rather than jointly, not surprisingly portrayed themselves as injured parties who deserved the assembly's sympathy and support. When women submitted divorce petitions, the seduction motif that was so popular in contemporary fiction often shaped their narratives.[17] Susannah Wersley informed the

---

15. Censer, "'Smiling through Her Tears,'" 37–43; Wyatt-Brown, *Southern Honor*, 283–91. The latter overstates the extent to which men's interests dictated divorce decisions. The responsibility of men to protect white women, at least theoretically, was an important aspect of southern patriarchy. See Fox-Genovese, *Within the Plantation Household*, 199–200, 207–11.

16. Petition of John Nelson and Elizabeth Kemp Nelson, 27 Nov. 1786, GASR, Nov. 1786–Jan. 1787, Nc-Ar.

17. Jan Lewis, "The Republican Wife: Virtue and Seduction in the Early Republic," *WMQ*, 3d ser., 44 (1987): 716–20; Cathy N. Davidson, *Revolution and the Word:*

Virginia legislature that she was the innocent victim of a man who "professed himself an officer of the North Carolina line." The pair married in 1781, but John Wersley abandoned his bride less than a month after their wedding. Susannah unsuccessfully petitioned for divorce five years later on the grounds that John had been "activated by a principle of convenience and deception alone in Marr[y]ing" her.[18] North Carolinian Teresa Butler likewise portrayed herself as an innocent seduced by a man who married her and made her pregnant—the order of these events is uncertain—despite the fact that he had at least one other living wife. Henry Butler deserted Teresa and their infant daughter within five months of their nuptials (Doc. 5). Rebekah Davidson also unwittingly married a man who turned out to be a bigamist as well as the perpetrator of other unspecified "felonious actions." In 1800, she entreated the North Carolina assembly to afford her the chance "to repair her broken fortune as far as the Smiles of Heaven, and her own prudence will admit of" (Doc. 15).

When divorce petitions failed, as they frequently did, unhappy couples resorted to other means to sever their ties to each other. Couples who had little property to divide or protect may have dissolved their marriages without any formal proceedings whatsoever. Some estranged couples, such as Thomas Smith and Sally Dobson, drew up their own "articles of separation" even before they sought a formal divorce, while others entered into separation agreements after the assembly rejected their petitions.[19] In 1800, the North Carolina assembly rejected the divorce petition of John and Rebekah Farrow, but three years later the couple entered into a contract, endorsed by two witnesses, by which they agreed to "Desolve the Marrage Contract once made between us . . . that Either of us may and Shall have Free and undenied Liberty to Live Single or to Entermarry again with any other person without any manner of hin-

---

The Rise of the Novel in America (New York: Oxford University Press, 1986), esp. 45–47, 101–12, 129–50.

Occasionally, men employed an inverted version of the conventional scenario, portraying themselves as seduced and then cuckolded by wicked women. See, for instance, Petition of John and Rebekah Farrow, 25 Sept. 1799, GASR, Nov.–Dec. 1800, Nc-Ar.

18. Petition of Susannah Wersley, 20 Nov. 1786, LP, Hanover Co., Vi-Ar.

19. Petition of Thomas Smith and Sally Dobson, 5 Nov. 1795, GASR, Nov.–Dec. 1795, Nc-Ar.

drance or denial of the adverce party . . . and . . . [that] all children hereafter Begotten by Either of us shall not in any wise be chargeable" to the
other.[20] As the case of Sarah Coakley Hawley demonstrates, the viability
of such agreements was less certain than that of an outright divorce, but
they provided the best available option to those whose divorce petitions
failed.

Separation agreements were impossible without the concurrence of
both spouses, but women who unsuccessfully sought to dissolve their
marriages on their own sometimes found other formal means to distance
themselves from unsavory husbands. Teresa Butler, an abandoned wife
whose divorce petition the assembly rejected in 1791, petitioned again
the following year to divest herself of the surname of her bigamist husband (Doc. 6). More commonly, abandoned or abused wives sought economic emancipation from their spouses, either after failing to obtain a
divorce or in lieu of requesting one. Between 1800 and 1832, North Carolina women filed 238 petitions for separate estates. Courts and legislatures were often willing to grant such requests, which encouraged
abandoned wives to support themselves and their children, when they
otherwise might become public charges.[21]

Even during the colonial period, under certain circumstances a wife
could maintain property separate from that of her husband. Most wives
preserved their separate estates by negotiating prenuptial settlements,
though some couples executed postnuptial agreements, often to guarantee the wife's control over property she inherited from her own family.
Both types of settlements were increasingly common in the nineteenth
century, when they were used primarily by wealthy families who vested
property in women at least partly to preserve it from their husbands'
creditors.[22] Other women, however, sought feme sole status, an option
that had precedent in English custom and one that statutory law explic-

20. Petition of John and Rebekah Farrow, 25 Sept. 1799, GASR, Nov.–Dec. 1800,
Nc-Ar; Indenture between John Farrow and Rebekah Farrow, 24 May 1803, quoted
in Johnson, *Antebellum North Carolina,* 220.

21. Johnson, *Antebellum North Carolina,* 220–22.

22. Julia Cherry Spruill, *Women's Life and Work in the Southern Colonies* (Chapel
Hill: University of North Carolina Press, 1938), 361–66; Marylynn Salmon, "Women
and Property in South Carolina: The Evidence from Marriage Settlements, 1730 to
1830," *WMQ,* 3d ser., 39 (1982): 655–68; Salmon, *Women and the Law of Property
in Early America* (Chapel Hill: University of North Carolina Press, 1986), 190–93;

itly recognized in colonial South Carolina. By claiming feme sole status, married women could escape the legal and economic disabilities they suffered under coverture. Controlling a separate estate enabled a wife to make binding contracts, to sue and be sued, and thereby conduct business independently of her husband. In colonial South Carolina, wives claimed feme sole status both to engage in business independently and to protect themselves and their children from their husbands' creditors.[23]

In the postrevolutionary era, feme sole status became a possible remedy for wives in other southern states who found themselves impoverished by irresponsible husbands. In South Carolina, women continued to seek formal feme sole status in the courts of equity, as they had done during the colonial era. Chancery courts in Virginia and Georgia also heard women's petitions for separate estates in the postrevolutionary decades.[24] In North Carolina, by contrast, wives attempted to secure their exemption from coverture by petitioning the state legislature. In 1798, Ruth Bell, Elizabeth Carter, and Elinor Perry—all of whom were abandoned wives—became the first North Carolina women to petition for separate estates. Seven more petitioned the following year, and seventeen did so in 1800, when the assembly responded by passing a statute collectively granting the requests of all the petitioners. Over the next three decades, an average of seven women per year petitioned the legislature for separate estates.[25]

Like wives who petitioned on their own for divorce, those who sought separate estates stressed their husbands' shortcomings and their own worthiness of the assembly's special consideration. Of the authors of fourteen extant North Carolina petitions for separate estates submitted through 1800, eleven asserted that their husbands abandoned them, and nine described their spouses more specifically as debt ridden and irre-

---

Suzanne Lebsock, *Free Women of Petersburg: Status and Culture in a Southern Town, 1784–1860* (New York: W. W. Norton, 1984), chap. 3.

23. Salmon, *Women and the Law of Property*, 44–48.

24. Eleanor M. Boatwright, "The Political and Civil Status of Women in Georgia, 1783–1860," *GHQ* 25 (1941): 310; Lebsock, *Free Women of Petersburg*, 55–56. Lebsock, however, argues that "women of the propertied classes" were most likely to use Virginia's courts of equity.

25. Committee reports on the petitions of Ruth Bell, Elizabeth Carter, and Elinor Perry, [Dec. 1798], GASR, Nov.–Dec. 1798, Nc-Ar. These petitions are not extant. For the 1800 statute, see North Carolina sessions laws, microfiche, 1800, chap. 83.

sponsible. In a political culture that valued independence, industry, and rationality, these characteristics presumably rendered such men unfit to exercise the extensive property rights that the common law vested in husbands.[26] Like those wives of Tories who carefully distinguished their own conduct from that of their spouses when they petitioned to recover confiscated property, these women sought to appropriate the property rights of their defective spouses, who, by virtue of their political or moral failings, could not be trusted to act appropriately.

Because their requests were unusual and seemed to undermine patriarchal authority, women petitioning for separate estates took special pains to portray themselves as exemplars of republican womanhood. These petitioners attempted to counteract conventional images of women as extravagant, idle, and irrational—and thus politically and morally suspect—by describing themselves as frugal, industrious, and self-reliant.[27] When Penelope Hosea requested a separate estate, she explained to the legislators that "by her honest industry" she had "accumulated some little property" since the departure of her drunken and profligate spouse, and she presented an affidavit signed by nine men who declared her "highly worthy [of] the clemency of the Legislature" (Doc. 14). Jenny Jarritt Thomas, also abandoned by a drunken and insolvent mate, asked the assembly to "enable her to appropriate the product of her own labor" (Doc. 12). Elizabeth Whitworth declared herself "anxious to support herself & family by her & their Labour" but worried that her "Gameing, Drinking" spendthrift of a husband would return to seize the property she acquired (Doc. 16).

Above all, those who sought separate estates did not claim that women's property rights generally should be identical to men's but, rather, that deserving women should be empowered to support themselves and their children in the absence of a viable male breadwinner. In so doing, they deferred to the patriarchal proclivities of the legis-

---

26. On the rhetorical fear of debt and the dishonor attributed to debtors, see T. H. Breen, *Tobacco Culture: The Mentality of the Great Tidewater Planters on the Eve of Revolution* (Princeton: Princeton University Press, 1985), 91–95, 186–210; Jan Lewis, *The Pursuit of Happiness: Family and Values in Jefferson's Virginia* (Cambridge: Cambridge University Press, 1983), 109–10.

27. For the politically significant image of woman as frivolous spendthrift, see Carroll Smith-Rosenberg, "Dis-Covering the Subject of the 'Great Constitutional Debate,' 1786–1789," *JAH* 79 (1992): 859–60.

lators while appealing to their practical interest in limiting the numbers of impoverished people who depended on public relief. Accordingly, Elizabeth Carter sought to "Prevent her Ungrateful Husband from Cumming Back and distressing of her what little She git by her Industry" so that she might support her "parcel of Suffering children."[28] Another petitioner, who claimed to have acquired "a Small Maintenance for me and my little Son . . . by Sore Work and frugality," requested "the privilege of enjoying the fruits of my Labour" (Doc. 13).

The influence of coverture, which stripped women of their autonomy on marrying and jeopardized the economic gains of abandoned wives, continued into widowhood as the rules of dower constrained a wife's economic activities even after the death of her husband. When a man died intestate, most states automatically granted his widow a one-third dower interest in his estate and divided the remainder among the children of the deceased. But the widow enjoyed only a life interest in the real property that constituted her dower portion, which meant that she might live off its proceeds but could neither alienate it nor alter it substantially. On her death, the widow's dower portion returned to her husband's estate and descended to his heirs. By writing a will, a man could endow his wife with more than the traditional "widow's third" of his estate, but even then he dictated the extent to which she controlled the property she received.[29]

These provisions survived into the postrevolutionary decades, when widows, either as a result of economic dislocation or a growing willingness to approach their legislatures, increasingly sought relief from wills and dower customs that bound them in ways they deemed detrimental to the welfare of their families. In the closing decade of the eighteenth century, such requests accounted for 12.2 percent of all North Carolina

---

28. Committee report on the petition of Elizabeth Carter, [Dec. 1798], GASR, Nov.–Dec. 1798, Nc-Ar.

29. For the best overview of dower rights in eighteenth-century America, see Salmon, *Women and the Law of Property*, 141–60. As Salmon shows, variations existed, even among the southern states. While Virginia defined dower as consisting of one-third of both the personal and real estates, South Carolina guaranteed widows only a life interest in a share of the latter while granting them full ownership of the personal property they inherited. After the Revolution, as we have seen, changes in North Carolina law undermined widow's dower rights, while widows may have benefited from legal changes in postrevolutionary South Carolina. See ibid., 168–72; Kerber, *Women of the Republic*, 146–47.

women's petitions and for 10.1 percent of those submitted by women in South Carolina. Legislators, however, were extremely reluctant to grant such petitions, which interfered with the rights of independent male citizens to use their property as they saw fit and to govern their domestic dependents.

Many postrevolutionary southern families were land rich but cash poor, and women, on finding that their husbands died deeply indebted, sometimes asked the legislature to empower them to sell land to satisfy their creditors. Thomas Odingsell Elliott left a "considerable" estate in land and slaves as well some "enormous" debts when he died in 1798. The law required his widow to preserve his real estate intact, thus forcing her to sell a portion of his personal estate, which included slaves, to pay his debts, though, as Mary Elliott observed, "the disposal of the negroes . . . would not only render the lands useless, but burthensome" to herself and her six young children (Doc. 10). Widows of less substantial means could face severe financial hardship as a result of the state's determination to preserve a man's real estate intact for the next generation. Sally King, the widow of an insolvent North Carolina physician, worried that satisfying her husband's debts would leave her little to maintain herself and her six children unless the legislature empowered her to sell some of his land.[30]

When a man died intestate and without heirs, his widow received her dower interest and assumed responsibility for his outstanding debts, while the remainder of the property reverted to the state. Because most men who did not make wills had little property, they usually left their widows with scant resources and sizable debts. Some of these widows petitioned, usually unsuccessfully, to recover property that was escheated to the state on the death of their spouses (Doc. 11).

Other widows petitioned to rectify oversights in their husbands' wills or related business transactions. One North Carolina woman found herself in a particularly difficult situation when her husband died in 1789. John Wilson recently had received payment for a tract of land but died before formally conveying it to the purchaser. John Wilson's death left his wife, Unity, in a double bind: as a widow, she lacked the power to transfer the land to its rightful owner, but, as the administratrix of John's estate, she was financially liable. The purchaser sued the estate of John Wilson to recover the purchase price, and Unity, who described herself

---

30. Petition of Sally King, Dec. 1795, GASR, Nov.–Dec. 1795, Nc-Ar.

as "Indigent," feared that paying the claim would "lay me under the Necessity of seeing my children bound out" as servants. Although the legislature granted her request, other petitioners were not as fortunate. Elizabeth Allen claimed that her husband mistakenly neglected to stipulate in his will his intention that a certain tract of land be sold to satisfy his creditors. Although Allen presented affidavits to support her claim, the legislature rejected her petition on the grounds that "the said tract of Land . . . [was] vested in the male Issue of the deceased, and . . . granting a power to sell the same to the widow, would deprive such Issue, of an interest to which by Law, they have an indefeasable title." [31]

The personal and economic dislocations of the revolutionary era caused special problems for women who lacked the legal authority to manage property in the best interests of their families. When Leonard Pattison died in 1782, he left his wife and children little besides 497 acres of land in Buckingham County, Virginia. Although Elizabeth Pattison was "Indigent," in 1788 the Virginia legislature refused to allow her to sell the land, even though by then she and her children had moved to Wilmington, North Carolina. [32] When Tory Andrew Cumming went into exile, he left his family "almost destitute" and unsure whether he was dead or alive. When his wife, Mary, tried to support her family by selling some property that she had inherited from her father, she discovered that coverture prevented her from controlling even that property while her husband might still live (Doc. 2).

Some of the most poignant cases arising from white women's tenuous access to property, even in widowhood, concerned their relationships with African Americans. Women who held property in their own right could make wills to dispose of it after their death, and fragmentary evidence suggests that they were more likely than men to emancipate favored slaves. [33] Nevertheless, several ill-fated early attempts of white women to manumit slaves suggest that their wills may have been vulnerable to challenge, at least when they undermined the institution of slavery. In 1775, North Carolinian Mary Clear wrote a will that freed her

---

31. Petition of Unity Wilson, 6 Nov. 1789, GASR, Nov.–Dec. 1789, Nc-Ar; Petition of Elizabeth Allen, 21 Nov. 1792, GASR, Nov. 1792–Jan. 1793, Nc-Ar; Committee report on the petition of Elizabeth Allen, 28 Nov. 1792, ibid.

32. Petition of Elizabeth Pattison, 6 Nov. 1788, LP, Buckingham Co., Vi-Ar.

33. Lebsock, *Free Women of Petersburg*, 136–38.

slave, Rose, and instructed her executors to buy a plot of land on which she could live as a free woman. Clear's executors and heirs disregarded her will, and Rose was still a slave in 1792, when forty-eight men submitted an unsuccessful emancipation petition on her behalf. Sarah Greene's mistress likewise sought to free a faithful slave who was hers by virtue of her marriage settlement, taking Sarah to Ireland to live for fifteen years as a free women and writing a will that affirmed her emancipation. Soon thereafter, however, a male relative forcibly brought Sarah Greene and her children to "Carolina," where he planned to "take the first opportunity of forcing them into Slavery." When Greene petitioned to preserve her freedom and to uphold the will of her former mistress, the Virginia legislature tabled her petition.[34]

Slavery was the most egregious injustice that remained virtually untouched by the Revolution's reforming impulse, at least in the southern states, where it was most profitable and most deeply entrenched. Although revolutionary-era legislation empowered Virginians to manumit their slaves by deed or by will and North Carolinians could free their slaves with court approval, they did not do so in impressive numbers. In fact, by the 1790s, a spirit of reaction set in as white southerners watched in horror as African Americans became increasingly assertive and as blacks in Haiti invoked the libertarian ideals of the American and French revolutions to overthrow their white enslavers. Fears of real and imagined slave conspiracies, coupled with African Americans' vocal support for the Haitian revolutionaries, resulted in the imposition of stricter controls on both slaves and free blacks in the postrevolutionary era.[35]

African Americans who either purchased their freedom or acquired it at their masters' or mistresses' behest clung tenaciously to their liberties in the postrevolutionary decades, sending unprecedented petitions to the assemblies to establish or to verify their status as free people (Doc. 7).

---

34. Committee report on "the petition in behalf of a Negroe Slave, Rose," Jan. 1792, GASR, Dec. 1791–Jan. 1792, Nc-Ar; Petition of Sarah Greene, 3 Dec. 1784, LP, Fairfax Co., Vi-Ar.

35. Sylvia R. Frey, *Water from the Rock: Black Resistance in a Revolutionary Age* (Princeton: Princeton University Press, 1991), 226–42, 285–96; Robert McColley, *Slavery and Jeffersonian Virginia* (Urbana: University of Illinois Press, 1964), 141–62; Douglas R. Egerton, *Gabriel's Rebellion: The Virginia Slave Conspiracies of 1800 and 1802* (Chapel Hill: University of North Carolina Press, 1993), 5–17, 45–48.

Ann and Margaret Rose, whose master had freed them and sent them to Scotland to live before the enactment of the Virginia manumission law, sought verification of their emancipation from both the courts and the legislature before returning to their native state after the Revolution.[36] Similarly, though a North Carolina court had issued a warrant confirming the emancipation of Nancy Handy, Princess Green, and John Caruthers Stanly by their owners, these three asked the assembly for an act that explicitly granted them "all powers, privileges and advantages which free people of color enjoy" because they worried that their freedom and any property they acquired would be insecure without it.[37]

Like their white counterparts, African-American women who petitioned the legislature sometimes alluded to their own political allegiance when they presented their grievances for consideration. In June 1777, a Virginia woman named Rachel submitted a manumission petition in which she complained that the brother of her late master threatened to kidnap her and her infant daughter and sell them into slavery "in foreign parts," despite the fact that the deceased had freed them both by will a year earlier. Rachel's master, however, had failed to obtain the license he needed to manumit his slaves officially, an omission she attributed to the political situation in 1776, when "Earl Dunmore instead of exercising any legal acts of Government in this Country, was in open arms against the same." By citing Dunmore as the chief obstacle to her emancipation, Rachel subtly reminded the legislators that she had not participated in the recent attempt to subvert Virginia's social order.[38] More pointedly, Grace Davis of North Carolina, who petitioned jointly with her son Richard in 1791, connected her legal claim to freedom to her son's willingness to fight in the Revolution. Requesting confirmation of her own emancipation and that of her children, Davis informed the legislators that Richard's status as a freeman inspired him to volunteer to fight "in defence of his Country & . . . in the cause of Liberty" (Doc. 4).

---

36. Petition of Ann and Margaret Rose, 5 Dec. 1783, LP, Halifax Co., Vi-Ar.

37. Petition of Nancy Handy, Princess Green, and John Carruthers Stanly, [Dec. 1796], GASR, Nov.–Dec. 1796, Nc-Ar. On Stanly, who eventually became the owner of 163 slaves and several plantations, see Loren Schweninger, "Prosperous Blacks in the South, 1790–1880," *AHR* 95 (1990): 41–42; and Schweninger, "John Caruthers Stanly and the Anomaly of Black Slaveholding," *NCHR* 67 (1990): 159–92.

38. Petition of Rachel and Rachel Jr., 6 June 1777, LP, Northumberland Co., Vi-Ar.

Having secured their emancipation, a few free black women and men appealed to the legislatures to protect them from the discrimination they often suffered, regardless of their legal status. In certain cases, a racist government could attempt to make all blacks subject to the slave codes, which prohibited group meetings and the possession of weapons, imposed curfews and travel restrictions, circumscribed economic activities, and virtually eliminated all civil rights. Consequently, in 1789, four South Carolina couples who recently had purchased their freedom asked the assembly to guarantee their legal rights as free people, especially their right to trial by jury (Doc. 3). Others petitioned to protest postrevolutionary statutes aimed specifically at free blacks, whose growing numbers appeared to portend social upheaval. In 1792, for instance, South Carolina imposed a special poll tax on free people of color. Twenty-three free black men from the Camden District petitioned to seek relief from the onerous tax, noting that they were "but a small remove from Slavery . . . [and] likely to . . . be reduced to Poverty and want itself."[39] Seventy-eight free blacks, including five women, from Liberty County also protested this tax and the hardships it caused for them and their families (Doc. 9). In these and in most other similar cases, however, the petitioners protested to no avail; the assembly either rejected or did not act on their petitions.

The Revolution did not eradicate entrenched inequalities of race and gender, but it may have raised the expectations of the disenfranchised, some of whom now sought equity, if not equality, from the propertied white men who were their governors. White women, most of whom previously had kept silent publicly on the issues of marriage and property rights, increasingly sought government intervention in instances when patriarchy malfunctioned. The nineteenth-century divorce laws and married women's property acts had their roots in the individual petitions of the postrevolutionary era.[40] Unlike their colonial predecessors, African Americans who became free during the revolutionary decades also appealed to the legislatures and the courts to recognize and to secure their

---

39. Frey, *Water from the Rock*, 240–42; Petition of William Morris et al., 3 Dec. 1793, LP, Sc-Ar.

40. On married women's property acts in the southern states, and the nonfeminist intent of these statutes, see Suzanne D. Lebsock, "Radical Reconstruction and the Property Rights of Southern Women," *Journal of Southern History* 43 (1977): 196–97, 200–204.

recently won freedom. Their sudden visibility as petitioners and plaintiffs demonstrates both their own assertiveness and the fragility of liberty in a society in which so many remained enslaved.

DOCUMENT 1

James and Mary Garrett

Residents of the Edenton District of eastern North Carolina, the petitioners had lived separately for roughly a decade when they requested a legal divorce on 21 November 1787. The legislature rejected their petition, but the Garretts probably continued to live apart. In 1790, James Garrett resided with a woman in Tyrell County. He predeceased his estranged wife, Mary Hofler Garrett, who moved to nearby Bertie County and wrote her last will and testament in 1823.[1]

The Petition of James Garret and Mary his Wife (late Mary Hofler) Humbly sheweth

That, some time in the Month of October, in the Year of Our Lord one thousand seven hundred and seventy two, Your Petitioners, being at that time Infants of tender years, to wit, the said James, of the age seventeen years or thereabouts, and the said Mary, of the age of fourteen years or thereabouts, were by the intervention of and concurrence of their Parents, intermarried agreeable to the Rites and Ceremonies of the Church of England: that, soon after their intermarriage as aforesaid, there arose a variety of Quarrels and Disputes, between them; which, in a short space of time, gradually grew into a mutual disgust and inveterate hatred: that, in this miserable state, they continued to live together, for the space of three long years; about which time, as their Reason approached to a state of Maturity, they discovered that their Tempers, were so dissimilar and discordant, that they must never hope to taste that Comfort and Happiness in Wedlock, which is only the Lot of congenial minds, formed to promote the mutual happiness of each other; one thing alone they could agree in, which was, to divide their substance, & live separate and apart,

---

1. *Heads of Families . . . in the Year 1790: N.C.*, 119; Will of Mary Garrett, 1823, Bertie County Will Book G, 122–23, Nc-Ar.

which, they accordingly by about that time did, and have lived assunder from that time hitherto.

Your Petitioner James farther shews that, being unable to endure the Solitude and other inconveniences of a single Life, after some considerable time prevailed upon another Woman, to marry him, tho' his former Wife was still alive; in consequence of which, he was involved in a most expensive & dangerous Prosecution, on the Statute against Bigamy & Polygamy;[2] from which, he was relieved, by the Death of his second Wife, and the Act of Pardon & Oblivion; after having expended large Sums of Money in his Defence, & suffering much trouble and vexation: and that he has since lived a most uncomfortable and solitary Life, at once exposed to all the inconveniences of Celibacy & deprived of all those blessings which arise from the happy Union of Kindred Souls.

And your Petitioner Mary, on her part, farther sheweth, that from the time she parted with her said Husband, she has languished in a Situation equally solitary and uncomfortable without any prospect of Relief, except from the Honorable the General Assembly, or from her final Dissolution.

Your Petitioners therefore humbly pray that the General Assembly will be pleased to take their unfortunate Case under their Serious Consideration, and pass an Act to dissolve their Marriage, the Source of all their Miseries and Misfortunes; and grant them such other & further relief, as to them in their Wisdom shall seem meet, and your Petitioners as in duty bound &c.

(DS, Nc-Ar)

DOCUMENT 2

Mary Cumming

The petitioner had been married for seven years when the state banished her husband Andrew as a loyalist, in 1782, leaving her and her daughter, Helen, in difficult financial circumstances. On

---

2. In 1749, North Carolina's colonial assembly adopted a seventeenth-century English statute that prohibited bigamy and polygamy, which remained in force until the state enacted a similar law in 1790 (*N.C. Recs.*, 25:74; Henry Potter et al., comps., *Laws of the State of North Carolina . . .* , 2 vols. [Raleigh: J. Gales, 1821], 1:628–29).

23 February 1788, unsure whether her husband was dead or alive, Mary Baker Cumming sought an exemption from the customary law of property, asking the South Carolina legislature for permission to sell some land she had inherited from her father, which Andrew ordinarily would have controlled by virtue of coverture. In March 1789, the legislature passed a private bill empowering Mary to sell the property. There is no evidence that Andrew ever returned to South Carolina.[3]

The Petition of Mary Cumming Humbly sheweth

That Your Petitioner's Father at the time of his death was seized and possessed in Fee Simple of and in a Lot of Land situate in King Street within the City of Charleston And likewise of and in a Tract of Land situate near the Town of Beaufort within this State And that he died Intestate leaving no other Children besides Your Petitioners and her two Sisters him surviving.

That, the said Estate being clear of all incumbrances, Your Petitioner to make provision for the Maintenance and support of herself and Daughter agreed with her two Sisters and her Mother (who agreed to renounce her claim of Dower therein) to join in the sale and conveyance of the said Lot situate in King Street to Mr. William Lee of Charleston aforesaid Watchmaker As well as in the Sale and Conveyance of the said Tract of Land situate near Beaufort unto Mr. Richard Bolan[4] who intermarried with one of Your Petitioner's Sisters, which accordingly took place. But it hath since been discovered that Your Petitioner's joining in the sale and Conveyance of the said Land is not a sufficient security to the said Purchasers for Your Petitioner's part or proportion thereof it being uncertain whether Your Petitioner's Husband Mr Andrew Cumming (who went off with the British at the evacuation of Charleston) is still living or not as Your Petitioner hath never heard any thing about him since that period.

---

3. *Biog. Dict. of S.C. House, 1775–1790,* 3:166; *S.C. House Journals, 1789–1790,* 247.

4. Bolan was a merchant and partner in the firms of Bolan, Godber and Company and William Godber and Company, both of which were based in Granby, Richland County, South Carolina (Edwin L. Green, *A History of Richland County, Volume 1: 1732–1805* [Columbia, S.C.: R. L. Bryan Company, 1932], 192).

As Your Petitioner was left by her said Husband almost destitute of the necessaries of life And is at present in a very distressed situation being very much in want of her share of the Purchase Money aforesaid for the support and Maintenance of herself and Daughter And as the said Andrew Cumming, if it was certain that he is still living, would only be entitled to a Life Estate in Your Petitioner's share or proportion of the said Premises.

Your Petitioner therefore humbly prays for the sanction of this Honorable House for the purpose of rendering the Sale and Conveyance of the said Land so as aforesaid made, as far as related to Your Petitioner's share or Proportion thereof, as compleat as possible, which Your Petitioner is advised cannot be done under the above Circumstance except by the Legislature of the Commonwealth.

And Your Petitioner will Pray &c.

(DS, Sc-Ar)

DOCUMENT 3

Francis, et al.

> *On 28 December 1789, these eight former slaves petitioned the South Carolina assembly for explicit recognition of their exemption from the slave codes, armed with a supporting letter from six white men and one white woman, who described them as "honest and industrious [persons who] have always conducted themselves in a manner becoming their station." The assembly granted this request, ruling that the special laws governing the conduct and treatment of slaves did not apply to these free black petitioners.*[5]

The humble Petition of Francis, Daniel, Hammond and Samuel (Free Moors) in behalf of themselves and their wives Fatima, Flora, Sarah and Clarinda. Humbly Sheweth

---

5. Certificate of Benjamin Legaré et al., 28 Dec. 1789, copy, LP, Sc-Ar; *S.C. House Journals, 1789–1790*, 374–75.

That your Petitioners some years past had the misfortune while fighting in the defence of their Country, to be captured with their wives and made prisoners of War by one of the Kings of Africa.[6]

That a certain Captain Clark had them delivered to him on a promise that they should be redeemed by the Emperor of Morocco's Ambassador then residing in England, in order to have them returned to their own Country: *Instead of which* he brought them to this State, and sold them for slaves. Since that period they have by the greatest industry, been enabled to purchase their freedom from their respective Masters: And now prayeth your Honorable House, That as freeborn subjects of a Prince now in Alliance with the United States, that they may not be considered as subject to a Law of this State (now in force) called the negro law:[7] but if they should unfortunately be guilty of any crime or misdemeanor against the Laws of the Land, that they may have a just trial by a Lawful Jury.

And your Petitioners as in duty bound will ever pray.

(D, Sc-U [Copy in LP, Sc-Ar])

DOCUMENT 4
Grace Davis and Richard Davis

In 1764, John Davis, a New Bern merchant, manumitted a slave woman named Grace. Twenty-seven years later, on 14 December

---

6. The Moroccan sultans employed both slaves and free blacks in their armies, which consisted mainly of Christian captives and Spanish renegades. These petitioners most likely served in the army of Sidi Muhammad Ibn r.Abd Allah (1757–1790), who spent most of his reign putting down revolts, securing his country's borders, and unsuccessfully attempting to drive the Portuguese out of Mazagan on Morocco's western coast (Charles André Julien, *History of North Africa*, trans. John Petrie [New York: Praeger Publishers, 1970], 249–50, 264–66).

7. The Negro Act of 1740, which remained South Carolina's fundamental slave code, stipulated that slaves would be tried for capital offenses by two justices and three freeholders. For other offenses, the court would consist of one justice and two freeholders, authorized to inflict "any corporal punishment, not extending to taking away life or member, as he and they in their discretion shall think fit" (John Codman Hurd, *The Law of Freedom and Bondage in the United States*, 2 vols. [New York: Negro Universities Press, 1968], 1:305).

*1791, perhaps sensing that her freedom was not secure, Grace peti-
tioned the assembly for the passage of a private bill recognizing her
own status and that of her offspring as free people of color. Grace
Davis based her appeal on the facts of the case and on her son
Richard's military service in the Revolution. The assembly granted
her petition. In 1800, Richard Davis headed an eight-member
household in Brunswick County in eastern North Carolina.*[8]

The humble Petition of Grace Davis & of her eldest Son Richard
Davis of Brunswick County Sheweth

That in the year 1764 John Davis Esquire late of the said County in
& by certain Instruments of writing did manumit them & that the said
Grace continued to live with her former Master 'till his death on or about
January 1790 since which She has continued to enjoy all the rights of a
free woman.

That the said Richard Davis after his arrival to man's Estate settled
himself without interruption & has ever enjoyed the Priviledges of a
Freeman. That As such he chearfully turnd out during the war in defence
of his Country & exposed his life as an Artilleryman[9] in the cause of liberty & that he behavd worthy of such a noble cause can be proved to your
honorable body.

That the said Grace since her manumission aforesaid has borne a
number of other Children[10] all of whom have & do continue to enjoy

8. "An Act to Emancipate certain persons therein named," North Carolina sessions laws, microfiche, 1791, chap. 46; Federal Census of Population, North Carolina,
1800, Brunswick County, 37. Neither Grace nor Richard Davis is listed as a head of
household in the 1790 census.

9. Two Richard Davises served in the North Carolina forces, one in the First North
Carolina Battalion of militia and another in the Tenth Regiment of North Carolina
Continentals. White southerners were reluctant to enlist black soldiers, but slaves and
especially free blacks served in the war's later years. As an artilleryman, however,
Davis was unusual. Most African Americans served in the infantry or in unarmed oc-
cupations (*N.C. Recs.*, 15:722, 16:1045; Benjamin Quarles, *The Negro in the Ameri-
can Revolution* [Chapel Hill: University of North Carolina Press, 1961], 74–78; Frey,
Water from the Rock, 78, 86, 136).

10. Grace Davis had five children in all: Richard, Harriot, Samuel, Rebecca, and
Elizabeth ("An Act to Emancipate certain persons therein named," North Carolina
sessions laws, microfiche, 1791, chap. 46).

their freedom. But She being advised, notwithstanding the County Court in consideration of her meritorious services & honest Character did confirm her manumission that the same is not perfect more especially as to her Children without an Act of Assembly.[11] She therefore on behalf of herself & Children & the said Richard humbly pray your honorable body to take such measures as in your great wisdom you shall think necessary & as in duty bound &c.

(DS [by marks], Nc-Ar)

DOCUMENT 5
Teresa Butler

> *This petitioner was an abandoned wife who, on 4 December 1791, requested a formal dissolution of her five-year marriage. The petitioner's father supported her attempt to obtain a legislative divorce, as did the magistrate who had officiated at her ill-fated wedding, who now wished that "a second tryal of the matrimonal state" would bring her "much happiness." Notwithstanding these endorsements, the North Carolina assembly rejected Teresa Butler's petition, asserting that, "should the Legislature enter into the business of granting divorces, it would be productive of evil and dangerous consequences."[12]*

The Petition of Teresa Butler of the Town of Wilmington Humbly Sheweth;

That Your Petitioner was married unto Henry L: Butler, sometime in the Year of Our Lord one thousand Seven hundred and Eighty Six (the first day of April); as will appear by a Certificate of James Parratt Es-

---

11. North Carolina statute gave the county courts full jurisdiction over the manumission of slaves, though the assembly received and granted petitions to verify emancipations as early as 1786 ("An Act to prevent domestic Insurrections, and for other Purposes," 1777, *N.C. Recs.*, 24:15; "An Act to Emancipate Caesar, formerly a servant . . . ," North Carolina sessions laws, microfiche, 1786, chap. 48; "An Act to Emancipate Hannah, alias Hannah Bowers . . . ," ibid., chap. 58).

12. Affidavit of Isaac Davis, 26 Nov. 1791, GASR, Dec. 1791–Jan. 1792, Nc-Ar; J[ames] Parrott to Teresa Butler, n.d., ibid.; Committee report on the petition of Teresa Butler, 29 Jan. 1791, ibid.

quire (the Magistrate by whom they were married) and by the Affidavit of her Father Isaac Davis both of which will be handed to your Honorable Body, that the said Henry L. Butler without having or assigning any just cause of complaint or disaffection about five months afterwards left the House of Your Petitioners father the said Isaac Davis where they (the said Henry L. Butler and Your Petitioner) had 'till then resided. That the said Henry L. Butler has never since that time given Your Petitioner the least Assistance nor even corresponded with her; On the contrary has abandoned her, and her Infant Daughter by him to poverty and distress; and was it not for the Paternal care of her Father she must have long ere this languished out her life in wretchedness and misery; That Your Petitioner is further credibly informed that prior to his the said Henry L: Butler's Marriage with her he had been married in Boston and that since his marriage with Your Petitioner he has again been married in the West-Indies. That Your Petitioner finds it impossible to force him to maintain her, and her daughter; he residing in a foreign Country (where, she cannot tell) that he has no visible property from which she may claim a support for herself and daughter. Under these considerations and circumstances Your Petitioner requests that Your Honorable Body will grant her the relief she is intitled to viz: a Divorce à Vinculo Matrimonii, by reason of the aforesaid Praecontract.[13] And that the said relief may be as speedy as possible.

And Your Petitioner Shall ever Pray &.

(DS, Nc-Ar)

DOCUMENT 6

Teresa Butler

In December 1792, a year after the assembly rejected her divorce petition, Teresa Butler sought to rid herself of the name of her estranged husband. She chose for herself the surname Dunbar— probably her mother's birth name—and this time the assembly

---

13. A *divorce à vinculo matrimonii* is an absolute divorce, which dissolves the marriage bond completely and allows the affected parties to remarry. A *praecontract* is an exclusive contract or engagement, such as marriage, into which a person can enter lawfully only if free of conflicting obligations or claims (*Black's Law Dictionary* [1990 ed.], 486, 1177).

granted her request. Teresa Davis Butler Dunbar never received a
legal divorce, but she did take a second husband, Benjamin Jacobs,
sometime before 1817. Either Henry Butler's death or his uninter-
rupted absence for a period of seven years would have allowed
Teresa lawfully to remarry.[14]

The Petition of Teresa Davis alias Butler humbly Sheweth—

That by the advice of her Parents & freinds She unfortunately contracted marriage with a certain Person of the name of Butler who appeared to be an honest reputable man but a few months after their
marriage the said Butler left her and married another Woman in So.
Carolina & that She has neither seen or heard from him for several years.
Your Petitioner further sheweth that She has had the misfortune to find
out that the said Butler previous to his marriage with her had a Wife &
Children in Philadelphia. In consequence of which She applied to the last
Assembly for a Divorce but failed to obtain the same and is informed that
the Legislature could not with propriety grant her such Relief. As a small
alleviation to her unhappy situation She therefore petitions that her name
may be altered from that of Butler to Dunbar and She as in duty bound
will ever pray &c.

(DS, Nc-Ar)

DOCUMENT 7

Charlotte Green

This Craven County woman was one of a growing number of
black North Carolinians who attained their freedom in the post-

---

14. "An Act to alter and confirm the names of certain persons therein mentioned,"
North Carolina sessions laws, microfiche, 1790, chap. 36; Will of Isaac Davis, 15 Oct.
1817, Brunswick County Wills, box 1, Nc-Ar. The petitioner was one of nine siblings,
one of whom was named Dunbar, probably to honor his mother's family.

A 1790 statute allowed remarriage in cases in which an absent spouse "shall continually remain beyond the sea for the space of seven years together" or if after any
absence of seven years the resident spouse did not know if the other was living or
dead ("An Act to restrain all married Persons from marrying again whilst their former
Wives or former Husbands are living," North Carolina sessions laws, microfiche,
1790, chap. 11).

revolutionary decades. Daughter of a white planter and a slave woman who purchased her own freedom and that of her children, Charlotte Green (b. 1772) asked the state assembly to verify her emancipation. On 11 December 1792, she petitioned, with the support of John Waite, a New Bern merchant and her former master, and the assembly granted her request, enacting a private bill that secured her freedom and permitted her to change her name to Elizabeth Johnston.[15]

The Humble Petition of Charlotte Green—Sheweth

That your Petitioner is a Native of this State and the daughter of a Free Woman who by her Industry & hard Labour purchased her Liberation,[16] but your Petitioner is yet in bondage, altho' by the Interposition of a kind Providence she has it in her Power to seek an Honest Livelyhood in the World on her own footing, and that she may be able to defend herself against unjustifiable or unwarrantable Provocation from Evil disposed Persons, as she has it in Contemplation to travel into Foreign Countries, she humbly prays that your Honours would take her case into consideration, & if you should see fit, to pass a Bill of Emancipation for her releif from Slavery, she will as in duty bound ever Pray &c.

(D, Nc-Ar)

DOCUMENT 8
James and Comfort Tomlinson

On 21 December 1793, this Guilford County, North Carolina, couple petitioned jointly for a formal dissolution of their marriage of eight years. Though James and Comfort Tomlinson had not lived together for the past six years and though their petition carried the

---

15. Schweninger, "John Carruthers Stanly," 168–69, 188; Certificate of John Waite, 10 Dec. 1792, GASR, Nov. 1792–Jan. 1793, Nc-Ar; "An Act to emancipate the persons herein mentioned," North Carolina sessions laws, microfiche, 1792, chap. 38.

16. Amelia Green (ca.1740–1807) secured first her own freedom and then that of her four daughters during the 1790s. She later helped her daughter Nancy Green Handy to purchase the freedom of her two daughters (Schweninger, "John Carruthers Stanly," 168, 188).

supporting signatures of five men, the assembly refused to grant them the divorce they requested.[17]

The petition of James Tomlinson and Comfort Tomlinson Humbly sheweth that your petitioners were Joined in the state of Matrimony about eight years past And that we your petitioners lived together Neare on Two years and had one Child And then one of your Petitioners to wit the said James Did take up with A single woman and absented him self from the Company of your petitioner, to wit, Comfort for some Time And being gilty of several other misdemeanors Which your Petitioner, to wit, Comfort Conceive not to be the Duty of a husband therefor Did not think proper To live with him any longer and as such by mutal Consent parted and has been parted about six year As will appear more fully by a paper which will Be produced to your Honours[18] if Requi[r]ed. And the said Comfort now have taken up with another man and Being lusty[19] by him therefore your petitioners both of us being still Desirous to Continue For ever Seperated And to be no more as man and wife therefore Humbley pray that your honorable body will Give a General Divorce[20] from this time forward that we May not be any longer Considered as man & wife. And as in Duty bound your Petitioners will ever pray &c.

(DS [by marks], Nc-Ar)

Document 9
Free People of Colour of Liberty County

Although free blacks in most states lacked the right to vote and other civil rights, they were compelled to pay taxes, and often they were taxed more heavily than the white population. In South Carolina, free black men and women alike paid a poll, or head, tax, in addition to the taxes they paid on their land and other property. Among whites only men who paid no other taxes were subject to

---

17. *Heads of Families . . . in the Year 1790: N.C.*, 152.

18. Not found.

19. Pregnant (*The Century Dictionary and Cyclopedia*, 12 vols. [1889; reprint, New York: Century Company, 1913], 5:3548).

20. A *divorce à vinculo matrimonii*, which permits the partners to remarry.

*the poll tax until 1788, when they, too, became exempt, making it a
tax for blacks only. On 30 April 1794, seventy-eight free blacks—
seventy-three men and five women—requested relief from this discriminatory tax. The assembly did not act on their petition.*[21]

The Petition of the people of Colour of the state [of South Carolina]
who are under the act intitled an Act for imposing a poll tax on all free
Negroes, Mustees and Mulattoes.[22]

most humbly sheweth that whereas (we your humble petitioners)
having the honor of being your Citizens, as also free and willing to advance for the support of Government any thing that might not be preju-
dicial to us, it being well known that we have not been backward on our
part, in performing any other public duties that hath fell in the compass
of our knowledge,

We therefore, being sensibly griev'd at our present situation, also
having frequently discovered the many distresses, occasion'd by your
Act imposing the poll tax, such as widows with large families, & women
scarcly able to support themselves, being frequently followed & payment
extorted by your tax gatherers.

These considerations on our part hath occasioned us, to give you this
trouble, requesting your deliberate body, to repeal an Act so truly mortifying to your distress'd petitioners—for which favor your petitioners will
ever acknowledge, & devoutly pray.

(DS [by fifty-eight signatures and twenty marks], Sc-Ar)

DOCUMENT 10

Mary Elliott

*When Thomas Odingsell Elliott died in 1797, he left his wife and
children a house in Charleston, 3,333 acres in St. Andrew parish,*

---

21. Judith E. Brimelow and Michael E. Stevens, *State Free Negro Capitation Tax
Books: Charleston, South Carolina, ca.1811–1860* (Columbia: South Carolina Division of Archives and History, 1983), 2; Hurd, *Law of Freedom and Bondage,* 1:301,
2:95; Frey, *Water from the Rock,* 240–41.

22. "An Act for raising Supplies for the year of our Lord one thousand seven hundred and ninety-three," 1793, *S.C. Statutes,* 5:226. Each annual supply law enumerated the taxes levied for the coming year (ibid., 5:25, 58, 130, 150, 189, 209).

and nearly 200 slaves. But Elliott died deeply indebted, and the law
of inheritance prohibited the alienation of real property to satisfy
outstanding debts. Being land rich but cash poor, Mary Pinckney
Elliott petitioned the legislature on 4 December 1798 for special
permission to sell some of her husband's land. The assembly did not
act on this petition, and Elliott did not resubmit her request in a
subsequent session.[23]

The Petition of Mary Elliott Widow and Relict of Thomas Odingsell
Elliott late of Charleston, in the State aforesaid, Esquire, deceased, as
well as and in behalf of herself as the maternal guardian of her children by the said Thomas Odingsell Elliott, to Wit, Benjamin in his
twelfth year—Frances Brewton in her tenth year—Mary Odingsell eight
years—Rebecca Pinckney in her seventh year Thomas Odingsell in his
fourth year, and Charles Pinckney Elliott an infant of nine months and
John Splatt Cripps[24] of Charleston aforesaid Administrator of all and Sin-
gular the goods and Chattels rights and credits which were of the said
Thomas Odingsell Elliott deceased at the time of his death.

Sheweth That the said Thomas Odingsell Elliott hath lately departed
this life largely indebted to divers persons and possessed of a considerable real and personal estate consisting chiefly of lands and negroes.[25]

That your Petitioners have already ascertained that the debts of the
Estate of said Thomas Odingsell Elliott amount to the enormous Sum of
eleven thousand Pounds Sterling, and are persuaded that the Same cannot possibly be extinguished without a Sale of Some part of the Estate.

That the disposal of the negroes belonging to the Estate would not
only render the lands useless, but burthensome.

That your Petitioners are persuaded it would advance the interest of
the Representatives of the late Mr. Elliott to dispose of a part of or even
the Whole of his lands in preference to his Negroes, but that by Law the
personal Estate is the only fund which can be Sold or disposed of, for the

23. *Biog. Dict. of S.C. House, 1775–1790,* 213–14; *Heads of Families . . . in the*
Year 1790: S.C., 34, 42.

24. Cripps, a merchant, was one of the Whigs the British captured and sent to
St. Augustine when they occupied Charleston (*N.C. Recs.,* 15:393).

25. In South Carolina, unlike in some other southern states, widows held a dower
interest only in real property, receiving absolute ownership of personal property,
which included slaves (Salmon, *Women and the Law of Property,* 156–57).

Satisfaction of the debts. Your Petitioners therefore pray Your Honorable House to take the premisses into Consideration, and to grant leave to the administrator of the Said Thomas Odingsell Elliott to Sell and dispose of the whole, or any part of the real Estate of the said Thomas Odingsell Elliott deceased to be applied to the payment and Satisfaction of his debts, Such Sale or Sales to be made on Such termes and Conditions as your Honorable House in their wisdom Shall think proper to order and direct: and as in duty bound they will pray.

(DS, Sc-Ar)

DOCUMENT 11

Amey Patterson

The common law guaranteed a widow a dower portion of her husband's property, but if a man died intestate and without legal heirs his wife was not entitled to his entire estate. After setting aside the widow's dower portion, the remaining property in such cases reverted to the state. On 26 November 1799, Amey Patterson petitioned to recover escheated property that once belonged to her husband, who had died intestate. The assembly rejected her petition, asserting that "legislative interference in the present, as well as all other cases similar to it, would be improper, as all escheated property is [since 1789], vested in the trustees of the University of North Carolina." [26]

The humble petition of Amy Paterson Widow of James Paterson lately deceased

Sheweth, that her said late husband having for many years resided in this State and bore a good character among his acquentance, who was suddenly taken sick and imediately departed this life without having it in his power to dispose of his property agreeable to his inclination, and agreeable to the Laws of this State his property became under the es-

---

26. Ibid., 141–42; Committee report on the petition of Amey Patterson, Dec. 1799, GASR, Nov.–Dec. 1799, Nc-Ar; "An Act for Raising a Fund for Erecting the Buildings and for the Support of the University of North Carolina," 1789, *N.C. Recs.,* 25:24–25.

cheated act after defraying all debts; Now may it please your Honors, in defraying the debts it has well near taken all the property, Land excepted, and it is hoped your Honors will have compassion on myself a poor Widow and do away the right of escheation in this particular and invest the title of the Land to my only use.

Therefore your petitioner (whom he has left a poor Widow) makes this her application that your Honors will be graciously pleased to grant to your petitioner the said Land to the sole use and benefit thereof to her and her assigns forever.

And your petitioner shall ever pray.

(DS, Nc-Ar)

DOCUMENT 12

Jenny Jarritt Thomas

In the postrevolutionary decades, growing numbers of abandoned wives sought relief from coverture by requesting separate estates. Jenny Jarritt Thomas's husband, Charles, drank heavily and squandered his property, abandoning her soon thereafter. At least one observer concluded that there was "little or no prospect of a reconcilation" between her and her estranged husband, who appeared "determined to follow the Dictates of his Drunken Disposition, which most probable will Terminate with his life." On 11 December 1799, Jenny petitioned for a separate estate. The North Carolina assembly granted her petition.[27]

The petition of Jenny J. Thomas wife of Charles Thomas of the County of Wake, respectfully sheweth:

That your petitioner intermarried with her said husband some years past; at which time, in addition to the portion given by your petitioners father,[28] her said husband was seised and possessed of a considerable es-

---

27. Affidavit of Nathaniel Jones, 11 Dec. 1799, GASR, Nov.–Dec. 1799, Nc-Ar.
28. The household of Thomas Jarrott of Wake County included himself, his wife, one white male between the ages of sixteen and sixty, and one white female between those ages—presumably his daughter Jenny—in 1800. Jenny's child was not listed in the census for 1800 (Federal Census of Population, North Carolina, 1800, roll 32, 741).

tate, both real and personal. But your petitioner states that her said husband through mismanagement and neglect, hath entirely wasted and expended all the property he possessed on Earth. Your petitioner further states and charges, that her said husband is, and for some years past has been, entirely regardless of your petitioner, nor has he made any provision for her support and maintenance, but she hath been compelled by dire necessity to return to the House of her aged parents to shield her from the inclemency of the weather and implore their charity for the necessaries of Life. Your petitioner further saith, that she hath one child by her said husband, who is now with her in the same wretched situation with herself; and here it is, that she begs leave to remark to your Hon[o]r[a]ble body that her father is possessed of some property and has expressed his inclination to bestow a part thereof on your petitioner, but being advised by Counsel learned in the Law, that on such gift, the aforesaid Charles, her husband of your petitioner, would acquire the Ownership; She has no relief to hope for from that Source, as there are at this time debts against her said husband to a much larger amount, than the property she has a right to expect from her father would pay and discharge.

Your petitioner further begs leave to observe to your honorable body, that she is advised should any property be given to her Child, her husband would probably be entitled to recieve it as natural Guardian which would defeat every purpose designed by her Charitable friends. Wherefore, She prays you, to take her case under your consideration, and pass a Law securing to her all such property as she may hereafter acquire; or so to remedy her present distressed situation as will enable her to appropriate the product of her own labor, towards relieving the necessities it is her misfortune to bear.

And she is in duty &c &c.

(ADS, Nc-Ar)

DOCUMENT 13

Catharine Dick

By the time she petitioned for a separate estate, in December 1799, Catharine Dick had been an abandoned wife for most of the past twelve years. She was a resident of Montgomery County, North Carolina, where she probably lodged in a house other than

her own, as she is not listed in the census for either 1790 or 1800.
The legislature granted her petition, which bore the supporting sig-
natures of five men and the marks of two others.[29]

Having been so unfortunate as to marry Joseph Dick, a Pedlar, from
Canada and by Birth a French man, who by foolish trading brought Distress and ruin upon his poor family, so, that every thing been taken from
us by the Constables, and after that my Said husband deserted me the
first time the 22d December 1787, and the Second time for good and all
in April 1790 and Since I heard nothing of him any more. I took therefore the Resolution to begin at a new to acquire a Small Maintainance for
me and my little Son John, which I attained by Sore Work and frugality,
but grown old and weak, I need it now very much and live in constant
fear, my husband might take from me again what little I have Saved; I beg
therefore most humbly the General Assembly may favour me with the
Privilege of enjoying the fruits of my Labour and Secure my Smal Estate
to me self free from any and all Claims of my dissipating husband, which
I will ever acknowledge with the Submissest Thanckfulness and remain
with the greatest Respect.

(DS [by mark], Nc-Ar)

DOCUMENT 14

Penelope Hosea

This petitioner was another abandoned wife who sought a sepa-
rate estate to preserve her earnings from the potential demands of
a profligate spouse. This petition, which the legislature heard on
21 November 1800, bore the supporting signatures of nine men,
who recommended Penelope Hosea as "highly worthy [of] the clem-
ency of the Legislature." The assembly granted Hosea's petition,
making her one of seventeen women to receive a separate estate dur-
ing this legislative session.[30]

---

29. Petition of Catharine Dick, [Dec. 1799], GASR, Nov.–Dec. 1799, Nc-Ar.

30. Petition of Penelope Hosea, 21 Nov. 1800, GASR, Nov.–Dec. 1800, Nc-Ar;
"An Act to secure to the persons therein mentioned such estate as they may hereafter
acquire," North Carolina sessions laws, microfiche, 1800, chap. 83.

The Petition of Penelope Hosea of the County of Pasquotank—
Humbly Sheweth—That some years ago she intermarried with a certain
Seth Hosea of the said county, who at that time was possessed of a very
considerable Real and Personal Estate, but by bad management and a
fondness for spiritous liquors was in the course of two ot three years
reduced to a state of Insolvency, when he absented himself from your
Petitioner.

That your Petitioner hath in the course of these years, that her said
Husband has absented himself by her honest industry accumulated some
little property that is highly necessary for her support and being apprehensive as a reconciliation is not likely to take place, that your Petitioners
said husband will deprive her of the little property she hath so acquired.

May it therefore please your Honorable Body, to pass a law authorizing your said Petitioner to hold such property as she hath acquired since
the seperation from her said Husband and all such as she may hereafter
acquire either Real or Personal by purchase or otherwise, in as ful and
ample a manner as if your said Petitioner had never been married to the
said Seth Hosea, clear from all the claim or claims of her said Husband,
or any other person or persons whatsoever—And your Petitioner as in
duty bound will ever pray &c.

(DS [by mark], Nc-Ar)

DOCUMENT 15

Rebekah Morrison

*On 28 November 1800, less than fifteen months after her wed-
ding day, Rebekah Davidson Morrison sought a formal divorce
from the North Carolina legislature. Although her husband was a
fugitive from justice and also a suspected bigamist, the assembly rejected her petition but, instead, empowered her to maintain a separate estate.*[31]

---

31. "An Act to secure to the persons therein mentioned such estate as they
may hereafter acquire," North Carolina sessions laws, microfiche, 1800, chap. 83. If
Rebekah Morrison asked for the right to maintain a separate estate, her petition is
not extant.

The Memorial of Rebekah Morrice Alias Davidson of Buncombe County most Humbly Sheweth.

That Your Memorialist did (unfortunately) marry a man[32] by the name of John G Morrice the 5th day of September 1799, who came into the Neighbourhood of Your Memorialists Father about the first of June Preceeding. About the first of October following there was reports began to circulate purporting that my Husband had been guilty of a number of felonious actions, and in a short time he was taken with a States Warrant, and committed to Jail, after some time he found Security for his appearance at Court, on the day for his tryal he disappeared, and your Memorialist has never seen him since.

Your Memorialist further inform your Hon[ora]ble] Body that said Morrice (both from his own confession, and Intelligence received from Major Evans of the State of Kentucky) had at the time of your Memorialists Marriage with him a wife and one, or two Children then alive. Major Evans I am Creditably informed was personally acquainted with said Morrice prior to my Knowledge of him.

Your Memorialist submits her situation to your Honourable Body, and prays you will take her case into consideration, and if upon mature Deliberation the Legislature should think my Situation merits their attention, Your Memorialist Humbly flatters herself you will grant her a Divorce from said Morrice and give her an Opportunity of endeavouring to repair her broken fortune as far as the Smiles of Heaven, and her own prudence will admit of.

And Your memorialist will ever Pray.

(DS [signed "Rebcah Davidson Alias Morrison"], Nc-Ar)

Document 16
Elizabeth Whitworth

Under coverture even the hard-earned wages of an abandoned wife could be seized by her husband or his creditors. On 29 November 1800, this North Carolina woman sought relief from cov-

---

32. The clerk initially wrote *gentleman,* which was crossed out and replaced in the same hand.

erture to protect the interests of herself and her children from her insolvent husband. The assembly granted her petition for a separate estate, which was supported by three men, two of whom were county magistrates. Elizabeth Whitworth's estranged husband, John, was still alive in 1835, when, at the age of seventy-four, he received a pension for his service as a private in the state militia during the Revolution.[33]

The Petition of Elizabeth Whitworth of Stokes County Humbly sheweth, that in the year 1786 She intermarried with a Certain John Whitworth, and that previous to her intermarriage with the said John, she was a Widdow with Two Children, and was in affluant circumstances, and immediately after the intermarriage, the said John betook himself to Gameing, Drinking & Contracting of Debts & thereby soon brought your Petitioner & family into indigent Circumstances, & in the year 1796 the said John deserted the said Elizabeth & has not yet returnd., and it is Currently reported that he is living in adultry with a woman in the State of South Carolina, and your petitioner further Sheweth, that at the time of the desertion of the said John he was excessively indebted by Judgments, Bonds, Notes &c—and that she being anxious to Support herself & family by her & their Labour & cannot do it without being Subject to the payment of the extravagant Debts of the said John—Now your Petitioner prays that your Honorable body, would take her case under Consideration, & if they can pass an Act, that the property she may hereafter acquire shall not be Subject to the payment of the said Johns Debts which he has already or may hereafter Contract, and that the said John shall have no more power or Authority to Sell or dispose of such acquired property, as your Petitioner may acquire, than any other Person Whatever.

and as in duty bound your Petitioner will ever Pray &c.

(ADS, Nc-Ar)

---

33. Affidavit of Benjamin Forsyth, Nov. 1800, GASR, Nov.–Dec. 1800, Nc-Ar; Statement of Charles Banner and Henry B. Dobson, Nov. 1800, ibid.; "An Act to secure to the persons therein mentioned such estate as they may hereafter acquire," North Carolina sessions laws, microfiche, 1800, chap. 83; [Hay et al.], *N.C. Soldiers*, 461.

Appendix 1

WOMEN'S LEGISLATIVE PETITIONS BY SUBJECT: NORTH CAROLINA, 1776–1800

	1776–80	1781–85	1786–90	1791–95	1796–1800
Debt Recovery	1	4	8	4	4
Debt Relief	—	1	5	4	2
Divorce	—	—	2	3	5
Ferries and Bridges	1	—	1	—	1
Military Arrears	—	—	5	4	3
Military Pensions	1	9	1	2	—
Property Disputes	—	2	3	1	2
Separate Estates	—	—	—	—	27
Slavery and Emancipation	1	1	1	4	1
Tory Laws	5	4	5	1	—
Wills and Inheritance	—	—	1	6	6
Other	1	—	1	2	4

Appendix 2

WOMEN'S LEGISLATIVE PETITIONS BY SUBJECT: SOUTH CAROLINA, 1776–1800

	1776–80	1781–85	1786–90	1791–95	1796–1800
Debt Recovery	—	4	6	23	7
Debt Relief	—	—	2	3	4
Divorce	—	—	—	—	—
Ferries and Bridges	—	2	2	1	6
Military Arrears	1	3	—	4	—
Military Pensions	1	6	3	1	—
Property Disputes	—	3	5	3	1
Separate Estates	—	—	—	—	—
Slavery and Emancipation	—	1	—	—	7
Tory Laws	1	53	8	13	3
Wills and Inheritance	—	4	5	3	7
Other	—	—	1	3	1

SELECT BIBLIOGRAPHY

The works listed below deal primarily with the history of petitioning, the southern states in the revolutionary era, and issues pertaining to women and gender which this study considers. Readers seeking more information on individual petitioners and their families or on other aspects of the Revolution should consult the footnotes for additional sources.

Primary Sources

Andrews, Evangeline Walker, and Charles McLean Andrews, eds. *Journal of a Lady of Quality: Being the Narrative of a Journey from Scotland to the West Indies, North Carolina, and Portugal, in the Years 1774 to 1776.* New Haven: Yale University Press, 1921.

Candler, Allen D., ed. *The Revolutionary Records of the State of Georgia.* Vol. 3: *Journal of the House of Assembly, From August 17, 1781, to February 26, 1784.* Atlanta: Franklin-Turner Company, 1908.

Cooper, Thomas, and David J. McCord, eds. *The Statutes at Large of South Carolina.* Columbia, S.C.: A. S. Johnston, 1836–41.

Dann, John C., ed. *The Revolution Remembered: Eyewitness Accounts of the War of Independence.* Chicago: University of Chicago Press, 1980.

Dewey, Frank L. "Thomas Jefferson's Notes on Divorce." *William and Mary Quarterly,* 3d ser., 39 (1982): 216–19.

Drayton, John. *Memoirs of the American Revolution as Relating to the State of South Carolina.* 2 vols. 1821. Reprint. New York: New York Times and Arno Press, 1969.

Gilman, Caroline, ed. *Letters of Eliza Wilkinson, during the Invasion and Possession of Charleston, SC, by the British in the Revolutionary War.* 1839. Reprint. New York: New York Times and Arno Press, 1969.

Hemphill, William Edwin, Wylma Anne Wates, and R. Nicholas Olsberg, eds. *The State Records of South Carolina: Journals of the General Assembly and House of Representatives, 1776–1780.* Columbia: University of South Carolina Press, 1970.

Hening, William Waller, ed. *The Statutes at Large: Being a Collection of All the Laws of Virginia from the First Session of the Legislature in the Year 1619.* Philadelphia: William Waller Hening, 1819–23.

Hurd, John Codman. *The Law of Freedom and Bondage in the United States.* 2 vols. New York: Negro Universities Press, 1968.

Johnston, Elizabeth Lichtenstein. *Recollections of a Georgia Loyalist.* New York and London: M. F. Mansfield and Company, 1901.

Marbury, Horatio, and William H. Crawford, comps. *Digest of the Laws of the State of Georgia, 1775–1800.* Savannah: Seymour, Woolhopter and Stebbins, 1802.

Moultrie, William. *Memoirs of the American Revolution.* 2 vols. New York: David Longworth, 1902.

Potter, Henry, et al., comps. *Laws of the State of North Carolina* . . . . 2 vols. Raleigh: J. Gales, 1821.

Ramsay, David. *History of South Carolina, from Its First Settlement in 1670 to the Year 1808.* 1808. Reprint. Newberry, S.C.: W. J. Duffie, 1858.

———. *The History of the Revolution in South Carolina.* 2 vols. Trenton, N.J.: Isaac Collins, 1785.

Robertson, Heard, ed. "Georgia's Banishment and Expulsion Act of September 16, 1777." *Georgia Historical Quarterly* 55 (1971): 274–82.

Rogers, George C., Jr., et al., eds. *The Papers of Henry Laurens.* Columbia: University of South Carolina Press, 1968– .

Saunders, William L., Walter Clark, and Stephen B. Weeks, eds. *The Colonial and State Records of North Carolina.* 30 vols. Raleigh, Winston, Goldsboro, and Charlotte, N.C.: State Printers, 1886–1914.

Schmidt, Frederika Teute, and Barbara Ripel Wilhelm. "Early Proslavery Petitions in Virginia." *William and Mary Quarterly,* 3d ser., 30 (1973): 133–46.

Thompson, Theodora J., et al., eds. *The State Records of South Carolina: Journals of the House of Representatives, 1783–1794.* 6 vols. Columbia: University of South Carolina Press, 1977–85.

Wells, Louisa Susannah. *The Journal of a Voyage from Charlestown to London.* New York: New York Times and Arno Press, 1968.

Secondary Sources

Ashe, Samuel. *History of North Carolina.* 2 vols. Greensboro, N.C.: C. L. Van Noppen, 1908–25.

Bailey, Raymond C. *Popular Influence upon Public Policy: Petitioning in Eighteenth-Century Virginia.* Westport, Conn.: Greenwood Press, 1979.

Baker, Paula. "The Domestication of Politics: Women and American Political Society, 1780–1920." *American Historical Review* 89 (1984): 620–47.

Barnwell, Robert W., Jr. "The Migration of Loyalists from South Carolina." In *Proceedings of the South Carolina Historical Association: 1937,* 34–42. Columbia: South Carolina Historical Association, 1937.

Basch, Norma. "Equity vs. Equality: Emerging Concepts of Women's Political Status in the Age of Jackson." *Journal of the Early Republic* 3 (1983): 297–318.

———. *In the Eyes of the Law: Women, Marriage, and Property in Nineteenth-Century New York.* Ithaca, N.Y.: Cornell University Press, 1982.

Benson, Mary Sumner. *Women in Eighteenth Century America: A Study in Opinion and Social Usage.* 1935. Reprint. New York: AMS Press, 1976.

Bloch, Ruth H. "The Gendered Meanings of Virtue in Revolutionary America." *Signs* 13 (1987): 37–58.

———. "American Feminine Ideals in Transition: The Rise of the Moral Mother." *Feminist Studies* 4 (1978): 101–26.

Boatner, Mark Mayo. *Encyclopedia of the American Revolution.* New York: D. McKay, 1966.

Boatwright, Eleanor M. "The Political and Civil Status of Women in Georgia, 1783–1860." *Georgia Historical Quarterly* 25 (1941): 301–24.

Bogin, Ruth M. "Petitioning and the New Moral Economy of Post-Revolutionary America." *William and Mary Quarterly,* 3d ser., 45 (1988): 391–425.

Bynum, Victoria E. *Unruly Women: The Politics of Social and Sexual Control in the Old South.* Chapel Hill: University of North Carolina Press, 1992.

Censer, Jane Turner. "'Smiling through Her Tears': Ante-Bellum Southern Women and Divorce." *American Journal of Legal History* 25 (1981): 24–47.

Chalou, George C. "Women in the American Revolution: Vignettes or Profiles." In *Clio Was a Woman: Studies in the History of American Women,* ed. Mabel C. Deutrich and Virginia C. Purdy, 73–90. Washington: Howard University Press, 1980.

Claghorn, Charles. *Women Patriots of the American Revolution: A Biographical Dictionary.* Metuchen, N.J., and London: Scarecrow Press, 1991.

Clark, Murtie June. *Loyalists in the Southern Campaign of the Revolutionary War.* 3 vols. Baltimore: Genealogical Publishing Company, 1981.

Coker, Kathryn Roe. "The Artisan Loyalists of Charleston, South Carolina." In *Loyalists and Community in North America,* ed. Robert M. Calhoon et al., 91–104. Westport, Conn.: Greenwood Press, 1994.

Coleman, Kenneth. *The American Revolution in Georgia, 1763–1789.* Athens: University of Georgia Press, 1958.

Cott, Nancy F. "Divorce and the Changing Status of Women in Eighteenth-Century Massachusetts." *William and Mary Quarterly,* 3d ser., 33 (1976): 586–614.

Crane, Elaine Forman. "Religion and Rebellion: Women of Faith and the American War for Independence." In *Religion in a Revolutionary Age,* ed. Ronald Hoffman and Peter J. Albert, 251–70. Charlottesville: University Press of Virginia, 1993.

Crow, Jeffrey J. "Tory Plots and Anglican Loyalty: The Llewelyn Conspiracy of 1777." *North Carolina Historical Review* 55 (1978): 1–17.

Cumming, Inez Parker. "The Edenton Ladies' Tea-Party." *Georgia Review* 8 (1954): 289–94.

Davis, Robert S., Jr. *Georgia Citizens and Soldiers of the American Revolution.* Easley, S.C.: Southern Historical Press, 1979.

DeMond, Robert O. *The Loyalists in North Carolina during the American Revolution.* Durham, N.C.: Duke University Press, 1940.

Eckenrode, H. J. *The Revolution in Virginia.* Boston: Houghton Mifflin, 1916.

Ekirch, A. Roger. *"Poor Carolina:" Politics and Society in Colonial North Carolina, 1729–1776.* Chapel Hill: University of North Carolina Press, 1981.

Ferguson, E. James. *The Power of the Purse: A History of American Public Finance, 1776–1790.* Chapel Hill: University of North Carolina Press, 1961.

Fliegelman, Jay. *Prodigals and Pilgrims: The American Revolution against Patriarchal Authority.* Cambridge: Cambridge University Press, 1982.

Frey, Sylvia R. *Water from the Rock: Black Resistance in a Revolutionary Age.* Princeton: Princeton University Press, 1991.

Gilpatrick, Delbert Harold. *Jeffersonian Democracy in North Carolina.* New York: Columbia University Press, 1931.

Gundersen, Joan R. "Independence, Citizenship, and the American Revolution." *Signs* 13 (1987): 59–77.

Harrell, Isaac S. *Loyalism in Virginia: Chapters in the Economic History of the Revolution.* Durham, N.C.: Duke University Press, 1926.

[Hay, Gertrude Sloan, et al.]. *Roster of Soldiers from North Carolina in the American Revolution.* Durham, N.C.: North Carolina Daughters of the American Revolution, 1932.

Higgins, Patricia. "The Reactions of Women, with Special Reference to Women Petitioners." In *Politics, Religion, and the English Civil War,* ed. Brian Manning, 179–222. New York: St. Martin's Press, 1973.

Hoffman, Ronald. "The 'Disaffected' in the Revolutionary South." In *The American Revolution: Exploration in the History of American Radicalism,* ed. Alfred F. Young, 273–316. DeKalb: Northern Illinois University Press, 1976.

———, and Peter J. Albert, eds. *Women in the Age of the American Revolution.* Charlottesville: University Press of Virginia, 1989.

———, et al., eds. *An Uncivil War: The Southern Backcountry during the American Revolution.* Charlottesville: University Press of Virginia, 1985.

Hudson, Geoffrey L. "Negotiating for Blood Money: War Widows and the Courts in Seventeenth-Century England." In *Women, Crime and the Courts in Early Modern England,* ed. Jennifer Kermode and Garthine Walker, 146–69. Chapel Hill: University of North Carolina Press, 1994.

Johnson, Guion Griffis. *Ante-Bellum North Carolina: A Social History.* Chapel Hill: University of North Carolina Press, 1937.

Kerber, Linda K. "A Constitutional Right to Be Treated Like American Ladies: Women and the Obligations of Citizenship." In *U.S. History as Women's History: New Feminist Essays,* ed. Linda K. Kerber, Alice Kessler-Harris, and Kathryn Kish Sklar, 17–35. Chapel Hill: University of North Carolina Press, 1995.

———. "The Paradox of Women's Citizenship in the Early Republic: The Case of Martin vs. Massachusetts, 1805." *American Historical Review* 97 (1992): 349–78.

———. "'I have Don . . . much to Carrey on the Warr': Women and the Shaping of Republican Ideology after the American Revolution." In *Women and Poli-*

tics in the Age of Democratic Revolution, ed. Harriet B. Applewhite and
Darline G. Levy, 227–58. Ann Arbor: University of Michigan Press, 1990.
———. *Women of the Republic: Intellect and Ideology in Revolutionary Amer-
ica.* Chapel Hill: University of North Carolina Press, 1980.
Kettner, James H. *The Development of American Citizenship, 1608–1870.*
Chapel Hill: University of North Carolina Press, 1978.
Kierner, Cynthia A. "Genteel Balls and Republican Parades: Gender and Early
Southern Civic Rituals, 1677–1824." *Virginia Magazine of History and Bi-
ography* 104 (1996): 185–210.
Klein, Rachel N. *Unification of a Slave State: The Rise of the Planter Class in the
South Carolina Backcountry, 1760–1808.* Chapel Hill: University of North
Carolina Press, 1990.
Lambert, Robert Stansbury. *South Carolina Loyalists in the American Revolu-
tion.* Columbia: University of South Carolina Press, 1987.
Lamplugh, George R. *Politics on the Periphery: Factions and Parties in Georgia,
1783–1806.* Newark: University of Delaware Press, 1986.
Lebsock, Suzanne. *Virginia Women, 1600–1945: "A Share of Honour."* Rich-
mond: Virginia State Library, 1987.
———. *The Free Women of Petersburg: Status and Culture in a Southern Town,
1784–1860.* New York: W. W. Norton, 1984.
———. "Radical Reconstruction and the Property Rights of Southern Women."
Journal of Southern History 43 (1977): 195–216.
Lee, Jean B. *The Price of Nationhood: The American Revolution in Charles
County.* New York: W. W. Norton, 1994.
Lewis, Jan. "The Republican Wife: Virtue and Seduction in the Early Republic."
William and Mary Quarterly, 3d ser., 44 (1987): 689–721.
Mayer, Holly A. *Belonging to the Army: Camp Followers and Community during
the American Revolution.* Columbia: University of South Carolina Press,
1996.
McCrady, Edward. *The History of South Carolina in the Revolution.* 2 vols. New
York: Macmillan, 1902.
Middlekauff, Robert. *The Glorious Cause: The American Revolution, 1763–
1789.* New York: Oxford University Press, 1982.
Morrill, James R. *The Practice and Politics of Fiat Finance: North Carolina in the
Confederation, 1783–1789.* Chapel Hill: University of North Carolina Press,
1969.
Moss, Bobby Gilmer. *Roster of South Carolina Patriots in the American Revolu-
tion.* Baltimore: Genealogical Publishing Company, 1983.
Nadelhaft, Jerome J. *The Disorders of War: The Revolution in South Carolina.*
Orono: University of Maine at Orono Press, 1981.
Nelson, William H. *The American Tory.* Oxford: Clarendon Press, 1961.
Norton, Mary Beth. *The British-Americans: The Loyalist Exiles in England,
1774–1789.* Boston: Little, Brown, 1972.

———. *Liberty's Daughters: The Revolutionary Experience of American Women, 1750–1800*. Boston: Little, Brown, 1980.

———. "'What an Alarming Crisis Is This': Southern Women in the American Revolution." In *The Southern Experience in the American Revolution*, ed. Jeffrey J. Crow and Larry E. Tise, 203–34. Chapel Hill: University of North Carolina Press, 1978.

———. "Eighteenth-Century American Women in War and Peace: The Case of the Loyalists." *William and Mary Quarterly*, 3d ser., 33 (1976): 386–409.

O'Donnell, James H., III. *Southern Indians in the American Revolution*. Knoxville: University of Tennessee Press, 1973.

Olson, Alison G. "Eighteenth-Century Colonial Legislatures and Their Constituents." *Journal of American History* 78 (1992): 543–67.

Pancake, John S. *This Destructive War: The British Campaign in the Carolinas, 1780–1782*. University: University of Alabama Press, 1985.

Pateman, Carole. *The Disorder of Women*. London: Polity Press, 1989.

Peckham, Howard H. *The Toll of Independence: Engagements and Battle Casualties of the American Revolution*. Chicago: University of Chicago Press, 1974.

Quarles, Benjamin. *The Negro in the American Revolution*. Chapel Hill: University of North Carolina Press, 1961.

Rankin, Hugh F. *The North Carolina Continentals*. Chapel Hill: University of North Carolina Press, 1971.

Riley, Glenda. "Legislative Divorce in Virginia, 1803–1850." *Journal of the Early Republic* 11 (1991): 51–67.

Rogers, George C., Jr. *Evolution of a Federalist: William Loughton Smith of Charleston (1758–1812)*. Columbia: University of South Carolina Press, 1962.

Royster, Charles. *A Revolutionary People at War: The Continental Army and the American Character, 1775–1783*. Chapel Hill: University of North Carolina Press, 1979.

Sabine, Lorenzo. *Biographical Sketches of Loyalists of the American Revolution, with an Historical Essay*. 2 vols. Boston: Little, Brown, 1864.

Salmon, Marylynn. *Women and the Law of Property in Early America*. Chapel Hill: University of North Carolina Press, 1986.

———. "Women and Property in South Carolina: The Evidence from Marriage Settlements, 1730 to 1830." *William and Mary Quarterly*, 3d ser., 39 (1982): 655–85.

Schulz, Constance B. "Daughters of Liberty: The History of Women in the Revolutionary War Pension Records." *Prologue* 3 (1984): 139–53.

Selby, John E. *The Revolution in Virginia, 1775–1783*. Williamsburg, Va.: Colonial Williamsburg, 1988.

Siebert, Wilbur Henry. *Loyalists in East Florida, 1774 to 1785*. 2 vols. Deland: Florida State Historical Society, 1929.

Smith-Rosenberg, Carroll. "Dis-Covering the Subject of the 'Great Constitutional Debate,' 1786–1789." *Journal of American History* 79 (1992): 841–73.

Troxler, Carole Watterson. *The Loyalist Experience in North Carolina.* Raleigh: North Carolina Division of Archives and History, 1976.

Walsh, Richard. *Charleston's Sons of Liberty: A Study of the Artisans, 1763–1789.* Columbia: University of South Carolina Press, 1959.

Ward, Christopher. *War of the Revolution.* 2 vols. New York: Macmillan, 1952.

Wilson, Joan Hoff. "The Illusion of Change: Women and the American Revolution." In *The American Revolution: Explorations in the History of American Radicalism,* ed. Alfred F. Young, 386–431. Dekalb, Ill.: Northern Illinois University Press, 1976.

Wyatt-Brown, Bertram. *Southern Honor: Ethics and Behavior in the Old South.* New York: Oxford University Press, 1982.

INDEX